THE ENGLISH VIEW OF ACCOUNTANTS DUTIES AND RESPONSIBILITIES 1881-1902

This is a volume in the Arno Press collection

THE DEVELOPMENT OF CONTEMPORARY ACCOUNTING THOUGHT

See last pages of this volume for a complete list of titles.

THE ENGLISH VIEW OF ACCOUNTANTS DUTIES AND RESPONSIBILITIES 1881-1902

Edited by
Michael Chatfield

With a Preface

ARNO PRESS
A New York Times Company
New York • 1978

Publisher's Note: This book has been reproduced from the best available copies.

Editorial Supervision: LUCILLE MAIORCA

Reprint Edition 1978 by Arno Press Inc.

THE DEVELOPMENT OF CONTEMPORARY ACCOUNTING THOUGHT
ISBN for complete set: 0-405-10891-5
See last pages of this volume for titles.

Manufactured in the United States of America

Library of Congress Cataloging in Publication Data

Main entry under title:

The English view of accountants duties and responsibilities, 1881-1902.

(The Development of contemporary accounting thought)
Reprints of 24 articles published between 1881 and 1975 in various journals.
1. Accounting--Great Britain--History--Addresses, essays, lectures. I. Chatfield, Michael. II. Series.
HF5616.G7E54 657'.0941 77-87312
ISBN 0-405-10925-3

CONTENTS

Whitehill, R.
SOME NOTES ON THE RESPONSIBILITIES OF CHARTERED ACCOUNTANTS WITH REGARD TO THEIR CERTIFICATES (Reprinted from *The Accountant*) London, January 2, 1897

Harvey, B. S.
THE LIMITS WHICH A CHARTERED ACCOUNTANT SHOULD PLACE ON HIS DUTIES AND RESPONSIBILITIES AS AN AUDITOR (Reprinted from *The Accountant*) London, April 3, 1897

Dicksee, Lawrence R.
THE LIABILITIES OF AUDITORS UNDER THE COMPANIES ACTS (Reprinted from *The Accountant*) London, May 14, 1898

THE LIABILITIES OF AUDITORS (Reprinted from *The Accountant*) London, May 21, 1898

Dicksee, Lawrence R.
LETTER TO THE EDITOR ON "THE LIABILITIES OF AUDITORS" (Reprinted from *The Accountant*) London, May 28, 1898

THE LIABILITY OF AUDITORS (Reprinted from *The Accountant*) London, June 11, 1898

Easton, J. M.
THE LIABILITIES OF AUDITORS OF COMPANIES, WITH ESPECIAL REFERENCE TO THE COMPANIES ACT, 1900 (Reprinted from *The Accountant*) London, April 27, 1901

Crewdson, Ernest
CODIFICATION OF AN AUDIT (Reprinted from *The Accountant*) London, February 22, 1902

Dicksee, Lawrence R.
LETTER TO THE EDITOR ON "CODIFICATION OF AN AUDIT" (Reprinted from *The Accountant*) London, March 1, 1902

CODIFICATION OF AN AUDIT (Reprinted from *The Accountant*) London, March 14, 1902

Dickinson, Arthur Lowes
THE DUTIES AND RESPONSIBILITIES OF THE PUBLIC ACCOUNTANT (Reprinted from *The Accountant*) London, July 26, 1902

THE ENGLISH VIEW OF ACCOUNTANT'S DUTIES AND RESPONSIBILITIES: 1881-1902

Michael Chatfield

PREFACE

Quite a few perennial accounting issues center around questions of accountant's duties and responsibilities. What comprises full disclosure in financial reporting? How many alternative accounting techniques should be permitted? What should be the scope of an audit examination? What is the meaning of the auditor's certificate, and what verbal formula best expresses that meaning? What ethical stance should accountants adopt in dealing with their clients and with each other? What responsibility can they safely assume for corporate estimates and prospectuses?

One difficulty in coming to grips with these questions is that none of them originated in American practice. Neither the issues involved nor their preferred treatments can be understood solely in terms of American experience. Beginning about a hundred years ago, British accountants confronted and debated these questions for the first time in their modern context. Their discussions produced a consensus about methods to be used in certain areas of practice, and agreement on a number of guides to professional conduct--conventions which we now call "generally accepted accounting principles". Add to this the fact that half the present Big Eight CPA firms were founded by English or Scots Chartered Accountants, and the nineteenth century British experience becomes even more relevant to an understanding of how the profession has defined itself and its duties. Yet the details of late Victorian accounting practice are not well known in the United States.

This book traces the evolution of auditing, ethical, and financial reporting standards in the words of some of the men who pioneered in these areas. The timespan (1881-1902) carries us from the appearance of the first article on accountant's duties in The Accountant, almost to the point where the Journal of Accountancy (founded 1905) began an independent American coverage of the subject. Editorial comments and letters to the editor have been included to capture the flavor of debate on these issues.

Any collection of historical articles represents a search for precedents. In selecting materials for this volume, no attempt was made to give a balanced picture of nineteenth century accounting thought. Rather I have tried to show our intellectual debt to our predecessors, and to reveal the thought processes which produced ideas on which we still rely. Though laws, social customs, and the whole industrial environment have changed, the perceived problems of accountant's responsibility have not greatly altered, nor have their proposed solutions. Problems which have been expressed in their present form for nearly a century are not apt to be solved by accountants of the present generation.

Finally, there are the authors themselves. It is likely that men such as Dicksee, Pixley, Cooper, and Lowes Dickinson have influenced modern accounting thought more than almost anyone alive today. They came on the scene just at the time when accounting practice required codification, and they seized a unique opportunity to set standards for future generations of accountants. Unlike today's accounting scholars, few of these men were academics. The majority were practicing accountants, often partners in firms, dealing very directly with problems they encountered in their daily work. Nearly all the articles in this book were originally speeches given to accounting society meetings. Those who offered opinions at these meetings were expected to defend them in the discussions which followed. The viewpoints which represent what A.C. Littleton has called "The survival of the satisfactory" were hammered out in sometimes violent debates. In this environment general theories were not highly valued; proposals had to be practical and applicable to the problems at hand. At its best this system produced a group of men whose technical knowledge, broad general culture and range of awareness may surprise the modern reader. They can justly be called our earliest contemporaries.

Michael Chatfield
Hayward, California
August, 1976

CONTENTS

Page

THE ACCOUNTANT'S RESPONSIBILITY IN HISTORICAL PERSPECTIVE (1975)

Richard P. Brief

This summary article compares nineteenth century English and twentieth century American practice with respect to (1) the scope of audits and the audit certificate, (2) the accountant's responsibility for forecasts and estimates, and (3) uncertainty and the corporate concept of profit.

The Accountant's Responsibility in Historical Perspective

Richard P. Brief

SEVERAL years ago it was reported (*The New York Times*, January 4, 1972) that many accountants, "like victims of an earthquake or the fist of Joe Frazier, . . . wander dazedly asking what happened; where did the force come from; why wasn't it foreseen; how could it have been avoided . . . ?" The article elaborated on the current state of the profession, indicating that "now, from within the profession itself, revolt is brewing . . . . And for more than 100,000 accountants themselves, the preservation of their professional credibility could not have higher significance. This credibility is under attack in the Congress, in the courts and within the profession itself." This revolt is not new. It has been brewing for nearly 100 years.

One way to gain insight into the vexing and unsettled questions connected with the responsibility of accountants is to approach the subject from an historical perspective. In the pages that follow we examine nineteenth and early twentieth century thought on various topics which have been, and continue to be, of concern to accountants. It will become evident that "history repeats itself" and that most of the basic problems considered by accountants now are also those which have perplexed the profession for nearly a century. Thus despite all the changes in the business environment, controversy within the accounting profession today has remarkable similarities to the discussion taking place decades ago. Why do certain accounting problems appear to be perennial and why has regulation and legislation apparently not solved many of the fundamental disputes in accounting?

The thesis of this study is that accounting controversy persists because profit calculations involve "uncertainty about the future." Legislation and regulation cannot reduce this controversy because they cannot eliminate the element of uncertainty from the problem of profit determination. Consequently, until the subject of uncer-

The original version of this paper was written while the author was a Visiting Professor of Finance, Dartmouth College. It was presented at the annual meeting of the American Accounting Association in August, 1974, during a session sponsored by the Academy of Accounting Historians. Comments and suggestions by the discussants, Professor David Green, Jr. and Mr. Leonard Spacek, and by Mr. Walter Oliphant, Professor Louis Goldberg, and the reviewers of THE ACCOUNTING REVIEW changed the manuscript in important ways. Their help is appreciated. In addition, some of the ideas expressed in this paper are a joint product of several years of discussion with my colleague, Professor Joel Owen. Research support was provided by the Tuck Associates Program, Dartmouth College, and it is gratefully acknowledged. Naturally, the author is solely responsible for this paper.

Richard P. Brief is Professor of Business Statistics and Accounting, Graduate School of Business Administration, New York University.

tainty is given a central position in accounting theory, the problems recognized in earlier times will continue to be deferred to later generations for resolution.

The paper is divided into three sections. The first surveys accounting thought on the subjects of disclosure and alternative techniques and questions concerning the scope of audit and audit certificate. Although there has been an enormous amount of legislation and regulation in these areas, many of today's problems are no different from those which preoccupied the profession during the last century. In the second section, the attitude toward the accountant's responsibility for forecasts and estimates is examined. Historically, an effort was made to minimize uncertainty-related problems by arguing that the accountant's main responsibilities was for "prosaic facts" and "dry realities." The third section concludes that this emphasis on the past rather than the future conflicts with the idea of profit as a return for risk bearing. However, the modern corporate concept of profit is a product of lawyers, not of accountants, and legislation governing the payment of dividends has had a significant impact on the development of accounting.

Legislation and Problems of the Accountant's Responsibility

This section considers two broad topics relating to the accountant's responsibility: full disclosure and alternative techniques and the scope of the audit and audit certificate. Nineteenth century accountants were concerned with the improvement of practice in these areas and many of them, like their twentieth century counterparts, advocated more effective regulation to reduce the degrees of freedom in accounting behavior. The profession was almost unanimous in its belief that accountants should take the lead in promulgating reform. However, there was a diversity of opinion on the specific changes in practice that were needed and some cautioned that certain kinds of regulation would have undesirable consequences.

Full Disclosure and Alternative Techniques

In the last quarter of the nineteenth century debate over the interpretation of the legal requirement that "dividends must not be paid out of capital" and the determination of "profits available for dividends" were inextricably connected to the depreciation problem and other familiar subjects (Brief, 1970). During this period accountants attempted for the first time to formulate theory, to codify methodology, and to clarify their responsibility. The development of accounting was marked by angry argument, caustic rhetoric, and more important, a very sophisticated and penetrating dialogue on a wide range of subjects.

Underlying much of the debate was the belief that reported profits had an effect on investor behavior. The nature of this relationship was boldly and sarcastically described in 1837 (*Railway Magazine*, p. 2): "Let it only be seen by six months working of that line [Grand Junction] that a profit will accrue to proprietors of 8 or 10 percent per annum and there is little hazard in predicting that other lines of great intercourse will be amply supported." Thus, when a railroad charged £14,625 to capital and paid a dividend by arguing that "the efficiency and the value of the engines have been materially increased" after the severe winter of 1838, the sufficiency of disclosure and capitalization policy were criticized by the *Railway Magazine*, which stated: "a more puny and meagre document we have never witnessed" (1838, p. 189). The subject of accounting error, its economic effect, and the accountant's responsibility for this error were a source of continuing argument throughout the period (Brief, 1965).

Many accountants advocated that the profession should take the lead in writing new legislation to improve business practices. One writer put it this way (*The Accountant*, December 12, 1885):

Is there a single word in the whole of the Acts restraining the payment of dividends out of capital? There is not; what is said seems to amount to this, that the payment of dividends out of capital can be made. . . . What are accountants doing towards drawing up formal suggestions on this and other equally important points on which the Companies Acts are notoriously at fault? Not going to sleep, let us hope.

In addition, a very competitive attitude towards others, notably lawyers, also is observed in the profession's formative years. This attitude is illustrated by the common complaint that "Existing law is deplorably defective, and . . . the Chartered Accountants acting through their Institute should be the first to move in the matter, and not allow the work to be done, and the honour to be appropriated by other and less capable hands" (*The Accountant*, December 19, 1885).

At an early date *The Accountant* (April 30, 1881) stated that "If a balance sheet be correct although condensed he [the auditor] is bound to sign it" because the auditor should not publicly disagree with management. But *The Accountant* also advocated full disclosure of the amounts charged to depreciation, the method of valuation, etc.:

A shareholder is entitled to know, not what is the true value of his shares, for that in most instances is a matter of opinion, but *how* the value of fixed assets has been estimated—whether at cost, at a valuation . . . , or otherwise, and what sums have been placed in reserve or written off for depreciation, running out of leases or other decreases in value . . .

However, although the editor argues that "Much of the information . . . might be given if the legislature made its publication compulsory upon all," he also believed that "it is difficult to enforce full information without committing an act of injustice towards companies, as opposed to private concerns, which need never print any balance-sheets" (June 4, 1881).

Although many accountants, in the nineteenth century as in the twentieth, argued that legislation which increases the amount of disclosure in financial statements and reduces the number of alternative methods is a desirable goal, others, like the editor of *The Accountant*, also considered some of the undesirable by-products of achieving these objectives. The extreme position was that "as I don't approve of too much grandmotherly legislation in a free country where a people should learn from their own experience how to take care of themselves, I don't approve of the State preventing undertakings being floated with an inducement of this sort" [returning interest on capital during construction] (*The Accountant*, December 4, 1886). In the same vein, when the editor of *The Accountant* discussed (October 8, 1881) the balance sheet of John Crossley and Son, Limited, which was criticized on the basis of inadequate disclosure by the *Citizen* newspaper, he reasoned, in effect, that inadequate disclosure would increase a firm's cost of capital:

Here, indeed, the entire assets are lumped together in one line, and we infer that no outsider is expected to take shares; in fact, none but a semiprivate concern would issue such a balance sheet. Any ordinary company would assuredly separate its freehold and plant, its stock-in-trade, its book-debts, and its cash, though it might include "minerals" perhaps with freeholds. The *et cetera* at the end of the liabilities means the reserves, no doubt, against discounts, bad debts and any other drawbacks. But the true answer of the public to such a balance sheet, however respectably audited, is to respectfully let the company's shares alone. *We therefore, consider that the "dissatisfied shareholder" must be deemed a goose.* (italics added)

Dicksee, doubtless the most influential nineteenth century accountant, also questioned the effect of legislating accounting practices (*The Accountant*, March 1, 1902):

. . . even with regard to such important questions as the value of assets, provision for depreciation, the assessments of profits earned, and the distribution of unrealised profits, the Courts have shown a marvelous disinclination [to provide] principles for the safe guidance of the auditor. . . . No doubt it has acted wisely in adopting this course, however, because any attempt to state explicitly what the duties of auditors are in all cases would afford the best possible excuse in such cases for the insufficiency of the audit that has been performed.

And seventeen years earlier Matheson, responding to a criticism of failing to specify exact methods in his book on depreciation, had the same apprehensive attitude about fixed rules (*The Accountant*, January 3, 1885):

. . . [regarding] the absence from my book of exact rates of depreciation for different classes of plant, I am more on my ground, and I venture to assert that any positive statements of rates would be more likely to mislead than inform . . . fixed rules are impossible, and examples, if offered for imitation, dangerous.

More recently, a strikingly similar view was expressed by the Chief Accountant of the Securities Exchange Commission, John C. Burton: "He was not happy with the old 18-man, part-time board. 'By writing precise rules,' he asserted, 'the board made it possible for people to observe the letter and avoid the spirit with the blessing—and often the assistance—of their auditors' " (*The New York Times*, June 25, 1972).

There were other arguments against regulation and they concerned the depreciation problem. For example, one writer said that legal requirements to charge depreciation before declaring dividends would be "injurious to companies and the public. . . . It would stop all enterprise because it would be absolutely impossible for companies to pay dividends in the early years of their existence" (*The Accountant*, December 14, 1889). Similarly, Lord Justice Lindley, in the landmark 1889 decision in *Lee* v. *Neuchatel* (41 LR Ch. 1, 19) went so far as to argue that the legal requirement to charge depreciation regularly and periodically would "paralyze the trade of the country."

Still another argument against legally requiring depreciation, which the business historian might usefully consider, was made by "an eminent accountant in the north of England." He argued (*The Accountant*, November 29, 1884) that the provision for depreciation ("money retained out of profits"):

enables managers and directors to undertake continual new work without consulting their shareholders. It is only another way of providing fresh capital or avoiding a call, which might be resisted by those interested if it came in that form; and further in cases where you have several classes of shares upon which the capital is not equally paid up, or where you have debenture holders as well as ordinary shareholders, the rights of the respective parties are prejudicially affected by what can only be styled the misappropriation of funds intended for a specific object.

There were differences of opinion among accountants over basic questions and they were vigorously debated. However, judicial and statutory authority did not play a significant role in resolving these differences (Brief, 1966). Rather, the profession attempted to establish the limits of its own responsibility and the aims were, according to Dicksee (1915, p. xiv), somewhat Utopian:[1]

If it should be thought that the standard I have throughout advocated is somewhat Utopian in character, and unattainable in practice, I can only reply that I maintain that, to me, an incomplete investigation seems worse than useless, and I am convinced that it is only by voluntarily accepting, and even increasing, the responsibilities of our position that we can hope to maintain and to increase the large measure of public confidence we at present enjoy.

Throughout the period, accountants

[1] The quote is taken from the preface to the first edition (1892) which was reprinted in subsequent editions.

fought to establish the profession as a permanent institution, but the battle still rages to determine whether "the honour [will be] appropriated by other and less capable hands."

It is now likely that unless accountants and their corporate clients take the initiative in reducing the number of acceptable accounting practices, financial disclosure will become much more a matter of law. There seems to be increasing pressure to limit the diversity of accounting methods by establishing an arbitrary set of rules. . . . If the accounting profession does not do so, "its position of eminence may be lost to those who seize the larger opportunity"[2] (Chatfield, 1974, p. 280).

Although the business setting has changed, nineteenth century debate on disclosure and alternative methods has a modern tone and many of the issues before the profession in the present day are those which concerned its original members. How can disclosure be improved? How much disclosure is desirable? How can the range of accounting alternatives be reduced? What are the effects of regulation? Then, as now, accountants were searching for satisfactory answers to these questions. Nineteenth century debate on the audit certificate is also relevant to today's problems.

Scope of Audit and Audit Certificate

The pure laissez-faire attitude in the last century towards the scope of the audit was illustrated in the early legal case of *Turquand* v. *Marshall* which was decided in 1869 (20 LT 766):

As to the publication of false balance sheets and including in them debts which were hopelessly bad, it was difficult to say where a debt was hopeless; and besides, if any shareholders were deceived into buying shares he might have his separate remedy, but each would have a different case, and the whole body could not sue.

The debtor in this case was the Confederacy! However, although the courts generally did not interfere in business affairs, accountants and other groups were more active in their advocacy of reform, and the audit and related problems quickly became a major issue which was actively discussed.

As early as 1883 there was an interesting controversy on the audit, sparked by a series of articles in a magazine called *Vanity Fair*. Significantly, *The Accountant* reprinted them in entirety, even though the comments were harshly critical of accounting practice.

Apparently, *Vanity Fair* thought that "auditors' certificates might be longer and better" and "legislation is needed" to achieve this objective. However, the editor of *The Accountant* argued that "In a simple matter such as an auditor's certificate we fail to see why any legal interference is called for. What the public and shareholders want is a readable assurance from the accountants, stating in plain English what they really have done" (October 27, 1883). With great sarcasm, the editor elaborated on this point (November 3, 1883):

We would suggest that in future the auditors' certificates should, in accordance with the defense now made for them, run thus:—We having been allowed to audit not from month to month, but only once a year; having had too little time to make an exhaustive report, because the documents are required for the printer; knowing that shareholders are generally impatient to get through the business; being paid a fee out of all proportion to the work required to be done; and being aware that the voting power is in the abso-

[2] Chatfield is quoting from Mautz and Sharaf (1961, p. 200). Similar comments can be found elsewhere. For example, Hawkins (1963, p. 168) commented, "Once more, the possibility of further government intervention in industrial reporting matters is imminent, principally because of the accounting profession's inability to narrow the areas of difference in accounting principles and management's resistance to its critics' demands for improved corporate disclosure." The same idea is echoed by *Business Week* (April 22, 1972). "Before such sweeping moves are widely demanded, the Wheat proposals give the accounting profession another chance to demonstrate that workable accounting and auditing procedures can be set in the private sector, with the broad-based cooperation of accountants, financial executives, security analysts, and educators."

lute control of the Board—certify that, so far as we, under these disabilities, can ascertain and dare disclose the facts, it is all right. This would at any rate let shareholders know from the certificate, as we know from the general chorus of certifiers, what the true meaning and value of the certificate really amounts to. Our complaint was and is that at present they do not know this, but that they are led and are meant to imagine that bladders are lanterns and auditors' certificates proofs of all excellences and complete solvency and security. . . .

We are not to be drawn off the scent by any invitation to discuss the powers of auditors or the technicalities of auditing. That is not the question. The question is—What is worth, and what, therefore, the use of an auditorial certificate in its various forms as it is now commonly given? We say it is worth next to nothing. Our critics say, not that it is worth much, but that it is very hard to make it worth anything. Very well. Then we and our critics are agreed. The certificate *is* worth next to nothing, and this being so, it is a delusion and a snare.

Then, in response to a letter, the editor of *The Accountant* argued that to remedy the audit's deficiencies, a direct approach was called for: "Cease making those damnable faces which are called Auditors' Certificates." Rather than paraphrase, these remarks are quoted in entirety in order to give the flavor of the lively debate which took place during the profession's first decade of development:

There is however one correspondent of *The Accountant* who signs himself "Anti-Twaddle," and who deserves special remark. He is very rude, but not more rude than illogical and ungrammatical. He too sets forth the difficulties of the poor auditor, and so feelingly that he has evidently suffered from them. The auditor gets no power, no time, and no money to talk of; he is not responsible except for the verification of figures put before him; he is the slave of the directors, who do not like to look at the worst side of affairs, and he has to satisfy also the shareholders, for we believe that if they have sometimes a strong objection to knowing the truth, they have at least as often as strong an objection to having lies told to them. And it is quite clear that, if this venerable Aunty were herself set to audit accounts and to frame thereon an auditorial certificate, she would unhesitatingly avoid any difference of opinion with directors, would carefully abstain from looking at the worst side of affairs, would very generously indulge the shareholders' strong objection to knowing the truth, and would, in spite of the insufficient time, power, and money, frame and publish a certificate that would make everything pleasant for everybody, and above all for Aunty. This is exactly what we complain of.

And yet, in spite of this injurious disclosure of the way in which certificates are moulded from the dirty mud of facts by the Sculptor-Director, and invested with artistic merit by the Ghost-Auditor, Aunty wants to have herself fastened on all concerns by an Act of Parliament which shall supersede directors and everybody else, and make Aunty a first charge on the concern, just as though she were an official liquidator or trustee. And she proposes that *we* should get her Act passed for her! No; we cannot do this. On the contrary, we say—Amend your certificates and not your Statutes; tell the truth if you know it, and shame the Director. If you don't know and can't find out—why say that; but in any case, cease making those merely damnable faces which are now called Auditors' Certificates. (November 3, 1883)

Some leading accountants took a constructive view of this criticism. Thomas Welton, President of the Institute of Chartered Accountants in England and Wales in 1891–2, believed that *The Accountant's* remarks on the auditors' certificate "would do great good even if they did no more than induce shareholders to more closely scan the wording of these documents . . . " (October 27, 1883). But the basic complaint was that accountants lacked authority to impose exacting standards. For example, the problem of requiring firms to charge "adequate" depreciation was of great concern in those days and Pixley (1887, p. 127) complained that "It is in the earlier years of a company's existence the auditor has the greatest difficulty in inducing Directors to charge an amount sufficient to provide for the past depreciation of the period." A similar comment appears in the preface to the second edition of the first book on depreciation (Matheson, 1910, p. ix–x): "Auditors, and especially those who have to deal with joint stock or other concerns, where the remuneration of the management is made wholly or partly dependent upon declared profits, know in what varied forms resistance to an adequate charge against profits for Depreciation is presented."

This conflict between the accountant and management, and its effect on the accountant's responsibility to shareholders, was recognized in the first years of the profession's existence, and questions relating to the auditor's independence were connected to the proxy system which permitted persons in fiduciary positions to vote on matters affecting their own interest. Once again, *The Accountant* (October 27, 1883) identified a critical problem:

> The audit of Public Companies' accounts was designed to control and check the action of directors in their administration of the affairs of Public Companies: and yet, as a rule, the auditors who are chosen for this purpose owe their employment to the very directors whom they are presumed so to control and check in the interests of the shareholders. This is one of the evils arising out of the proxy system, which I trust we may some day see abolished, as being utterly pernicious and vicious in root and branch. It should be laid down as an invariable rule that directors, trustees, or other persons in fiduciary positions should never be allowed the direct or indirect use of proxies in voting, or in fact to vote personally, on any subject affecting the performance of the duties imposed upon them by the trusts under which they act, or on the passing of the accounts as presented by them to their proprietary or *cestui que* trust.

This problem of the auditor's autonomy remains a topic of current interest, and recent suggestions for reform (Hawes, 1974) echo *The Accountant's* earlier argument:

> At a time when auditors are subject to a staggering number of lawsuits, intense pressures from managements to adopt accounting treatment that will put the best face on the financial statements and the difficult task of codifying accounting principles, legislation is needed to make stockholder approval of the appointment of auditors mandatory.
>
> Such legislation would underscore the fact that the auditor's client is the stockholders and thus would have an important therapeutic effect on the corporation.

This historical review of the audit certificate and scope of audit has demonstrated that many modern problems are not new. From the first, accountants recognized the limitations of the audit certificate and they raised questions concerning the auditor's independence. Many recommended more effective regulation but some took a more straightforward approach: "Amend your certificates and not your statutes." In summarizing this section, one conclusion is inescapable. After nearly a century of debate,

> . . . there is still no comprehensive, integrated statement of concepts on which accountants and statement readers can agree and rely. There is still no consensus as to the exact meaning of the standard audit opinion that financial statements present the results of operations "fairly" in accordance with generally accepted accounting principles. One result is that accounting methods have changed much more slowly than the accounting environment. And the profession has not solved its basic problems of disclosure, consistency and statement comparability (Chatfield, 1974, pp. 298–99).

The thesis of this paper is that accounting controversy persists because profit calculations involve "uncertainty about the future." The next section surveys the attitude toward the accountant's responsibility for estimates and forecasts.

Attitude Toward Accountant's Responsibility for Estimates and Forecasts

In the discussion that follows it should be borne in mind that a formal framework for studying decision problems under uncertainty has become generally available only in the last decade or so. Therefore, nineteenth century accountants quite naturally made an effort to avoid uncertainty-related problems. Nevertheless, these early theorists did begin to discuss topics related to the subject, and their attitude towards them had a significant influence on the progress in accounting.

Historical Attitude Toward Uncertainty

One of the earliest references to the problem of uncertainty in accounting can be found in a series of articles on audits which appeared in several 1881 issues of *The Accountant*. Referring to balance sheet audits, the editor asserted (April 23, 1881) "that the real object to be aimed at is such a verification that will be practically sufficient." The auditor's task is then compared to a judge and jury who are often obliged to be content with "little more than a reasonable probability." Thus, at the end of a period "some matters outstanding . . . must be introduced by estimation . . . to make the apparent profit a real measure of what has been accomplished in the period under review." However, the auditor should not "indulge in forecasts or in expressions of feeling, but rather adhere as coldly and impassively as he can to facts—hard, dry realities."

This logical contradiction between the necessity to make estimates and the adherence to dry realities is not resolved, but the writer does suggest a "trend analysis" for specific problems like estimating "probable losses" such as "bad and doubtful debts." Since the facts "keep changing almost hourly," the auditor should study past trends and advocate reserves in good years to be used in years when losses exceed the average. However, when a loss is certain, "no rule can be laid down," but "broad principles" which "favour moderation in the distribution of dividends, and . . . ample reserves is [sic] desirable. Yet he should likewise remember the possibility of excess in the latter direction" which might induce shareholders "to part with their shares at an insufficient valuation."

The principle of conservatism and the auditor's responsibility for estimates is discussed again (June 4, 1881):

> Generally he [the shareholder] should be enabled to see in the balance sheet which of the assets are matters of opinion, and which are matters of fact. When this part of the subject is clear, little doubt can rest upon the estimate of profit or loss, which may be deemed correct or otherwise according to the spirit in which matters of opinion are apparently handled.
>
> Estimates are often proper things to make use of, where they relate to subsidiary matters, and enables the balance sheet to be speedily prepared, but all estimates should be slightly to the disadvantage of the company, rather than tending the other way.

In the first paper on the ethics of accountancy in 1888 (*The Accountant*, December 12, 1888), John Mather flatly opposed any idea of chance or uncertainty in accounting However, once again, the views on this subject are not perfectly consistent:

> What is called the "glorious uncertainty of the Law"—illustrated not only in the varying interpretations of enactments, but often in the evidence of opposing experts in law suits—conveys an idea that rarely attaches to the figures, statements, or certificates of Chartered Accountants. And it is our hope and belief, that as we succeed in gradually raising the standard of the skill and the ethics of the profession, any such idea of chance or uncertainty will be still more foreign to its work in the future.

In other words, "There seems a general agreement that . . . the accountant may not prophecy 'unless he knows' . . . he must avoid the tempting region of fancy and stick to the prosaic facts." Stated differently, "in most cases an accountant is no better able than other people to forecast the business prospects of an undertaking which, however sound at the outset, may ultimately fail through mismanagement, change of fashion, invalidity of patents, or numberless unforeseen causes." Yet, according to Mather, the accountant, "in the opinion of many . . . is fully justified in dealing with those facts in their bearing upon the future . . . ." But how can the accountant do this if he must stick to the prosaic facts?

Further insight into the accountant's conflicting attitudes towards uncertainty is provided by Dickinson twenty-six years later. In concluding a discussion of the accountant's responsibility for earnings projections Dickinson (1914, pp. 226–27) said that:

It should be clear, therefore, from the above considerations that any estimate of future earnings must necessarily depend upon so many contingencies that it would hardly seem desirable that it should be put forth without calling specific attention to the assumptions involved; and an estimate with such qualification attached would hardly be of much service to the promoter and would not be incorporated in the prospectus.

However,

In as much as the community is being educated to consider that statements emanating from a public accountant deal only with facts, it may be said in conclusion that in such a case as that supposed, the accountant's duty should end with the submission on request of a carefully prepared estimate, accompanied by all necessary qualifications, without, however, any certificate there to . . . . (italics added)

Even though Dickinson rejects the inclusion of estimates in the prospectus, his proposal that all estimates should be accompanied by the assumptions on which they are based reflects modern thinking on the subject. Of greater significance, however, is his remark concerning the effort *to educate* the community that financial statements deal only with facts. It suggests that a conscious attempt was made by the profession to convince the public that the accountant is responsible only for "facts," and it also helps to explain why so many generations have come to regard accounting as an essentially historical discipline.

At the same time, accountants understood the tenuous nature of their argument. Even Dickinson (p. 236) recognized that "Every balance sheet is a matter of opinion." But he failed to make any explicit connection between the problems which require the accountant to exercise his "opinion" and the conditions which give rise to these problems—namely, uncertainty about the future.

These references to the uncertainty problem are generally in terms of estimating balances in asset and liability accounts at the end of each period. This perspective is consistent with a balance sheet approach to income determination. However, there were also discussions about another class of estimation and forecasting problems in accounting and they concerned the relationship between reported profits and future profits.

The first of these provides an amusing illustration of the "interim reporting problem." In 1883 The Hotels and City Properties Share Trust, Limited issued a four-month report and estimated the year's results by doubling the figures for the interim period. *The Accountant* (October 27, 1883) published a scathing criticism of this report:

Mr. Daniels has furnished the public with the result of working the Royal during the best four months of the year. But are we to understand that he pledges his professional reputation that *any* appreciable profit can be made during the remaining eight months, when Southend is little better than a howling wilderness, and when a stray Londoner at the Royal is looked upon with as much curiosity as if he were a friendly Zulu? During those dark and dreary months is there not an entire absence of excursionists, and as a rule are not the only occupants and best customers of that spacious bar which the prospectus says is a great source of profit, the neglected piermaster and the boatman?

In another reference to this general subject, Montgomery (1909, p. 324) seems to argue that the purpose of reporting the results of operations in past periods is to predict profits of future periods:

the certificate, therefore, should be a clear and unconditional certificate of accomplished facts, and not a mere estimate of possible—or even probable—future results, misnamed a "certificate." To the limited extent already mentioned it may be permissible, and even desirable, to modify the past results so that they may more usefully serve the purpose for which they are primarily intended—namely, provide a reliable index of future profits. But at the same time a certificate should relate not to the future, but to the past. . . .

Although Montgomery argues unequivocally that financial statements should reflect "accomplished facts," i.e., financial statements should be historical, he also points out that the primary purpose of reporting past results is to provide an index (estimate) of future profits. Clearly, the methods used to calculate past performance will influence this "index," but questions about this relationship were not raised.

Effect on Modern Accounting Thought

The early ideas on uncertainty and its relevance to accounting have not changed very much in the twentieth century. There are few extended discussions of the subject in modern texts and theoretical treatises and most references to the uncertainty problem are vague and ambiguous.

For example, van Pelt (1972, pp. 13–4) defines profitability as the "excess of revenues . . . over *known* costs . . . " (italics added), but also states that "estimates . . . will be required for the purpose of allocating costs." The *APB Accounting Principles* (1973, 1, p. 15) states that "Accountants have considered themselves primarily historians, not prophets . . . . However, *even* present accounting practices require estimates of the future" (italics added). How are estimates used in allocating costs? Which accounting practices require estimates of the future? What quantities must be estimated? What assumptions are the estimates based on? What estimating procedures are used? Questions such as these, and there are many others, have rarely been asked.

This historical review of the accountant's attitude towards uncertainty shows that the profession has always recognized that many of the numbers in financial statements are based on estimates of uncertain future events. At the same time, it also indicates that many accountants repeatedly stated that the accounts should reflect "prosaic facts" and "dry realities." This attitude toward uncertainty dominated thought; accountants, as well as the public, have been educated to believe that financial statements are essentially historical.

In the final section this attitude towards uncertainty is at least partly explained by the legal origin of the modern corporate concept of profit.

Uncertainty and the Corporate Concept of Profit

It is uncertainty about the future that makes profit a return for risk bearing (Edwards and Bell, 1961, p. 9). It is also uncertainty about the future that provides the *logical* motivation for calculating the "profit of a period," and the common procedure in accounting of assuming certainty about the future completely obscures the information content of period earnings reports (Brief and Owen, 1970, p. 167). Thus, by assuming that the future is known with certainty (or by deemphasizing and minimizing the importance of uncertainty), accountants have eliminated, or at least have obscured, that which they set out to measure.

However, as a practical matter, the origin of the modern corporate concept of profit is in dividend law, not accounting, and the purpose of this legislation was to protect the rights of creditors and different classes of shareholders. This legal origin of the profit concept had an important influence on accounting.

Kehl (1941, p. 14) indicates that "During the 1600's charters began including dividend regulations among their provisions. The most common limitation required that dividends be paid from profits. Such was the restriction used in 1620 in the charter of James I to the New River Company." And "By 1700, there had already been adopted in England two statutory standards, one or the other of which still controls dividend distributions under present day statutes in a great many American states" (Kehl, p. 4).

This legislation governing the payment of dividends produced the "capital impairment rule" and the "profits tests" which were the first statutory references to the modern corporate concept of profit. Dividends cannot be paid out of capital and/or dividends must be paid out of the *profit of a period.*

Historically, railroads, utilities, and other quasi-public enterprise used a cash receipts-less-disbursements method of calculating profit. This method implied that the value of assets was "permanent." And although it became evident that this assumption was not valid, the cameralistic origin of the method seems to have blocked accounting reform for this class of enterprise.

The profit calculations of other firms are more difficult to assess. At the beginning of the nineteenth century the "inventory method" was employed. This method was a balance sheet (direct valuation) approach to profit determination. Eventually, this method was replaced by the modern accounting concept of profit that assumes a going concern and computes profit by "matching" revenues and expenses. All of these approaches have been sanctioned by the courts at various times (Brief, 1966).

Leake (1912, p. 2) correctly observed that "when commerce was carried on by individuals, each on his own account, in a vast number of small undertakings, and there was no regular income tax, it was a matter of small moment . . . whether the surplus of receipts . . . was economic profits." On the other hand, the coming of modern corporation and the development of capital markets interacted with dividend law to make the concept of a year's profit one of the most important ideas in economics and, as May (1936, II, p. 307) put it, "the central question of modern accounting." Yet, Hatfield's comment (1927, p. 241) about the profit concept is as valid today as it was nearly fifty years ago:

> It is a peculiar fact that while all business is carried on for the purpose of securing profits, while the distribution of profits is continually the subject of controversy in the courts, while the ascertainment of profits enters largely into the discussion of every economist, the term is still vaguely and loosely used and without definition by either economist, man of affairs, jurist or accountant.

Thus, whereas dividend law conditioned businessmen, investors, and creditors to think in terms of the concept of "profit of a period," traditional accounting models that attempt to explain operationally the meaning of this concept in the context of the modern firm have been unsatisfactory. And as long as the term, "profit," is vaguely and loosely used and without definition, all areas of accounting responsibility that touch on questions concerning profit calculations must be a continuing source of controversy and dispute. This controversy will not subside until accountants become willing to acknowledge that in theory it is uncertainty about the future, not dividend law, that gives rise to the problem of determining the profit of a period.

Conclusion

Accounting thought in the nineteenth century is especially relevant to contemporary issues because the laissez-faire business environment produced a free and uninhibited exchange of views. The courts at this time were reluctant to interfere in business affairs and, unless fraud were an issue, business practices were determined by businessmen. Similarly, the statutes did not lay down specific rules governing accounting practices, and quasi-judicial administrative bodies such as the Securities Exchange Commission did not yet exist.

The last two decades of the nineteenth century were a "golden age" in accounting and most of the major issues connected with the subject of the accountant's responsibility were brought out in the period. Questions concerning full disclosure, alternative techniques, scope of audit and the meaning of the audit certificate were widely discussed in the first few years after the profession was formally established.

However, nineteenth century accountants did not "solve" most of the problems which they debated. One explanation for the perennial nature of controversy is the accountant's early attitude toward uncertainty. During the last century, the profession began to emphasize the historical nature of accounting calculations even though many theorists recognized that forecasts and estimates were inherent in most problems.

Thus one explanation for the persistence of accounting controversy is the failure to recognize that profit calculations involve uncertainty about the future. But given the legal origin of the profit concept, it is not surprising to find that accountants became more concerned with statutory and judicial references to profit than with the more abstruse questions associated with an uncertain future. What implications can be drawn from this historical study of the accountant's responsibility?

First, many modern proposals for reform can be traced directly to the nineteenth century. Indeed, the basic perspective of the accountant's responsibility has not changed very much, and recent suggestions for improving practice often repeat earlier ideas. Thus even though the economic environment was very different 100 years ago, the basic problems in accounting today closely resemble those which confronted the profession in the last century. Therefore, regulation and legislation do not seem to have produced many of the improvements in practice which were expected.

Second, there is recent evidence that the accounting profession's attitude toward uncertainty may be changing. The report of the Study Group on the Objectives of Financial Statements (1973) gives explicit attention to the problem of forecasting future cash flows. And the Forecasting Task Force of the MAS Development and Liaison Subcommittee of the AICPA (1974) considered questions concerning past profit as an "index" of future profit. This work could produce a radical change in the concept of profit.

If direct forecasts of cash flows and other information about the future are given in financial reports, the modern corporate concept of profit might become obsolete as a measure of either past performance or as an index of future performance. In the last analysis, a firm's performance depends on its cash flows, and if information about cash flows were provided by accountants, what purpose would be served by reporting profit figures that are based on conventional methods in accounting? And what purpose would be served by forecasting future profits, if direct estimates of future cash flows already were available? Questions like these will inevitably arise when more attention is devoted to the subject of uncertainty.[3]

Third, if the traditional opposition to forecasting and estimation overrides the current effort being made in some quarters to integrate forecasting and estimation problems within the mainstream of accounting theory, then the lesson of history will not have been learned. For most de-

[3] See, e.g., Thomas (1974).

bate in accounting inevitably must lead to a discussion of uncertainty about the future. This is the one area of thought which nineteenth century accountants were unable to deal with, and twentieth century accountants have not yet faced the problem squarely.

REFERENCES

Committee Reports:

American Institute of Certified Public Accountants, Study Group on the Objectives of Financial Statements, *Objectives of Financial Statements* (1973).

American Institute of Certified Public Accountants, Forecasting Task Force of the MAS Development and Liaison Subcommittee, March 28, 1974 Exposure Draft, *Standards for Systems for the Preparation of Financial Forecasts* (1974).

Journal Articles:

Brief, R. P., "Nineteenth Century Accounting Error," *Journal of Accounting Research* (Spring 1965), pp. 167–77.

———, "The Origin and Evolution of Nineteenth Century Asset Accounting," *Business History Review* (Spring 1966), pp. 1–23.

———, "Depreciation Theory in Historical Perspective," *The Accountant* (December 26, 1970), pp. 737–39.

——— and Owen, J., "The Estimation Problem in Financial Accounting," *Journal of Accounting Research* (Autumn 1970), pp. 167–78.

Hawes, D. W., "Towards a More Muscular Audit," New York *Times*, April 14, 1974.

Hawkins, D. F., "The Development of Modern Financial Reporting Practices Among American Manufacturing Corporations," *Business History Review* (Autumn 1963), pp. 135–168.

van Pelt III, J. V., "The Future of Accepted Accounting Principles," A Digest of the 1971–72 Gold Medal Award Winning Article, *Management Accounting* (August 1972), pp. 11–14.

Books:

Chatfield, M., *A History of Accounting Thought* (Dryden Press, 1974).

Dickinson, A. L., *Accounting Practice and Procedure* (Ronald Press, 1914).

Dicksee, L. R., *Auditing*, 10th ed., (Gee & Co., 1915).

Edwards, E. O. and Bell, P. W., *The Theory and Measurement of Business Income* (University of California Press, 1965).

Hatfield, H. R., *Modern Accounting—Its Principles and Some of Its Problems* (D. Appleton & Co., 1927).

Kehl, D., *Corporate Dividends—Legal and Accounting Problems Pertaining to Corporate Distributions* (Ronald Press, 1941).

Leake, P. D., *Depreciation and Wasting Assets* (Henry Good & Son, 1912).

Matheson, E., *Depreciation of Factories*, 4th ed., (E. & F. Spon, 1910).

Pixley, F. W., *Auditors: Their Duties and Responsibilities*, 4th ed., (Henry Good & Son, 1887).

Edited Books:

May, G. O., *Twenty-Five Years of Accounting Responsibility 1911–1936*, B. S. Hunt, ed. (American Institute Publishing Co., 1936).

Montgomery, R. H. ed., *Dicksee's Auditing*, 2nd ed. (New York, 1909).

Series:

APB Accounting Principles, Current Text as of June 30, 1973 (Commerce Clearing House, 1973).

Mautz, R. K. and Sharaf, H. A., *The Philosophy of Auditing*, American Accounting Association Monograph Number Six (American Accounting Association, 1961).

Thomas, A. L., *The Allocation Problem: Part II*, Studies in Accounting Research #9 (American Accounting Association, 1974).

ON THE PROGRESS OF ACCOUNTANCY AND THE DUTIES WHICH COME WITHIN THE SCOPE OF AN ACCOUNTANT'S PRACTICE (1881)

Adam Murray

In this earliest published article on accountant's responsibilities, the author surveys the principal accounting duties--bankruptcy and liquidation, company winding up, auditing, estate and trust accounting--and describes the qualifications and knowledge practitioners must have to perform these tasks.

MANCHESTER SOCIETY OF CHARTERED ACCOUNTANTS.

At a meeting of the members, held on the 13th inst., an address was delivered by the President (Mr. A. Murray) "On the Progress of Accountancy and the Duties which come within the scope of an Accountant's Practice." The following is the text of the address:—The grant to Public Accountants of a Royal Charter of Incorporation, by the name of "The Institute of Chartered Accountants in England and Wales," marks an epoch in the history of accountancy, and it is believed that such a public recognition of the profession will undoubtedly secure for the community the existence of a class of persons trained and well qualified to undertake the responsibility devolving on public accountants; while it will, at the same time, be attended with advantages to accountants themselves. The history of public accountancy extends over a comparatively recent period, having been but little practised as a distinct occupation previous to the end of the last century. At that time the trade and commerce of the country were limited in extent as compared with what they are in our day, and the work now undertaken by accountants would then be entrusted to solicitors and others, as it was not sufficient to find employment for those who would have been prepared to follow accountancy as a separate calling. In entering upon the history of accountancy, reference ought not to be omitted to that admirable system of book-keeping which came to us from the Italians, when Venice was the great entrepôt of Eastern commerce, before the English were heard of on the ocean. Upon book-keeping on the Italian or double entry method some hundreds of treatises have been written from about the middle of the sixteenth century to the present time, chiefly upon mercantile accounts. Of the efficacy of this system—which is simplicity itself combined with perfection—evidence is given by the adoption of it by so many. Into every well-regulated establishment this system of accounts has forced its way, and any business without it is imperfect. Except on such a system our banking, insurance, and all other large establishments, could not be assured of the accuracy of their accounts, and without it the departmental accounts of any large manufacturing or other concern would be unreliable. The title of "Accountant" in its more restricted sense seems to have been applied (as indeed it is now) to those who were at the head of large departments or offices, such as the India House, banks, and other establishments. In Bailey's Dictionary, under date 1770, the meaning attached to the word was—"One well versed in adding up accounts;" but the profession of public accountant seems then to have been unknown. As the population of England increased, and, what is more important to our subject, the trade of the country began to develop, necessity would, no doubt, arise for public accountancy, which is supposed to have been taken up as a separate business about the year 1790 by a few individuals in the principal towns. According to the directory for 1825, there were then in Manchester only 13 practising as public accountants. Contrasting the number at that time with those at present following the profession, the increase may appear large, but it is, in all probability, only in proportion to the growth of the commerce and wealth of the country. The great increase has taken place within the present century, our various industries being developed and extended by the discoveries and inventions of modern times. Public accountants have now for many years been admitted to be a necessity as much as lawyers and medical men. Those having the control of accounts of large undertakings, such as railways, banks, and other institutions, are well entitled to be styled accountants by reason of their ability to manage the accounts relating to the particular business with which they may be connected; and although some of them may be able to apply their knowledge in another direction, it is the province of the public accountant, from the special training which he has had, and the wider range of his knowledge of accounts, to inaugurate or improve systems of accounts, and to deal with accounts of the most complicated nature. Our Scotch brethren, more than 25 years since, obtained the distinction which was only last year accorded to English accountants, a Charter being granted to the accountants of Edinburgh in 1854, and to those in Glasgow in 1855. At that time, accountancy was practised by a comparatively small number; and it is to be regretted that the English accountants did not then take steps to place themselves in a position equal to the Scotch Chartered Accountants. It was not until the year 1870 that the London and provincial accountants took any action with a view to the improvement of the status of the profession. The London Institute and Liverpool Society were established in 1870, the Manchester Institute in 1871, the Society of Accountants in England in 1872, and the Sheffield Society in 1877; and by their combined action a Charter was obtained, the members of those societies becoming the first members of the Institute of Chartered Accountants in England and Wales, the number admitted up to a recent date being 1,150. It was part of the petition for incorporation that those becoming candidates for admission into the Institute shall have had a liberal education, both general and professional, and shall also pass examinations in arithmetic and mathematics, general knowledge, languages, science, book-keeping and accounts, the principles of mercantile law, the law of bankruptcy, the winding-up of companies, and general business of accountants. A course of education comprising the above subjects would be valuable, not only as being adapted to the cultivation of the mind, but as furnishing the student with important aids to the efficient discharge of the duties of an accountant. Consequent on the incorporation of accountants as the Institute of Chartered Accountants in England and Wales, the accountants of Manchester and the district agreed to amalgamate the old Manchester Institute of Accountants and the Incorporated Society of Accountants into one society, under the title of "The Manchester Society of Chartered Accountants," having similar objects to those of the Chartered Institute; it being a condition of membership that no person should be eligible for admission to the Manchester society unless at the time of the application he was a member of the Institute. There are now 171 Chartered Accountants in the City and district who are members of the society. A high standard of attainments being thus set up for the future, it will follow that the most important business and appointments will be entrusted to those who, by virtue of their training and qualifications, may be admitted as Chartered Accountants. With the accountants in Edinburgh and Glasgow this has proved to be the case, the number of Chartered Accountants in practice being less than one-half of those accountants who are not Chartered, all important business in connection with the Courts or otherwise being entrusted to the Chartered Accountants; and this will, no doubt, ere long, be so in England. The change will be a great advantage to the community, by whom it will in the course of a few years not only be realised but appreciated, and the importance of it will be readily admitted, inasmuch as the duties which accountants are now called upon to perform, and the various matters upon which they have to advise, are such as to command ability of a high order. It is now proposed to refer shortly to some of the duties which come within the scope of an accountant's practice, without attempting to place them in the order of their importance. By the public we are chiefly recognised as being associated with the misfortunes of others, in the position of receivers and trustees in the estates of bankrupts and liquidating debtors; and in this department our services have been required for many years past, more particularly since the Bankruptcy Act of 1869. There is a mistaken notion that accountants are almost altogether occupied on this class of business, the fact being that of the entire returns of some of them not more than five or ten per cent. arises from being so employed. It may with truth be said that some of the duties connected with the bankruptcy and liquidation department are not of a pleasant kind, and that accountants (preferring good times rather than bad) would willingly aid in reducing the number of liquidations and bankruptcies, but this is a matter which more immediately concerns debtors and creditors. So long as credit is given to the extent to which it has grown, there must of necessity be failures while the present law of bankruptcy exists. In the large number of small liquidations there is evidence of over-credit and over-trading, and accountants, no less than others, must desire that the time will come when credit may be on a sounder basis, so that there may be fewer bad debts. Accountants throughout the country have made suggestions from time to time with a view to the improvement of the Law of Bankruptcy; and the Manchester Society in June last sent to the Prime Minister, the President of the Board of Trade, and others, suggestions on the Bill introduced into the House of Commons during last session. The opinion of the Manchester accountants is that in the Act of 1869 there is little improvement to be made beyond a few amendments indicated by them, viz.:—The regulation of votes by proxy; A complete system of local official audit; Separate banking accounts for all estates exceeding £50. Of the above suggestions that of an audit is probably the most important, and it might be either local or by the Comptroller, as in the case of bankruptcies. In addition to this, the system of rendering summary accounts to the creditors, showing the realisation and the expenses, has been received by creditors with much satisfaction. Complaints are made as to the excessive costs which are incurred in connection with liquidations and bankruptcies; and there may be cases in which this is true, but we know, and so do creditors, of liquidations in which important questions have been settled without litigation, and thousands of pounds of costs have been saved. It must be a satisfaction to many that they have been associated with solicitors who have effected compromises, where they could properly do so, and thus secure the largest possible dividends to creditors. Cases of bankruptcies and liquidations could be instanced in which the costs and charges of solicitors and trustees have not exceeded from two to five per cent. on the assets. Whatever changes may take place in bankruptcy law, the services of accountants are not likely to be entirely dispensed with; as in mercantile estates of any magnitude, with complications in connection with bill transactions and otherwise, they will no doubt still be required. In estates in bankruptcy or in liquidation by arrangement, an accountant has not only to be well acquainted with the law of bankruptcy, but he must also know something of the law of partnership; of principal and agent; of general and specific liens; stoppage in transitu; appropriation of payments; principal and surety; of fraudulent preferences; the right to follow goods purchased on commission, and the distinction between such purchases for an English customer and for a foreign customer; also the rights of creditors where goods have been purchased on joint account. He must likewise be familiar with the rights of creditors to prove on bills of exchange, and the course to be taken where a proof has been made on the English as well as the foreign house of a failed firm, in which case the dividend from the latter may have to be brought into hotchpot. He should also be able to distinguish between direct security and collateral, in order to determine whether the security ought to be deducted from a debt or not. In considering these and other questions, he will have frequent occasion to refer to "Robson on Bankruptcy," or some other similar work. The rights of mortgagees to fixtures attached to the freehold have also to be considered, the law in connection with which has been altered as regards mortgages since the Bills of Sale Act, 1879. It also becomes needful in the course of his practice to make himself acquainted with the legal decisions which take place from time to time on the various questions which arise as to the rights of creditors. Without special experience and knowledge of this kind, he would be met with difficulties in preparing an important statement of affairs, including the accounts,—not only of an English house, but it may be of one foreign house or more, together with a deficiency account explaining the losses which may have taken place for a period of years. He may also have to make himself acquainted with the currency and exchange of various countries. This branch is a very important one, and there is probably a greater variety of knowledge to be acquired in connection with it than any other. Each new case that may be taken up reveals some new point which has not arisen in our previous experience. Should the Bill of the President of the Board of Trade be introduced again, and become law, the bulk of estates in bankruptcy and liquidation may pass into the hands of official receivers. Whether this will be attended with advantage and satisfaction to the creditors, is a matter of doubt. The result is more likely to be as predicted by Lord Sherbrooke, who, after describing the Court of Bankruptcy as "a temple of ruin and failure, into which "vast sums were poured, but comparatively little ever came out," goes on to say—"The President of the Board of Trade would add "yet one more to the tragical list of unsuccessful experiments." And again—"I see no reason to lead me to suppose that a "different fate awaits it from that which has overtaken so many "of its predecessors." If asked what he would propose instead, Lord Sherbrooke answers—"Nothing," and would leave debtors and creditors to the common law of England, with a shortening of the Statute of Limitations. The result, in his opinion, would be a great reduction of credit, with improved management of business; but we shall probably all be agreed that it would be simply impracticable to dispense altogether with bankruptcy law. The winding-up of companies of various kinds requires an entirely different class of experience, including an acquaintance with the Companies Acts, and such books as that by Buckley and others, the law of companies being entirely distinct from that of bankruptcy, except where assimilated by the Judicature Act of 1875. In this branch we have some times to take part in what may be describedas a *post mortem* examination, going back to the formation of the company to see that shareholders have had all that was promised by vendors, and reporting upon the causes of disastrous results, which may lead to the prosecution of vendors, directors, and others. This class of business is not free from the disagreeable element any more than bankruptcy practice, there being duties in connection with it which we have to discharge regardless of consequences, or, it may be, hardships in individual cases, the liquidator being for the time an officer of the court. There is a provision in the Companies Act, 1867, that shares shall be deemed to be held subject to the payment of the amount in cash, unless otherwise determined by contract in writing filed with the Registrar of Joint Stock Companies at or before the issue of the shares. Many questions have arisen upon this section, and shareholders who held shares under an agreement which had not been registered have been compelled to pay the amount of their shares when companies have gone into liquidation. There are other duties of a pleasanter nature, and to which many accountants have devoted much attention. That of audits requires special care and experience. As the accounts of which an audit is now required include those of banks, insurance companies, and various companies connected with so many of our manufacturing industries, it will be apparent that it is an advantage to an auditor to have a wide range of knowledge of business which he may readily bring to bear upon the accounts of any company whose affairs may come under his review. He should be careful to see that additions to property and plant, as well as depreciation, are shown on the balance sheets, so that shareholders may see for themselves and form an opinion as to the deductions made. On the subject of depreciation a great deal may be said: for instance, it is sometimes asked whether it is correct to write off depreciation as a percentage calculated upon the original value or upon the reduced amount only; or again, whether the right course is not to estimate the life of an article, then deduct from the cost what may be considered the value of the article at the end of the term, and write off the balance by a uniform half-yearly or yearly amount during the entire period, after taking into account interest on the original cost, or on the balance as reduced from time to time. In the case of a colliery lease, the latter mode appears to be the only sound principle of depreciation; and although we seldom see it carried out in practice, it at once commends itself to our approval, because the duration of the lease is known, whereas the life of a machine is uncertain, and any mode of depreciation of machinery is at the best arbitrary, and ought to be tested at intervals by a valuation, as is the practice in many large concerns. Mr. John Mather wrote a very able paper some years since upon depreciation which is well worthy of perusal, and in which there is much matter for thought for accountants. It is also for an auditor to see that a balance-sheet is in a form not open to objection, and that it may not be misleading. It is, however, the case that some balance-sheets cannot be considered otherwise than unsuitable—to say the least—being only in a transition state between a trial balance and a balance-sheet; some such balance-sheets being issued to shareholders showing on the one side thereof the gross profits for the period without deduction, the expenses being entered on the other side of the balance-sheet as an asset. Now it can scarcely be contended that a balance-sheet is perfect until the expenses have been written off, and only the net amount of profits shown in the balance-sheet; but the printed balance-sheet of one company goes even further than this, the profits being shown without deduction of expenses, which do not appear on the other side of the balance-sheet as a specific item, but are included either under the head of property, book debts, cash, or some other asset. An auditor must be perfectly independent, being appointed in the general interest of the company, and between the directors and the outside shareholders. He has sometimes occasion to confer and advise with the directors upon questions which may arise, and, although it very rarely happens, he may feel bound—as has been the case—to decline to sign a balance-sheet. The office of auditor is one of great responsibility, as he has not only to verify the profit and loss account, but examine the securities by enumeration; and he must be careful to ascertain that outstanding debts are not upheld after they are either bad, doubtful, or may have been received, the cash not having been accounted for. There was an extraordinary instance of the latter kind a few years since, in which arrears apparently outstanding had really been received, the defalcations in that case amounting to many thousands of pounds. Allowances, returns, &c., should be carefully verified.

Some extraordinary blunders were discovered in the accounts of a company in this neighbourhood a few years since. Errors were found to have been made in the stocktakings of previous periods, there not being a balance-sheet; and finally a payment of £4,000 was taken into account *twice*, in the property and asset items—not intentionally, but in the most perfect innocence,—the result of course being, that the accounts showed a surplus—*apparent* only, not real,—and dividends were paid on the assumption that the accounts were correct, although some connected with the company doubted their accuracy. The officials and auditors were not experts at accounts, or they would have found out the error by a comparison of the balance of floating assets at the beginning of the period and as they existed at the end of the period. The over-payment of dividends was corrected out of subsequent profits. In dealing with the balance-sheet of a limited company, an auditor would be expected to know that it is illegal to add interest to the cost of buildings during construction, and to allow such interest to shareholders by crediting them with the same as received on account of calls; but this is the practice with many companies. If he should have the misfortune to sign a balance-sheet, the accuracy of which was afterwards doubted, he would be liable with directors to a criminal prosecution, whether he signed the balance-sheet innocently or knowing it to be wrong. There is a wide field for this branch of accountancy in the audit of corporation accounts, it having become more general within the last few years to have a professional audit of such accounts, not only because of irregularities and defalcations which have taken place, but for the purpose of having such accounts placed upon a better system. In most cases the statements issued by corporations are little more than summaries of the treasurer's accounts, with the addition of balance-sheets for some of the departments, the latter, however, being imperfect and without any connection between the balance-sheet for one year and that of the previous year. It has not been thought needful to have a revenue account showing the actual income and expenditure, but to accept the treasurer's account of receipts and payments, which has been misleading, if supposed to show the revenue account for the year. Due regard also has not been paid to the creation of sinking funds for the redemption of capital and interest, as required by the various Acts of Parliament, the provision for which ought to be clearly shown, as having been made out of the various revenue accounts. The treatment of the accounts for life annuities, which are granted by some corporations, is also but imperfectly understood by those having the control of the department, as may be seen by the perusal of the accounts relating thereto. It is incredible that the accounts of some corporations should have been allowed to go on for so many years without attempts being made to place accounts of such magnitude upon a complete system, so as to bring the entire accounts into an amalgamated balance-sheet, showing at one view the whole of the liabilities, property and assets, with the changes which have taken place therein from year to year, and the additions to sinking fund and surplus fund. It is somewhat difficult to believe that there are not among corporation officials those who are competent to undertake such a task, and yet it would appear to be so, or that those who have the capacity are not allowed to use it for that purpose. There are, no doubt, able business men among the members of town councils, who, being familiar with accounts, have desired an improvement in those of their corporation, but who have had a difficulty in persuading others of the importance and necessity of accuracy and clearness in their accounts. The time, however, seems to have come when ratepayers will not be content with anything less than such information in a summary form as to their municipal affairs as they would require in connection with their own business as individuals.

There is another branch in which accountants have probably been more continuously and steadily employed than in any other, that is in the management of and in the keeping of accounts of executorship and trust estates. This portion of their duties might suitably have received special notice in the petition for the Charter, but it seems to have been entirely overlooked. There are some accountants in Manchester who are almost altogether occupied with this class of business, the number of estates in their care varying, it may be from 10 to 100 or upwards, and this part of the occupation of accountants with that of auditing are, perhaps, more deserving of attention than any other, and certainly there is as much or more care and accuracy required in these departments. In the first place, in an important estate, the accountant usually takes part in the preparation of an estimate of the personal estate of a testator, in order to the proving of the will, and he should know what personal estate is subject to probate duty; what foreign property ought to be included, and what is exempt. It is not unusual to fall into the error of including property which will never come into the hands of the executors; and a case which has happened may be mentioned, that of including personal property which was subject to a limited power of appointment, the result in that case being that, when the error was pointed out, probate duty was returned to the amount of some hundreds of pounds. In addition to looking to the return of probate duty on the ground of error, it has been part of the duty of the accountant to see that duty has also been returned on account of debts. In the case of important trusts including life interests, he has to see to the apportionment of rents, interests, and dividends, up to the death of a testator as well as that of a life tenant, and of accruing dividends included in the purchase of stocks for investment as well as in the sales of stocks. In connection with this subject, those having practised for a considerable time past, must have had some acquaintance with the various Apportionment Acts, including those of the years 1834 and 1870. It is also important to see that the capital to which those in remainder may be entitled is preserved for them, as executors have been known to make the mistake of paying to life tenants the full income received, without deducting outgoings; and the result would have been—if this state of things had gone on sufficiently long without being discovered—that the capital would have been materially reduced. In the case of leasehold property for short terms—bequeathed for a life interest—provision should be made for so much of the rent as is capital. Then the preparation of legacy and succession duty accounts devolves upon the accountant, that he may submit such accounts to the solicitors for approval. For this purpose he must necessarily be acquainted with the Legacy Duty and Succession Duty Acts, and the decisions on the cases arising thereon from time to time, which are to be found in the annual reports of the Commissioners of Inland Revenue.

In charging legacy duty paid upon legacies or residue, including accumulations, it is frequently overlooked that the whole of the duty should not be charged to capital, the duty on accumulations being in effect interest upon the duty on the capital, such interest being payable out of income. For the purpose of guiding executors and trustees, and conferring with solicitors, he should also know, in the case of life interests, what interest a life tenant is entitled to, because it has been held in the case of unauthorized investments that the dividends received from certain securities are not applicable to the full extent as income, unless the will has so provided in distinct terms. In connection with executorship estates an accountant will find frequent occasion to refer to such books as "Williams on Executors," and the various books on probate, legacy, and succession duties, including those of Gwynne, Hudson, Thring, Trevor, and the present Comptroller. Material changes have been made as to the probate and legacy duties by the new Act of the last session. The Real Estate Charges Act of 1854, and a subsequent Act, made an important alteration as to the payment of mortgage debts which previously were payable out of personal estate. Where trust estates are the subject of a suit in Chancery, the accountant has to prepare for the court the usual accounts which are required, together with the vouchers for payments. He may also have to attend counsel and the chief clerk to give explanations, and he should be well versed in the practice of the Court. In Chancery suits, where a receiver is required to collect debts and income, an accountant is usually appointed. Among the various duties for which the services of accountants are sought, they are not unfrequently asked to place the accounts of a business upon an improved system, not only for the purpose, it may be, of the satisfaction of partners, and to secure accuracy, but to prevent those irregularities which may arise where the accounts of a business are not kept upon a method which checks itself. As a rule, there is unwillingness on the part of those principals who have very little knowledge of accounts to have any change made in the system until some necessity has arisen. Not unfrequently it is found that at a stocktaking some important asset has been altogether overlooked, or there may have been some irregularity in the cash; and then principals begin to consider whether some change should not be made. There have been cases in which irregularities extending over years have been discovered which might have been prevented had proper precautions been taken in time. Double-entry is a bogie to many which they take fright at, on the ground that it would involve important changes; whereas nothing more is required than the entries which are in their books in order to prepare a profit and loss account, to prove the accuracy of the whole of the accounts; but many prefer to continue on the old-fashioned "stocktaking," and are content to assume that the correct result is the difference between the apparent capital at the beginning of the period, and at the end, without any proof of the accuracy thereof; and there are numerous large concerns the accounts of which are not on any better system. In actions before the courts involving questions of account, references are frequently made by the judges of both divisions of the High Court of Justice to accountants that they may report; and in other cases they are appointed arbitrators to settle partnership and other differences. The accounts of firms in voluntary liquidation also come before accountants for adjustment. In such cases the outstanding assets, as well as the nominal capital of the partners, have to be treated in a special manner for the allowance of interest to the respective partners on their capital. Accountants are also instrumental in negotiating partnerships, the affairs of which they may be acquainted with. In partnership changes it is not unusual for solicitors to submit draft articles of partnership to accountants for their opinion whether they are consistent with the balance-sheet and accounts of the firm. A knowledge of the Income Tax Act of 1842 and subsequent Acts is valuable to an accountant, that he may assist his clients in making their returns, or in making a claim for repayment of duty overpaid. There are many other ways in which the services of accountants are useful which might be mentioned, but to do so would extend this address to an unsuitable length. Accountancy is not a science in which it can be said that any great improvements have taken place, the scope of it being limited, and not capable of being advanced to any considerable extent. The old-fashioned journalising and elaborate system of bookkeeping have to a great extent been dispensed with or shortened, being found so cumbrous. As far as possible, preference is now given to the use of books in which original entries are made, bookkeeping being simplified thereby, and by the columnised invoice book, day book, cash book, and other books. A great saving of labour is thus effected, while at the same time greater accuracy is secured. The difficulty in obtaining a balance of books containing a large number of accounts is reduced by the introduction of check books or sheets by which a ledger or series of ledgers may be balanced separately, as is the practice in banks, savings banks, &c. In this address it has been attempted to draw attention to accountancy in its various branches, not at length, but with a general reference to each, in the hope that others may take up such of the subjects as they may be specially interested in. Sufficient, however, has probably been said to show the importance of the duties which an accountant may have to perform, and to induce those whose intention it is hereafter to follow the profession to fit themselves for it in its several departments. Accountants now occupy such positions of trust and confidence, the books of many companies, firms, and individuals being open to them, securities to large amounts being in their possession, and having the collection of assets it may be to the amount of some hundreds of thousands of pounds even in one liquidation without giving any security, that they must be men who have been tried, or whose habits are such as to command the respect and confidence of the public. In a business having a general practice, it will also be evident that they must have the aptitude to apply their knowledge to a great variety of matters, and this is one feature of accountancy which makes it enjoyable, that there is a constant change of occupation and thought. Any one preparing for the profession will find the advantage of studying such tables as those of Inwood, making himself thorough master of them, if need be, by compiling other tables at rates of interest which are not given in Inwood, because he will certainly, in the course of a long and varied experience, frequently be called upon to settle questions in which those tables are required; for instance, in dealing with instalments for wagons hired on deferred payment, there is often a great difficulty raised even with accountants, as to the proportion thereof to be charged to capital and to revenue. Now, as to this, there need not be any difficulty; the personal account in the books of a purchaser of wagons on hire ought to be dealt with as an ordinary purchase, adding the interest charged thereon, and writing off the instalments, so that at the end of the term the account would work itself out. In such a case as this Inwood's tables would be found to be useful, as well as in ascertaining the instalments to be written off the value of a lease over an unexpired term, including interest thereon: also in connection with sinking funds for the redemption of capital and interest, and in estimating the present value of reversions—these calculations properly come within actuarial science, which must not be considered as having reference only to matters connected with life assurance, annuities, &c. The word "actuary" seems to be understood now as applying only to insurance management, more particularly in connection with life insurances, but the earlier meaning of the word was "shorthand writer." The study and practice of actuarial science will be invaluable, and will be brought into frequent requisition in the higher branches of accountancy. It may be supposed from what has preceded that accountants may take too much legal responsibility upon themselves; but this is not the intention, and it is not found to be so in practice. It is a consequence of their calling to acquire a legal knowledge in the course of their experience, and questions of law are so constantly arising in connection with accounts, that the two are inseparable. It is *expected* by solicitors from accountants that they shall have a legal knowledge, which, of course, becomes useful, and without which they would not, for instance, be able to prepare a reliable statement of the affairs of a mercantile firm having English and foreign houses, because the preparation of such a statement would depend upon the law of the country in which the foreign house was situate, and whether the liabilities of that house would be payable out of the foreign assets or otherwise. It being the practice for accountants to present to a meeting of creditors such a statement of affairs, the legal position has of necessity to be referred to in the course of explaining such a statement, in order to make it intelligible. Many legal points arise in such an important case, and, indeed, in many ordinary liquidations. Again, an accountant becomes familiar with wills, and is usually able to read them correctly; and the same with articles of partnership, with which he will have to do in the settlement of partnership accounts. It must not be supposed from this that accountants will go beyond their province; they will rather confer with the solicitors and take their instructions. An old solicitor used to say—"You find facts and accounts, and I will find law;" and this being the true view to take, accountants will be careful to observe it. Their knowledge of law will assist them in finding such facts as they know will be wanted, and in arranging those facts in a suitable way in order that the solicitors may deal with them and advise upon them. Our old Manchester Institute did some good work in its time, and among the papers read were contributions from Mr. Chadwick, Mr. Thomas, Mr. C. F. Richardson, Mr. Mather, and Mr. Owen, as well as an exhaustive synopsis of proposed bankruptcy changes by our indefatigable Honorary Secretary, Mr. Trevor. We ought not to neglect the use of our Society as the medium of giving expression to our opinions upon all questions incident to the business of our profession, thus distributing the information we possess. In each of our offices the experience we have acquired is spread over and gained concurrently by those whose valuable assistance we willingly acknowledge; and it must be an advantage when individual experience is extended to as many as possible, because in that way our general usefulness is promoted. The pleasant duty must not be overlooked of a reference to the *Accountant* newspaper, which has now been issued weekly for some years past, containing valuable reports and information on matters pertaining to accountancy. The conductors of that journal are at all times ready to open its columns to us, and its usefulness will be increased when other subjects are discussed by some of its contributors. This interchange of views and experience is one of the pleasures we have in the pursuit of our profession, which is not devoid of agreeable associations—apart from the money result to us, in which there is only satisfaction to us when we have the consciousness of duty discharged—and another pleasure is the feeling of usefulness which we have in all that we undertake. Along with our legal knowledge, and partly arising out of it, we have to exercise judicial functions in dealing out even-handed justice, as there are very few, if any, of our duties in which we have not various interests to consider, and to endeavour to do what is right and best for all. Our younger members would derive great advantage from attending the law and jurisprudence and other classes at the Victoria University. From the limited business of the few who initiated public accountancy, there has been created a numerous distinct class who have set themselves apart to its study and practice, and who deservedly enjoy the confidence of the public, gained by their business qualifications and honourable conduct. It would be difficult to select a calling with greater attractions than accountancy, and those who intend to follow such an honourable occupation may well be encouraged to do so. Public accountants have now a legal status under the Charter, and those who may in future avail themselves of its privileges will occupy a higher position than others, by reason of the length of service required from them as articled clerks, and the strict examinations—preliminary, intermediate, and final—which they must pass, and that, before being admitted as a Fellow, each must have been in practice for five years as a public accountant. For the due prosecution of accountancy—ranging as it does over a wide field—varied attainments are required. These need not be brilliant, as moderate ability will achieve much when accompanied with steady application—an important essential—without which there will not be much accomplished. The work in the early years of practice is arduous and attended with anxiety, but as experience increases, the duties of our profession become lighter and pleasant, gaining as we do habits of self-reliance by the need which is placed upon us of looking at important questions for ourselves. To the community there will hereafter be a guarantee of the efficiency and respectability of chartered accountants as a body. To individual members the future will, in a great measure, be what each may make it for himself; and it is important to every one that his career shall be such as will bring satisfaction to himself in the confidence and approval of the public, which will certainly attend the conscientious discharge of the important interests intrusted to us.

Mr. Thos. Browning: Before we enter upon any discussion of this paper, there is an obligation which will be felt by every one present, and I rise to move a vote of thanks to our worthy President for his interesting and comprehensive paper. [*Applause.*] It embraces a wide and complete view of the business and duties of accountants, and his large experience, extending over so many years, has enabled him to give an amount of information which probably is almost peculiar to himself.

Mr. David Smith, Vice-President of the Society: I second the motion. I do not think any of us ever listened to a more elaborate resumé of the capabilities necessary for an efficient discharge of our duties. I think the paper has touched upon every form in which experience may be required. We have been told what an accountant ought to know; but the subject of what an accountant ought not to know has been avoided. There is a field there for some one to write a paper upon. [*Laughter.*] One thing struck me while Mr. Murray was speaking, and it is this,—that since we got a charter, we are often called upon to look at accounts for the sake of getting our signatures. It is useful to some people sometimes to say that their accounts have been looked over by Mr. so and so, chartered accountant. ["*Hear, hear.*"] I think we ought to make up our minds that no more superficial examinations of accounts or signing of our names shall be tolerated. [*Applause.*] That unless we have the books placed properly in our hands, and we are allowed to satisfy ourselves of their accuracy, we shall not, for the sake of earning a small fee, attach our names as chartered accountants to any document at all. [*Applause.*] And also as regards partnership matters, I think Mr. Murray's remarks were very happy. In times past, the preparation of partnership deeds was begun the wrong way about. I think the heads of a partnership deed ought to be set down by the accountant, who knows the business, and who could very often put down under a few heads what the lawyer would like to have, instead of the loose and not altogether easily understood statements of the people who go to give instructions.

Mr. Popplewell: I rise to support the motion, and to suggest that our President be asked to allow his paper to be printed. [*Applause.*]

Mr. Browning: I gladly adopt the suggestion, and I am sure Mr. Smith will support me in doing so.

The motion as amended was carried unanimously.

The President: I thank you very much for your vote of thanks. I had great pleasure in preparing the address, and I am, naturally, glad if it should be of any use whatever to any of the members. I am afraid it was a little lengthy; but still, on entering upon the subject, it seemed difficult to do otherwise than go over the whole of the branches. I have long wished to do something of this kind, as I thought there might be use in it, and my principal object has been, that it might lead others to take up the various subjects referred to. I think it would be very interesting at our meetings to have papers read, and unless this be so I do not see as much advantage in our meetings. I just omitted one or two points which I had intended to mention, and I am glad Mr. Smith has referred to some of them. In our business despatch is very important, and that I had overlooked. We sometimes get into a little discredit, I think, through not getting matters closed up quickly. I do not think it pays any of us to keep work. (*Applause.*) The sooner we get it out of hand, I think, the better, and it leaves room for something more to come. (*Applause.*) As to Mr. Smith's remarks on partnership articles, they are just the experience of myself and of many others. I have no doubt that when we get draft articles submitted to us, they rarely have to be very materially altered. ("*Hear, hear.*") I have only to thank you again for your vote of thanks. As to printing the paper, it will be very pleasing to me, if you think there is anything in it to make it worth printing. (*Applause.*)

"ACCOUNTANTS" AND ACCOUNTANTS (1884)

Editorial from The Accountant

Concerning the perennial question of professional identity.

"ACCOUNTANTS" AND ACCOUNTANTS.

DURING the last few days, persons claiming to be accountants have come before the public in ways which do not redound to the credit of the profession, in at least three instances.

The most noteable of these is Mr. John Yates Mawson, of Wigan, who styled himself an accountant and sharebroker. This gentleman was in the confidence of his neighbours and held various public positions. He was secretary to the Wigan Tramway Company; secretary to the Wigan Provident Permanent Building Society; a town councillor; and, as a sharebroker, was entrusted to make investments for the Lancashire and Cheshire Miners' Permanent Relief Society. Urgent private affairs suddenly requiring Mr. Mawson's presence abroad, he hurriedly departed, forgetting in the haste of his departure to account for sums of money which had been placed in his hands for investment, and his former friends and business acquaintances are so anxious to know his whereabouts, that several warrants have been issued, and descriptions of the fugitive are posted at the various police stations. It is supposed that he has fled to Spain. We are glad to say this gentleman was not a member of the Institute, and we are informed his defalcations were brought to light by the strict audit of the Miners' Relief Society's accounts, by a firm of Chartered Accountants.

The next instance is that of the defendant company, in the action of Gantlett v. The Grosvenor Bank and Discount Company. In this case, some curious revelations as to the *personel* of those connected with the above so-called bank, together with their mode of conducting business, were made to the outside public. The plaintiff however won the day, and a verdict in his favour with heavy damages was given. We do not propose to comment on the whole case, but the sub-manager's cross-examination is noteworthy. It was elicited that he was formerly a greengrocer, and he modestly added that he had had some experience as an accountant. In the celebrated case of Bardell v. Pickwick, Serjeant Buzfuz led the jury to believe that there was some hidden meaning in the words "chops and tomato sauce," inferring that the epistle containing those words was a fervent declaration of love, but we think it would puzzle even the learned serjeant to show the connection between greens and accountancy. Does the retailing of bunches of turnips and pounds of potatoes with the consequent book entries therefor, entitle a person to call himself an accountant? Hardly, we should imagine. We need scarcely say that the Charter has not been elastic enough to include him among the members.

The effrontery with which gentlemen, at a loss to know what business title to assume, take that of accountant, is on a par with that of those ladies of easy virtue, who when found brawling in the Haymarket in the small hours of the morning, and subsequently having an interview with the magistrate at Marlborough Street, in response to the latter's query as to their profession, or occupation, invariably reply "Please, your worship I am an actress."

The third case is that of an accountant summoned by the Incorporated Law Society, for pretending to be a solicitor, and which resulted in a fine of forty shillings with one guinea costs. This case somewhat differs from the two others, as the defendant stated that he acted in ignorance of the law, and doubtless took what he supposed the best steps in the interest of his client. He however, was not a Chartered Accountant.

It however, raises a point which, although decided against accountants, is of some importance: and that point is, as to whether accountants employed in the exercise of their profession in getting in accounts, should not be allowed to charge the cost of their services to the debtor instead of the creditor. Lawyers have this privilege, why not Chartered Accountants?

These repeated attempts to pose as members of an honourable profession, should induce all who have not yet availed themselves of membership of the Institute, to do so, and then the term "Accountant" will gradually give way to "Chartered Accountant," when anyone wrongfully describing himself by the latter title will doubtless be prosecuted by the Institute for usurping a title to which he has no claim.

ACCOUNTANTS AND THE PUBLIC (1885)

J.G. Griffiths

<u>As members of a relatively new profession, accountants must educate clients and the public concerning their duties and powers. This applies especially to those "dangerous clients" who expect more of the accountant than he can or should perform.</u>

CHARTERED ACCOUNTANTS' STUDENTS' SOCIETY OF LONDON.

AN ADDRESS BY THE PRESIDENT (MR. J. G. GRIFFITHS, F.C.A.)

In addressing you this evening, I have not taken as my subject any of the special branches of the work entrusted to the members of the profession to which you are ultimately to belong, nor have I thought it desirable to endeavour to give you any instruction on the many matters of business and practice which have had your consideration during the past year, and to which the various lecturers to whom you have listened have directed your attention.

I have thought that, as your president, I might speak to you with some hope of being of use on a subject less directly affecting the training you are now receiving, but having a distinct bearing on the nature of the profession and upon the duties you will eventually be called upon to perform.

Our profession is one which can hardly yet be considered to have taken a good hold of the opinion of the public, being at present but very little understood except in our own ranks, and immediate surroundings. I regret to say that outside of this country it is still less appreciated, there being countries in Europe of which the languages possess no real equivalent for the name we bear.

In the English Colonies, but few of our profession exist; in the United States the vocation we follow is hardly known; and in our own country, a large portion of the press, and a considerable number of the educated community, have very little idea of our duties and responsibilities, and are inclined to treat us with a lack of consideration and ordinary fairness which, to those who strive to do their duty, is at times very disappointing.

It is to this position of affairs, and with regard to the steps members of one body should take to remedy this state of ignorance and misconception, that I have ventured to claim your attention to-night.

I wish, therefore, to ask you to consider with me the position we occupy towards the public, and the means we ought to adopt individually to elevate our profession to the rank we should occupy, and to obtain for ourselves the consideration to which, I think, the nature of the duties we fulfil towards the community entitles us, and which, after all, it depends upon ourselves eventually to secure.

It must be admitted that the comparative novelty of our occupation has had much to do with the poor esteem in which we are held by those who, probably in the majority of instances, have never come across a well-trained and able accountant, and only know of us from what they gather from reports of some of our failures; where a skilful forger has, perhaps, evaded the careless audit of an inexperienced beginner; or where, as I regret to admit has happened in the short existence of our Institute, some prominent member of the profession has not met his engagements, or has otherwise failed in the performance of his duties.

We have been very unfortunate, I must confess, in this respect; but I have real hopes for the future.

It should be widely known that, whereas at the formation of the Institute the qualifications for membership were comparatively slight, obliging us to admit at once to our body many individuals we should probably have preferred to submit to some tests, and others we should have gladly excluded had we possessed the power, the present method of recruiting our numbers is by election, after a course of study, and a series of vigorous examinations which will certainly tend to eliminate the inefficient, and will, I venture to assert, in a very short time create a vast improvement in the average class of men engaged in our vocation, and in the quality and character of the work they perform.

And. yet, although I have to admit the failures and misconduct of a few, I feel that I have still good reason to be proud of the profession to which I belong.

Althought hardly known and quite unrecognised a comparatively short time ago, accountants now occupy a most prominent and responsible position in every branch of industry and trade; their assistance is sought, and their advice taken by those responsible for the conduct of all the most important institutions in this country. I find the great banks, railway, telegraph and other important corporations are now, almost without exceptions, audited by Chartered Accountants, and where, in rare instances, other persons are appointed to the duties, they generally have the wisdom to obtain the assistance of Chartered Accountants to enable them to acquit themselves of the responsibilities attaching to the serious duties they undertake.

The duty of conducting the liquidation of Joint Stock Companies and of bankrupts' estates is mainly entrusted to Chartered Accountants, notwithstanding the reckless charges made against them when the last Act affecting Bankruptcy legislation was introduced.

Chartered Accountants are sent all over the Kingdom and to all parts of the World, to examine and report on the affairs of undertakings either in progress or in contemplation, and the most intelligent and far-seeing of our merchants and investors are in the habit of relying, and with great advantage to themselves, on the reports so obtained; investing their money, withdrawing, or with-holding it, according as the accountants' certificates are favourable or the reverse.

It is then a very responsible profession, that of an accountant, and its duties should not be undertaken lightly, nor carelessly performed.

It behoves every member of this Students' Society to remember that when he becomes a member of the Institute, his individual work will be taken by his clients as the index of the merit or otherwise of the work performed by Chartered Accountants as a body, and I would therefore ask you all to bear in mind that each member of the profession can do it harm even if it does not lie in his power to do it, or himself, any good; and that work carelessly performed is not only likely to cause loss to our clients, but is fatal to the reputation of those guilty of neglect, and reflects a stigma on our profession and the Institute.

I will now glance at some of the duties and obligations it will eventually be your privilege to undertake, and endeavour to point out what are the limits within which these should be performed.

Much of the criticism to which we have of late years been subjected has resulted from an ignorance, shared, I fear, by many of our less experienced members, as to what it is possible for a skilled accountant to do and what impossible.

I would draw your particular attention to this, as it will be very essential that this question should invariably be before you whenever you are called upon to conduct any audit or investigation; or to undertake the management or liquidation of any business or estate.

It appears to me to be the rooted opinion of an unenlightened public and of the ignorant portion of the press that an auditor must have failed in his duty if a fraud has been effected, whether it is eventually discovered or not.

It would be as fair to hold doctors responsible for every death, and lawyers for every suit they may fail to gain for their clients.

The result of this ignorance has been that in cases where such frauds have been discovered, an immediate outcry is raised for the dismissal of the auditor. Without any careful investigation of enquiry into the facts, his utter ruin is decreed, and the whole profession is attacked and menaced. Audits performed by us are described as useless, wasteful and dangerous; as deceitful and fraudulent pretences, and as traps laid to catch fees and deceive confiding clients and the public. The society papers publish some satirical observations, the press generally is very severe in its strictures, and the ignorant public find some amusement in condemning us as a body; while, in the end, although we probably individually lose no clients, a real damage is done to us by the depreciation of the general confidence in the thoroughness of our work, and the ability we bring to bear in the performance of our audits.

Now, while all this unreasoning outcry is most cruel and unjust, it would be well to consider whether and to what extent we are responsible for the ignorance that certainly exists as to our powers of control, and our ability to prevent and detect fraud by the process of audit we perform.

Do we avail ourselves of the opportunities we have to make clear to our clients the limits within which it is possible for us to look after their interest? And do we always take care to advise them in what respects the management of the business carried on by them is deficient in safeguards, and of provisions for due check on officials and servants having the control of money, or the manipulation of books and securities?

In many cases this point does not receive the necessary consideration from auditors: and some are inclined to omit this important duty, either because it has never occurred to them as being a part of their work, or because they have not felt disposed to depreciate in the minds of their clients, the absurd estimate they may have formed of the efficacy of the professional accountants' audit.

In my experience I have found men of ordinary business ability holding the most ridiculous opinions as to the power of a professional accountant to detect fraud or error; not having the smallest notion of the nature of the work the auditor undertakes, but carrying on their business with the grossest laxity and without the least personal or other effective control, relying on the auditor, whose fee has been carefully fixed at as low a figure as possible, and expecting, that no matter how reckless may be the management and supervision of the business, the fee paid to the auditor is to be regarded as in the nature of an insurance premium, and is to hold them harmless and free from loss. The auditor, by some magic or by some other means (they do not know or care how) is to prevent any evil result occurring to them in consequence of their own or their subordinate's irregularities, and should any loss occur the auditor is to be blamed, and if possible made to pay.

Now such clients as these are very dangerous ones, and an accountant must be very reckless or careless if he permits himself to be put in this position.

It is the distinct duty of an auditor in such cases to point out to his clients in what respect he has noticed the business to be carried on under deficient management, and how far it lacks the ordinary prudent provisions against losses and frauds; and I would recommend him to put his objections and suggestions in writing, so that in the event of no notice being taken of them, and the evils he anticipated consequently occurring, it may be clear that he did all that lay in his power to enable his client to prevent them, who would moreover be shown to have been forewarned by his responsible adviser, and would be prevented placing the blame where it had no right to lie.

I fear that this course is not adopted by some of the members of our profession, and that consequently a false and most improper sense of security is felt in cases where no security exists; and there occasionally comes a rude awakening, resulting in a feeling of bitter disappointment, and a reckless denunciation of Accountants as useless, and even fraudulent.

On the other hand, I find people who, in the most utter ignorance of what would be the use or nature of the labour they consider necessary, hold strong views as to what is, at any rate, indispensable in any and every audit, whether the business being audited is financial, manufacturing, trading, mining, or professional. The most startling theories are propounded as to the extent of examination an auditor should make before passing accounts submitted for his examination, but I am bound to add that I have not noticed any tendency on the part of the theorists either to extend the time usually allotted to an auditor, or to increase his fees proportionately to the work they urge him to perform.

The fact is, that, as a rule, the fees paid to auditors are fairly adequate having regard to the work they can do with real advantage to their clients, within the time allotted to them, which is usually fixed so that the auditor's report may be received and acted upon while the accounts with which he deals are of real interest, and before they have become a matter of ancient history.

As an instance of the ignorance of some of our advisers, I will ask you to consider the position of the auditor of any of our largest Joint Stock Banks, and the scope of the duties he is called on to perform by some who pretend to lead public opinion.

I have actually seen it stated that the auditor should count all the cash, critically examine all the bills in hand, examine and check all the securities, whether belonging to the bank, or held in respect of advances to customers, or on their account for safe custody, and, in addition to satisfying themselves of the proper statement of the balance-sheet and accounts, as prepared for submission to the shareholders, they are to carefully and completely audit the transactions of the whole year, and should not attach their certificate to the accounts until this colossal work has been fully completed.

I am far from saying that there are not occasions where all this, and more, might prove to be necessary: but it is a little short of ridiculous to state that it is indispensable to an effective audit.

Consider for one moment what would be the position of affairs if this were invariably done. It would be necessary to close the bank on December 31st, and not re-open it until all the securities had been examined, for you cannot examine securities which are being changed from minute to minute.

I should like to ask our critics to tell me what would be the legal position of an auditor who took the keys of a bank's safes and refused to permit the removal of any securities belonging to customers until he had satisfied himself, by actual counting and comparison, that the contents of the safes agreed with the records in the books. Even were this desirable, it would, in my experience, be impossible, except after weeks of incessant labour, with the assistance of as large a staff as the premises would accommodate. In the meantime, customers might apply for their securities in vain, and the whole business of the bank must stop until the auditor's examination had been satisfactorily completed. On these terms, I think, few of the Joint Stock Banks would long require our services; in fact, the suggestion is based on that thorough ignorance of what is practicable, which seems to some people a qualification to advise, rather than a reason for silence, and an occasion for painstaking enquiry and self instruction.

I need hardly tell you that while in small institutions, where the internal control is limited in consequence of the business effected requiring but a small staff, a full and complete examination on somewhat similar lines to those suggested is necessary; but in large institutions where the work is distributed between a great number of employés, it is the province of the auditor to satisfy himself that the checks in existence controlling the operations of each department, and particularly those affecting the custody and manipulation of cash and securities, are in the highest state of efficiency, and when he has satisfied himself on this point, he will find plenty of work, which it is indispensable that he should perform, before he is able to certify the accounts of the bank's operations, without following the directions of these self appointed instructors.

I have taken the example of a bank, because the attention of the public has on several occasions been prominently directed to disclosures of an unsatisfactory nature in the affairs of banking companies.

It is certain that there are no business undertakings in which the services of a Chartered Accountant are more necessary than in the audit of the accounts of banks; and I am desirous to impress upon you where you can be of real value; and, at the same time, I would show you where an examination might be a waste of time, and a serious inconvenience.

The most prominent duty of a bank auditor, as indeed of an auditor of any undertaking, is, that he should take every possible means to satisfy himself of the existence and value of the assets stated on the balance-sheet; he should see that the liabilities are not understated; that the debts are well secured, and of a realisable character; that proper reserves have been made for bad debts, or other contingencies; and that he is not hoodwinked by the introduction among the assets of accounts which an investigation would prove to be valueless.

It is impossible to lay down any fixed rules by which this scrutiny can be effectively performed; nothing but long experience, and assiduous attention, can instruct an auditor fully in this part of his duty, and the method of arriving at the results will have to be varied according to the circumstances and the facilities of examination and enquiry in each separate case; but I would point out that nothing should be taken for granted, and that a strict investigation is essential.

Above all things, an auditor should satisfy himself that the statements to which his certificate is appended, are clear and accurate; there should be no possibility of shareholders and the public being misled, and, while nothing should be disclosed which might be detrimental to the real interests of the undertaking, and of those interested, there should be no chance of the accounts being misunderstood by the intelligent reader.

It is, of course, impossible to avoid misapprehension on the part of ignorant or careless persons, and similarly one cannot prevent wilful misconstructions of statements capable of being easily understood.

At the same time, I have noticed a tendency, particularly with younger members of our profession, to employ technical phraseology where ordinary language would have answered the purpose better; and I have often seen accounts submitted by public accountants which have contained much unnecessary obscurity, and involved statement of account, which a little intelligent care, and thoughtful consideration of what is presumably the occasion of the presentation of accounts, would easily have avoided.

I have, of course, nothing to say to those who intentionally obscure accounts they prepare for the information of the public, or for presentation to persons interested. I trust there are none such connected with this society; but I think you will agree with me that sometimes a little pride is taken by wrong-thinking, but otherwise well-meaning persons, in the puzzle they are able to put together, from originally intelligible accounts, for the mystification of those who are entitled to information and enlightment at our hands.

I cannot too earnestly impress upon such persons that

this is a prostitution of their intelligence, and I would ask you to bear in mind that shareholders and the public have a right to demand from every Accountant, and it is essential to the honour and credit of his profession, that he should state the facts he has to present in a clear, simple and easily understood form; so that those least informed on accounts and their preparation, may be able to understand them, and cannot be misled if they bring to their examination ordinary intelligence and perspicuity.

I think if more attention were given to this point, we should hear less ignorant criticism and should be told less frequently that figures can be made to show anything, and that accountants are in the habit of manipulating and distorting them so as to mystify and mislead rather than instruct.

There is one other point I should like to mention to you before I have done, and this is a very delicate matter, but deserving of your consideration.

It is, be careful how you criticise the work of your colleagues.

Bear in mind that we are now a large and important body, with much of mutual interest; and while I would not have you shield those guilty of negligence, displaying ignorance, or presenting statements evidently prepared for the purpose of misleading; I would ask you to fully inform yourselves and satisfy yourselves that you *are* acquainted with all the facts before you either bring or support a charge against anyone, particularly members of our profession.

Beware also of frivolous fault finding, and do not draw attention to un-essential and minute errors of statement or of judgment; we are all liable to them, and accountants as a body are damaged by differences of opinion between us on matters of no importance.

I ask you to be careful in these respects, because I think it important that we should stand before the public as a united body, having a pride in our profession and the Institute, and jealous of the individual character of its members, and of their reputations.

Let us be open and frank with the public and our clients, endeavour to create a true public opinion of the value of our services, and the scope and limits of our capacity. Let us present ourselves as we are; a specially trained and skilled class of professional men with a natural and educated aptitude for figures, and the preparation and elucidation of accounts. Let us be painstaking and earnest, honest, straightforward, and fearless in the performance of our duties, careful of the reputations of others as well as of our own; anxious to do justice to our clients, to defend them from robbery, fraud or loss; qualified to advise them on the conduct of their business; to inform them of the results of their work and the condition of their affairs; not pretending to extraordinary powers, but patient and industrious, seeking out the truth and stating it clearly and frankly.

By this course and in this manner, I hope to see our profession more widely known, more highly esteemed and more largely employed; and it is to the younger members of the profession, and to those who are training to enter it, that we must look for the full realisation of these most reasonable wishes.

CHARTERED ACCOUNTANTS AS AUDITORS OF COMPANIES (1886)

Ernest Cooper

Legal precedents and statutory requirements did not adequately define the auditor's duties. After giving a history of auditing, the author lists auditor qualifications, which include a knowledge of accounting, law, foreign exchange and actuarial science.

THE

INSTITUTE OF CHARTERED ACCOUNTANTS IN ENGLAND AND WALES.

AUTUMNAL MEETING—(*Continued*).

CHARTERED ACCOUNTANTS AS AUDITORS OF COMPANIES.

By Ernest Cooper, F.C.A.

On the members re-assembling on Friday, Oct. 15, the following paper was read:—

In a profession so varied and complex as that of a Chartered Accountant, there should be little difficulty in finding subjects of interest for consideration at a meeting of members of the Institute.

The three principal branches of our duties, namely, Bankruptcy, Liquidation of Companies, and Auditing, offer a wide field for selection.

Bankruptcy has hitherto engaged the largest share of attention. Royal Commissions and Select Committees have produced bulky Reports containing a mass of evidence available to support every conceivable form of opinion on the subject.

During the past 50 years no less than 30 large Bankruptcy Bills, and many smaller and amending measures have been printed, and some 26 Acts of Parliament have been passed.

Bankruptcy Treatises and works of practice, legal decisions almost innumerable, and pamphlets, newspaper articles and correspondence have appeared, and still appear in an almost continuous stream upon this never-resting subject.

The Law of Companies too has had its Royal Commissions and Select Committees, Blue Books, abortive Bills and Acts of Parliament. The Modern English Company Law may be said to have originated with the Banking Companies Act of 1826, and since then the development has been continuous and rapid.

No less than 50 Public Acts of Parliament relating to Joint Stock Companies have been passed during the past 60 years.[1]

Many treatises have been written and an enormous number of legal decisions have elucidated and settled the law of Companies.

Auditing also is too extensive a subject to be treated as a whole even superficially in a paper of this description, but auditing differs from the two other branches mentioned in having a very limited literature, and never having, I believe, been subjected to a special parliamentary or public enquiry.

The House of Commons Select Committee on Joint Stock Banks in 1836, to which I shall make further reference, and the careful enquiry by the 1864-5 Bankruptcy Committee of the House of Commons into the Audit of Official Assignees and other Bankruptcy Officials' accounts, are the only approximation to public enquiries with which I am acquainted.

Moreover when the nature of the duties and the serious responsibility involved in the office of an auditor are considered, it has remarkably seldom been the subject of judicial decision. The Law Reports for the last 20 years contain, I believe, only 2 or 3 cases which relate directly to the Office of an Auditor.

In Nicol's Case[2] Lord Justice Turner in 1859 held that Auditors were within the scope of their duty as much the Agents of the Shareholders as the Directors were, and that a shareholder was bound by the knowledge of the fraudulent representations which were discoverable by the auditor, and having had the means, through the auditor, of obtaining knowledge, the shareholder could be in no better position than he would have been if he had actual knowledge.

In *Spackman's Case*,[3] before the House of Lords, Lord Cranworth, evidently commenting on the remarks of Lord Justice Turner in Nicol's Case, said "the auditors may be "the agents of the shareholders so far as relates to the audit "of the accounts. For the purpose of the audit the auditors "will bind the shareholders;" and he held (with a qualification) that any special matter contained in the auditor's report as to the state of the accounts and the assets of the company, must be considered as having come to the knowledge of every shareholder. Lord St. Leonards, dissenting generally from the judgment of Lord Cranworth, points out that the report of the auditors would clearly place a *boná fide* purchaser upon enquiry. Lord Chelmsford, dissenting from the view of Lord Justice Turner (and presumably also from that of Lord Cranworth), held that it would be an unreasonable conclusion that the auditors were constituted agents, so as to conclude the shareholders by their knowledge of any unauthorised act of the directors. "It would," he said, (having in view the regulations of the Company in this particular case) "be no part of their office to enquire into the validity "of any transaction appearing in the accounts of the "company."

In *Steele* v. *The Sutton Gas Co.*,[4] it was held that one of joint auditors has power to appoint accountants under Section 108 of the Companies Clauses Act, without the consent of his co-auditor. It was stated in argument, and apparently

(1.) Lindley on Partnerships and Companies, pp. 1525-9.
(2.) 3 De G. & J. 387 & 441.
(3.) L. R. 3 H. L. 171.
(4.) 12 Q. B. D. p. 68.

adopted by the Court, that it is the duty of each auditor to examine the accounts independently of the other, and Baron Huddleston held that each auditor may make a special report, in a case they differ.

In *Bloxham* v. *The Metropolitan Railway*,[5] it was decided that the certificate of the auditors under the Companies Clauses Act, 1845, could not justify the transfer to capital of any charge which belongs to revenue.

In *Holgate* v. *Shutt*,[6] it was held that an account which had been audited, and under the Rules of the Building Society was to be held binding and conclusive, could still be impeached and re-opened on the ground of fraud.

There seem to be few authoritative decisions specially to guide an Auditor as to his duty, or as to his responsibility for negligence, or his liability to damages.

In an action for negligence by a firm of Estate Agents against a firm of Chartered Accountants in 1884 in Birmingham tried by Mr. Justice Wills,[7] some remarks of the Judge as to the measure of damages appear to point to the Auditors being in law liable for the whole amount of loss arising out of their negligence.

Further judicial decisions seem to be wanted on the question how far one of joint Auditors is responsible for the negligence or malversation of his colleague and to what extent one auditor may arrange with his colleague to divide the work, especially in cases where Auditors are resident at a distance from each other in the locality of branches of the concern.

The Audit of the Accounts of Companies and Charities is already to a large extent entrusted to Chartered Accountants, but auditing is still in great part and probably in a large majority of instances, in the hands of unskilled or at least unduly qualified persons.

I have found no reliable means of testing the comparative number of professional and untrained Auditors. In the case of Banks probably a far larger proportion of the Auditors are Chartered Accountants than in other businesses. Out of 128 Banks employing Auditors whose accounts I have referred to, in 99 cases the Auditors are professional accountants, and in 29 cases the auditors are non-professional.

In the Directory of Building Societies a list of 914 Societies in England and Wales is given of which only 81 are audited by Chartered Accountants, or say only 1 in 11.

So long as Companies are claiming confidence in their Balance Sheets and Charities are extracting money from the public on the faith of an audit by persons unqualified for the duty, no apology can be needed for attempting to show cause against the existing state of things.

I propose by examining the nature of the office of an Auditor of a Company to endeavour to ascertain what qualifications the proper discharge of the duties demands, and by examining the nature of the profession of a Chartered Accountant to seek to show that those qualifications are provided in our profession.

First let me do justice to a number of Co-Auditors joined with professional Accountants who have by close attention to the accounts of particular concerns acquired knowledge and training, rendering them amply qualified. Reasons may be advanced in favour of the practice of joining with the professional Auditor one or more shareholders, and I wish to be understood as expressing objection only to audits in which no Chartered Accountant is employed. There seems too small need to make objection in cases where the Auditors are empowered to, and do, employ Chartered Accountants to assist them, or, in other words, to do the technical work for them, but the advantage to Companies of this peculiar arrangement is not easily seen.

Whilst seeking to show that Audits by others than Chartered Accountants cannot in most cases be expected to be efficiently conducted, I shall refrain from any attempt to indicate the manner in which an Audit should be conducted. It seems undesirable, and even impossible, to lay down rules for guiding an Auditor in his work. The objection arises not only in the varied circumstances of each Audit, but also in the different qualities possessed by each Auditor.

(5.) L. R. 8 Ch. 337.
(6.) 27 Ch. D. 111.
(7.) Lea & Son v. Wenham Brothers—*Accountant*, 1884, No. 506, p. 11.

HISTORICAL AND STATUTORY POSITION.

The Office of an Auditor is of some antiquity. It has been said that the use of the word as applied to an examiner of accounts originated with the practice in early times of rendering accounts by word of mouth.[8]

The earliest mention I have found of an Auditor is the following in a Statute of Edw. I. 1285[9] :—

"It is agreed and ordained that when the masters of "such servants do assign Auditors to take their account, "and they be found in arrearages upon the account, all "things allowed which ought to be allowed, their bodies "shall be arrested, and by the testimony of the Auditors "of the same Account shall be sent or delivered into the "next gaol of the King's in those parts."

By an Act of Hen. VIII., 1541-2,[10] a Court of Receivers of the King's Lands was established, and among various officers appointed were Auditors.

More than 300 years ago an Auditor was defined as "an "officer who by yearly examining the accounts of all under "officers accountable, makes up a general book that shows "the difference between their receipts or charges and their "payments or allowances."[11] Audits or Auditors are referred to in this sense in seven of Shakespeare's Plays.[12] The Auditors of the Imprest are described as ancient officers of the Exchequer. They were remunerated in a manner, not, I believe, ever adopted in regard to modern Auditors, by a percentage on the amount of expenditure audited. The post was an honourable, or, at least, a lucrative one. When their office was abolished in 1785, each Auditor received a pension for life of £7,000. The duties included the collection of Taxes. They were succeeded by Commissioners for auditing Public Accounts.

Various subsequent statutes provided for the Audit of the Government Accounts, and these were in turn superseded by the existing system created by the "Exchequer and Audit Departments' Act of 1866," which provided for the appointment of a Comptroller and Auditor General, an Officer accountable direct to Parliament.[13]

A statute of 1705 provided for the Audit of Accounts in Actions for Account at Common Law.[14]

By the Bankrupt Law Consolidation Act of 1825, provision was made for the Audit of the Creditors' Assignees' Accounts by the Commissioners, and this form of Audit was with unfortunate results extended to the accounts of Official Assignees.[15]

The Bankruptcy Act, 1861,[16] required the Official Assignees to render an account to the Creditors' Assignees, who had to audit the Account in the presence of the Registrar.

The Audit of Trustees' Accounts under the Bankruptcy Act of 1869 was placed in charge of the Comptroller in cases of Bankruptcy, and left to the Creditors in liquidation cases.

Under the Bankruptcy Act, 1883, separate Audits, both by the Committee of Creditors and Board of Trade, are required.

The Municipal Corporations Act, 1835,[17] and the Public Health Act, 1875, provide for the appointment of Auditors.

(8.) Chambers' Encyclopædia.
(9.) 13 Edw. I. c. 11.
(10.) 33 Hen. VIII. c. 39.
(11.) Termes de La Ley. Temp. Hen. VIII.
(12.) Macbeth i. 6; Henry VIII. iii. 2; Coriolanus, i. 1; Cymbeline v. 4; Hamlet iii. 3; I. Henry IV. ii. 1; Timon of Ath. ii. 2.
(13.) 29-30 Vic. c. 39.
(14.) 4-5 Anne c. 16 s. 27.
(15.) 6 Geo. IV. c. 16.
(16.) Sec. 119.
(17.) 5-6 Wm. IV. c. 76.

In regard to Companies, the Companies Clauses Act, 1845, requires the appointment of Auditors of Companies formed by Act of Parliament whose Acts embody this Statute.

The Gas Works Clauses Act, 1847, the Waterworks Clauses Act, 1847, and the Metropolitan Water Act, 1871, provide for the appointment of Auditors.

The Building Societies Act, 1874, requires that the rules of the Society shall provide for an Audit.

We have seen what a very small proportion of the Auditors of Building Societies are Chartered Accountants. The connection between this fact and the frequent disclosures of frauds on Building Societies is significant. Mr. Henry F. A. Davis, in his work on Building Societies, says, "it is to "be feared that in too many Societies no accurate system of "keeping the books is adopted, and that in consequence "Balance Sheets are prepared which are perfectly untrust-"worthy."

The Friendly Societies' Act, 1875, and the Industrial and Provident Societies' Act, 1876, require an annual Audit.

The Education Act, 1870, provides for the Audit of the Accounts of School Boards.

But Companies registered under the Companies Acts, are the most important branch of the subject to our profession.

The Companies Act, 1862, contains in the body of the Act no reference to an Audit. Section 60 provides for the appointment by special resolution of Inspectors, whose duties are somewhat similar to those of an Auditor. This section has, I believe seldom, if ever, been acted upon.

Prior to the Joint Stock Companies' Act, 1856, it does not appear to have been the rule for Companies to appoint Auditors. The older Chartered Companies rarely, I believe, included provision in their Charters or Bye-Laws for an Audit. Companies formed by Deed of Settlement in many cases provided for the appointment of Auditors.

The Select Committee of the House of Commons of 1836 on Joint Stock Banks, addressed enquiries to the Banks, one of which was "the nature of the Audit and examination to which the accounts are subjected." The answers show that in a majority of cases there was no audit. Out of 107 Banks only nine had auditors. 14 others had power in the Deed of Settlement to appoint Auditors, but the power seems not to have been exercised.

The Committee examined a considerable number of witnesses upon the question of Auditing, and the majority were strongly in favour of an Audit.

At the present time, out of 159 Banks as to which I have been able to obtain information, 128 appoint Auditors.

The present almost invariable practice with newly formed Companies of providing for the appointment of Auditors, would seem to be largely referable to the form of articles of Association Table B., scheduled to the Joint Stock Companies' Act, 1856, which included clauses providing for the appointment of Auditors. With minor modifications Table B. of the 1856 Act is identical with Table A. of the Companies' Act, 1862. These Clauses are embodied in substantially similar form in the Articles of Association of nearly all newly-formed Companies.

A further important stimulus was given by the Companies' Act, 1879, passed to enable banks to register with limited and reserve liability. This Act makes Audit compulsory for all Banking Companies registered as Limited after the passing of the Act,

It is seen there is ample statutory recognition of the office of an auditor. But this recognition must be considered by our profession as deficient in one respect. In none of the cases mentioned is reference made to Accountants. In the appointment of an Auditor no restriction is placed upon the selection, beyond the exclusion of interested persons. I know of no statutory reference to Accountants in connection with the appointment of Auditors. In the Lunacy Act Amendment Bill brought into the House of Lords in February last by the Lord Chancellor, a clause was included requiring that the accounts of institutions affected by the Act be audited by a Member of the Institute of Chartered Accountants, but later re-prints of the Bill provides simply that an Accountant be the Auditor, and the Bill has not yet become law.

DESCRIPTION OF OFFICE AND QUALIFICATIONS.

The office of an auditor is an honourable one. He is second to none in the company. He is accountable direct to the general body of shareholders. The office, too, is one of authority. The directors and officers have no power over the auditor, but have to submit their actions to his examination. The office is one of confidence. Every transaction of the Company must be laid open to the Auditor, and he may decide on his sole responsibility what use he will make of the information he acquires as between himself and the general body, or in effect what he will make public.

An auditor of a Company I understand to be an officer appointed by the general body for the purpose of examining and reporting upon the account rendered by the administration.

It is evident the whole body of Shareholders to whom an account is presented cannot properly examine the account which they are asked to approve. It would be inconvenient at the meeting to depute the examination, as this would involve an adjournment. The more convenient course is to appoint Officers beforehand to examine and report upon the account. By this plan the Directors would seem to obtain a more effectual release, and the Shareholders obtain from an officer in whom they have confidence, appointed expressly for the purpose, the assurance that what they are asked to approve is in order.

The first essential qualification of an Auditor is that he be independent of the administrative body whose actions and accounts it is his duty to examine. The difficulty of insuring this qualification at once presents itself. First it is evident the Directors and the staff of the Company should have no hand in the appointment. But the general body of Shareholders are unfitted to initiate anything. They can only, as a body, by voting express an opinion upon what is proposed. Clearly the appointment of so important an officer as the Auditor ought not to depend upon the chance proposal of an irresponsible member. To insure a satisfactory appointment, either a Committee must be constituted for the purpose of selecting persons to be proposed, or the initiation of this, as of other important business of the Company, must rest with the Board of Directors. In practice this is what usually takes place. But the difficulty of making a satisfactory appointment surely emphasises the importance of the quality of independence.

The qualification which next suggests itself as essential to an Auditor is an acquaintance with Bookkeeping and Accounts. The necessity for this is so evident that no comment is needed. But so varied are the methods and forms of Book-keeping that an acquaintance with one class of accounts will be inadequate. A knowledge of various systems is called for.

A third essential to the Auditor is knowledge of the law affecting Companies. Not only of the so-called Company Law, but some acquaintance with the law of Partnership and of Ultra Vires and the Commercial Law generally. It has been truly said that "Accountants live in an atmosphere of law."

It may here be well to define the character of the legal knowledge which seems to be requisite. A Chartered Accountant's knowledge of those branches of law which specially concern him need only be an extension of that general knowledge of the law specially affecting his particular business, which should be, and usually is, possessed in more or less degree by every business man. Not a knowledge which will enable a Chartered Accountant to advise or guide others, nor cause him to usurp the functions of solicitors, or to dispense with their advice and assistance.

Those acquainted with the subject will know that some knowledge by Chartered Accountants of the law affecting their business is found in practice to be the reverse of prejudicial to the business of solicitors.

A leading London Accountant, withdrawn I believe from active practice, whose name has been for very many years, and still is probably, more familiar than any other, is said to have attributed his success to the possession of a sound knowledge of law.

A fourth qualification for an Auditor is the possession of a general knowledge of business. To be able to form an opinion upon questions of special business customs and practices, or even to understand them, a business training is essential.

Lastly, to the efficient examination of the transactions of a Company, an Auditor should be able to bring a knowledge of the internal working of a variety of other concerns. Failing this his criticisms will lack weight.

I will not discuss the question whether an Auditor should be a Shareholder. Reasons can be urged on both sides of this question, which seems unimportant if the Auditor possesses all the requisite qualifications. The balance of argument appears to me to be in favour of an Auditor being free from all interest in the Company.

In the examination of the accounts and transactions of Companies, questions of difficulty will frequently present themselves, acquaintance with which can hardly be looked for in an untrained Auditor.

In testing the correctness of the liabilities in the Balance Sheet, a competent Auditor may detect various omissions. Contingent liabilities and outstanding accounts are frequently lost sight of—Liability upon Bills discounted, or in Financial concerns, Bills re-discounted—Liability on Guarantees on Re-insurance by an Insurance Company, and other matters constituting a Contingent Liability—Rebate of Interest on Bills Receivable should be reserved, and the converse on Bills payable—Questions as to whether Liabilities may be deducted or set off against assets and the reverse.

The important question whether borrowing powers have been exceeded in Loans on Debentures, or otherwise, and the issue of Debentures or Shares at a discount may have to be considered.[18] The Company's powers of lending and investing funds, making gratuitous payments, granting pensions, and giving to Charities, may also require consideration.

In the examination of assets also, the training and experience of a qualified Auditor are essential.

The proper valuation of Stocks, whether at cost, sale or other value, is an important question. This subject has been ably dealt with in a paper read by Mr. Trevor before the Manchester Chartered Accountants' Students' Society.[19] The deduction of Discounts from Book Debts and the provision for Depreciation from wear and tear of Plant, Machinery, Shipping, Furniture, and other Capital outlay. The amortization of Leaseholds, Patents, and other property held on a term are also important questions.

The necessity referred to of an acquaintance with a variety of concerns is here seen in the different principles which govern the Capital Account of Companies owning Railways and Tramways or factories, and Companies formed for Mining or other speculative ventures.

An Auditor should understand the distinction between various kinds of Reserve Funds, and what are sometimes inaccurately called Reserves, but which really are provisions for Depreciation of Assets or for doubtful debts.

The need of special training is illustrated by the dangers attending the valuations of the advances of Building Societies.

Another question which has given rise to discussion is under what circumstances Goodwill may properly be included as an Asset.

But one of the most important questions is the distinction between Capital and Revenue, and the different principles applicable to Companies formed by Act of Parliament for Public Works, and manufacturing and other Companies' Connected with this subject is the question which has recently been the subject of much controversy, the payment of Interest on Capital (and with it the apportionment of expenditure) during construction. Those who seek for guidance on this question may read with advantage the able address of Mr. Guthrie on the subject to the Manchester Chartered Accountants' Students' Society.[19]

A knowledge of Foreign Exchanges is essential to the efficient audit of the accounts of Companies working in Foreign Countries, or in India, or some of the English Colonies. An Auditor without this knowledge would be at a serious disadvantage one may say in some respects helpless, in examining the accounts for instance, of an Indian or an Austrian Bank, where large fluctuations in the Exchange, no trace of which will usually appear in the books, may materially change the financial position of the concern.

This subject of the questions arising in the examination of Accounts might be pursued indefinitely, but probably sufficient has been said to establish that special knowledge and training are required to the efficient discharge of an Auditor's duties.

NON-PROFESSIONAL AUDITORS.

Having indicated what qualifications are essential to the efficient discharge of the duties of an auditor of the accounts of a Company, let us now see where it may be expected those qualifications are most likely to be found.

The chief qualifications demanded, I repeat, are:—

(1) Independence.
(2) Knowledge of Bookkeeping and Accounts.
(3) Knowledge of the Law affecting Companies.
(4) General knowledge of business.
(5) Acquaintance with the internal working of a variety of concerns.

Of the different classes of persons from whom the non-professional Auditor is selected, I must, from lack of time, dismiss those which seem to me to possess, in the smallest degree, the essential qualities. A Clergyman possesses few of the needful qualifications, and cannot be looked upon as a candidate in commercial concerns. Merchants and Traders, generally, may be expected to possess the qualities of a knowledge of accounts and general knowledge of business, but there is no reason to look to them for a special knowledge of Company Law, or a knowledge of the internal working of a variety of concerns.

An actuary possesses, in part, one essential, familiarity with figures, but although not less than a chartered accountant a man of arithmetic, there seems no reason to expect a knowledge of business, or of a variety of concerns in a person skilled in the law of probabilities, and in calculations for Insurance Companies and kindred concerns. Skill in calculation constitutes a small part of the essentials of auditing. Accounts have been said to be "a business more of reason than arithmetic,"[20] and the duty of an auditor does not stop at examining figures.

A Barrister may be expected to possess the qualification of a knowledge of Company Law, but as regards the essential of a knowledge of accounts, in no class is this knowledge more frequently disclaimed than in this branch of the legal profession.

It is rare indeed to meet with a Barrister to whom accounts are readily intelligible. Then, can a Barrister be expected to possess a knowledge of business?

A Solicitor is, although in perhaps a less degree, open to the same objections as a Barrister, with the additional objection of his connection, actual or prospective, with the Company in his professional capacity.

CHARTERED ACCOUNTANTS.

If it may be assumed that in no other class are the qualifications for the post of auditor to be expected, it re-

(18.) See Stannaries Act, 1869, Sec. 12, as to Discount on Shares.
(19.) Transactions, 1885.
(20.) Locke on Education.

nains to consider whether our profession satisfies the requirements.

Probably the profession of a chartered accountant is the 'oungest of those which are fairly entitled to be so designated.

What is the precise status of our profession at the present ime I will not attempt to determine. We may fairly claim hat it has advanced with exceptional rapidity of recent ears, and is still advancing both in status and in the cope of its duties, and also in the qualifications of its mem-ers.

It does not appear that the profession of an accountant an lay claim to a long history. Mr. Chalmers addressing he Liverpool Chartered Accountants' Students' Association n 1883, expressed an opinion that "the profession of accountants took its rise about the middle or end of the ast century,"[21]

The earliest mention of a professed accountant I have ound in the London Directory is the firm of Shortney and Iillne, Merchants and Commercial Accomptants, who first ppeared in 1776. In 1778 the firm appeared as Shortney nd Co., Commercial Accomptants and Agents; in 1779 as '. Shortney. In 1785 as Shortney and Son. In 1789 the usiness of Agents took precedence of the business of ccountants. Neither the name of Shortney nor that of Iillne, so spelt now appears in the London Directory.

In the year 1820, according to the Directory, 44 accountants were in practice in London. In 1843 there were 160 ccountants, the remarkable increase being possibly attriutable to the Bankrupt Law Consolidation Act of 1825. In 843 there were several firms which are still in existence nder altered names. In 1860 the number was 310. n 1869, the year when the recently repealed Bankuptcy Act passed from which owing to the abolition f officialism a large increase of business accrued to our prossion, the number was 453; and in 1870, when the Institute Accountants in London was formed, 464. In 1883 when e new Bankruptcy Act passed, 757, showing the stimulang effect of the 1869 Bankruptcy Act. In the present year 886) there is a slight falling off, (pointing to the depressing fluence of the Bankruptcy Act of 1883) the number ing 752, of whom 475 are chartered accountants, and in dition there are 97 chartered accountants in London not practice.

The Census of 1841 shows in England and Wales 4,260 ccountants, and that of 1881, 11,517. Showing a growth in e 40 years of 170 per cent. against an increase of populaon of 62 per cent.[22]

Probably the Census figures include a large proportion of ookkeepers and other persons not professional accountnts.

The growth of the Institute, according to the List of embers, has been from 1,025 in 1881 to 1,431 at present, or y, 40 per cent. in five years. In Manchester there were in 81, 126 members, and in 1886, 161 members, or an inease of 28 per cent. in the five years.

In the matter of Incorporation Accountants in Scotland ve been in advance of England. Societies of Accountants Edinburgh, Glasgow, and Aberdeen obtained Charters of corporation in 1854, 1855, and 1867.[23]

In order to understand the profession of a Chartered ccountant, let us glance at the principal duties he is lled upon to discharge.

In addition to the audit of every description of concern, int Stock, Charitable or Private, the duties of which have en already to some extent indicated, a Chartered Accounnt in regard to accounts generally is looked to for advice as to forms and modes of Book-keeping, and for assistance in unravelling confused accounts, and the detection of obscure errors, preventing the balance of the books, which have eluded the search of the Book-keeper. He is expected to take charge of books and accounts, either permanently or in the absence of the Book-keeper. In cases of fraud and defalcations he is called in to trace with more or less or no assistance from those acquainted with the books the details of the defalcations.

In litigation or compensation cases he has to prepare accounts and attend as a witness.

In criminal prosecutions, Chartered Accountants are employed on behalf of the Treasury, and otherwise, to examine and give evidence on Accounts.

Upon the failure of a firm or a Company, a Chartered Accountant has to prepare the Statement of Affairs, compressing into a document in an intelligible form the details of the position of the concern, its property and obligations, and into a deficiency account its history for a given period of years.

He is called upon to examine the accounts of businesses, and certify profits upon their being formed into Companies, or upon the introduction of a partner, or obtaining financial assistance, and to advise as to the prudence and safety of the advances.

He has to prepare accounts of Executors and other Trustees of property in accordance with the terms of the Trust, and the requirements of the Chancery Division, to prepare returns for Income Tax, and to assist in appeals against assessments.

As Trustee or Special Manager in cases of Bankruptcy or failure, or as Liquidator of a Company, or Receiver under Decrees or Private Appointments, he is called upon to take charge of the concern at home or abroad, often of wide extent and complication and beset with financial embarrassments, and to assume responsibility for all details of the business, its English or Foreign correspondence, whether a Railway, or Bank, or an Insurance Company, or a trading concern with Factories, Mines, or Works of any conceivable kind.

Probably a large number of business concerns of very varied description in many countries are at this moment in full operation under the Control of Chartered Accountants.

As Liquidator, a Chartered Accountant must be qualified to act as Director, Manager, and Secretary, for as a Liquidator the duties and responsibility of all these offices devolve upon him.

As Trustee in Bankruptcy, he is vested with the property of the Debtors, and with it has often to take serious risks of personal loss, which probably few Chartered Accountants in large practice have wholly escaped, under leases and other contracts.

In his capacity of Trustee and Liquidator, a Chartered Accountant gains valuable experience on the one hand in examining claims made upon the estate, testing their validity, and with the assistance of the Solicitor resisting unjust demands, and on the other hand, in asserting with the same assistance, the rights of the estate against those withholding property and indebtedness.

A Chartered Accountant has also to act as Arbitrator and Referee.

Thus it is clear the practice of the Profession of a Chartered Accountant qualifies its members exceptionally in three of the chief requirements of an Auditor above indicated, viz., Knowledge of Accounts, general knowledge of business, and acquaintance with a variety of concerns.

An additional guarantee of the possession of the qualifications referred to is furnished by the Institute of Chartered Accountants' Examinations for Membership requiring candidates to pass an examination in the following subjects:—

Book-keeping.

Auditing.

(21.) *Accountant* 1883, No. 431, p. 12.
(22.) Population 1841 16,035,198, 1881 25,968,286.
(23.) Edinburgh 23rd October, 1854.
Glasgow 15th March, 1855.
Aberdeen 18th March, 1867.
England & Wales. } 11th May, 1880.

The adjustment of Partnership and Executorship Accounts.
The Principles of the law relating to Joint Stock Companies.
The Principles of Mercantile Law.
The Principles of the Law of Bankruptcy.
The Rights and Duties of Liquidators, Trustees and Receivers.
The Principles of the Law of Arbitrations and Awards.

A further advantage possessed exclusively by Professional Auditors is the disposal of the services of a staff of clerks trained in audit work. Without assistance from his clerks it would be impossible for a Chartered Accountant to discharge effectively his duty of examining details in large Audits.

There remains the quality of Independence. In regard to this, a Chartered Accountant may claim exceptional qualification. When it is borne in mind that a large part of the business of Chartered Accountants lies in the audit of accounts, it follows that their professional repute is staked upon the efficient discharge of their duties as auditors.

Sufficient has, I trust, been said to show that our Profession, properly followed, is one which affords scope for full exercise of the faculties.

It was said by a late leading accountant of great experience, who lived beyond the usual span of life, that to learn thoroughly the profession of an accountant required a life-time, and that few days passed in which he failed to learn something in his profession.

An enquiry of some interest might be made, if time allowed, into the comparative history of Companies audited by professed accountants, and those Companies whose accounts are not audited at all, or are subjected only to a formal audit by untrained auditors. It is hardly conceivable that such a state of things as was disclosed in the disastrous failures of the City of Glasgow and West of England Banks could have arisen or been continued if the certificate of a qualified auditor had been required. More recent are the calamitous failures of the Oriental Bank Corporation and the Munster Bank. Both these Companies resorted at the last moment to the appointment of a professional auditor, but only when too late to be of service.

The still more recent disclosures in the liquidation of the Briton Medical Life Association would seem to have been impossible if a qualified auditor had been employed to examine the accounts.

In contrast with these misfortunes we may place with some satisfaction the discovery by the auditor, an eminent chartered accountant, of the extensive embezzlement of securities by the Secretary of the London and River Plate Bank in time to prevent the defalcations reaching a sum beyond the Bank's means.

CONCLUSION.

I have given facts and figures showing a remarkable growth of the profession, and also some particulars pointing to a similar satisfactory growth in the practice of employing chartered accountants as auditors.

All the great Banks, with one notable exception,[24] registering under the Companies Acts employ chartered accountants as auditors. Many of the larger Insurance Companies have in recent years employed chartered accountants as auditors, or to make a supplemental and continuous audit of the accounts. Most of the great railway Companies now employ chartered accountants, either as auditors or to assist the auditors.

Although the development of auditing of late years has been steady and rapid, the position remains unsound and unsatisfactory. We must rely mainly upon time and the operation of natural forces to remedy the existing state of things.

(24.) London and County Bank.

To the Council of the Institute we are, I think, under obligations for much able and well directed labour in the interest of the profession. I do not doubt they are fully alive to the importance of watching legislation, with a view to introducing provisions for efficient auditing into new Acts of Parliament. Something more seems possible to keep the Institute before the public. In connection with this—a small matter—the circulation of a list of members and the Bye-Laws at a price not so prohibitive as at present, if not gratis, seems practicable.

Some more active encouragement to students by the offer of prizes out of the large funds, or in other ways, and the stimulating of the production of sound literary work on subjects of interest to the profession seems possible to the Council.

But more may be done by individual action of the 1,400 members of the Institute by introducing method into audit work and by enforcing accuracy and neatness in our work, so much of which is made public.

I will not presume to indicate to members how the interests of the profession in the matter of auditing may be advanced, as the advance of the profession being the advance of its individual members, the subject is in safe hands.

AUDITING
(1887)

F.W. Pixley

The mechanical portion of an audit examination, which tests for errors and fraud, requires less skill than the judgemental analysis of accounts for "errors of principle".

CHARTERED ACCOUNTANTS' STUDENTS' SOCIETY OF LONDON.

AUDITING.

MR. FRAS. W. PIXLEY, F.C.A.

The following paper was read by Mr. F. W. Pixley, F.C.A., on the evening of the 25th October, 1887. Mr. E. E. Price, F.C.A. presiding:—

Having already lectured to this society on the subject of auditing, I naturally referred to my last lecture in order to avoid repetition as much as possible; but I saw Mr. Hanson, who informed me that I need hardly take that into consideration, as probably few present would have heard my former lecture.

It is, of course, quite impossible to give a fresh lecture on auditing without going over the same ground; and it is also impossible in a lecture to give more than a general idea of an audit and the principles which should guide an auditor in his duties, as of course every business varies from other businesses, both in the manner of conduct and in the manner of recording the result of the transactions. My remarks, however, will apply to any audit, as it is only experience which can show how the various books of account should be examined, and the statements of accounts arrived at, which it is the duty of the auditors to examine.

Auditing forms the main portion of the duties of chartered accountants, for although various matters are transacted in their offices which do not bear this name, still they nevertheless come under this branch of the profession, for example: investigations of accounts of every description; the majority of the work connected with official liquidators of companies, trusteeships in bankruptcy; reporting upon the accounts of executors and trustees of the estates of deceased persons; giving evidence as experts or qualified witnesses; compensation cases; or any other matters before the courts which require a knowledge of auditing; and, therefore, it may be said that it is the mainstay of a chartered accountant's practice.

Until within the last few years, the only qualification for the appointment of auditor to a joint stock company was the holding of a certain number of shares—at least one—in the undertaking. Previously, appointments were made without reference to any other qualification, and therefore, one of the largest shareholders would be appointed, but the revelations which have been made in the courts of the results of this kind of auditing has so started the financial world that I think the amateur auditor is fast dying out.

It is not necessary for me to discuss the training which is required for an auditor, this being prescribed by the Institute of Chartered Accountants, and you have all of you no doubt in your possession the list of subjects which are required for the various examinations.

The only subject with which I am at all concerned in this lecture is, that with which I presume you are all thoroughly acquainted: the principle and practice of book-keeping, for without this knowledge it would of course be absurd to attempt auditing which is the object of ascertaining whether the accounts kept by others are or are not correct.

Audits may be divided into two classes: the first, where the auditor performs the work at the request of a client who gives certain directions as to the nature of the audit required which the auditor carries out, his responsibility being limited to ascertaining that the accounts are in accordance with the instructions of his client, and prepared in the form required by him. Such, for example, are the accounts of individuals either their trade or their private accounts, or of firms engaged in business. The second, are those where the duties are defined, either by Act of Parliament or by general custom; such, for example, as public companies, executors or trustees of deceased persons estates, and in all matters generally, where capital is invested not under the entire control of the parties interested.

In the first case, the responsibility of the auditor is limited to his instructions—if his clients say they only require a partial audit, and wish him to take certain entries for granted, he is of course at liberty to undertake an audit of this sort, and his responsibility is limited. In the other case, his acceptance of the appointment involves the highest responsibility, and he must not allow himself to be influenced in any way by the wishes of the parties giving him instructions, but has to perform his duties strictly and impartially, having regard to the interest of all the parties concerned.

Before commencing an audit of the first class, the auditor has merely to request his clients to state distinctly the nature of the audit they require, and then his duty consists merely in verifying the books of account, and either certifying the statement of affairs already prepared in the form approved of by his clients, or else preparing the accounts himself in the required form.

In audits of the second class, the auditor must make himself thoroughly acquainted with the legal documents forming the basis upon which the accounts are prepared. For example, in the case of a firm where no special instructions are given to the auditor, but he is required to make a complete investigation, he must peruse the deed of partnership making extracts therefrom of all sections referring to the accounts, and his responsibility is the more increased in every respect, if there be a sleeping partner in the concern whose information is only conveyed through the auditor's report and accounts. In the audit of accounts of executors and trustees, the auditor should peruse the will and codicils (if any) and he should also be acquainted with the general law relating to executors and trustees, more particularly the Apportionments Act of 1870. In the case of accounts of public companies, he must be acquainted with the various Companies Acts, and if the company be incorporated under special Act of Parliament, he must also be provided with a copy of the special act. In the case of companies incorporated under the Act of 1862, he must see the articles of association, or if there be none, he is already supposed to be acquainted with the table A, which are the regulations applying to every company registered under that act not provided with details of association.

It is, perhaps, as well to give the various Acts of Parliament relating to the books, accounts, and auditors of Joint Stock Companies, including those of Building Societies, Friendly Societies, and Industrial and Provident Societies. They are as follows:—

The Companies Act, 1862.
The Companies Act, 1879.
The Companies Act, 1880.
The Companies Colonial Register Act, 1883.

The above acts refer entirely to what are known as Limited Liability Companies. The Companies Colonial Act, of course, as its name implies, refers to those companies who transact business in the colonies, and gives them power to keep a colonial register or branch register of members resident in the colonies.

The Companies Clauses Consolidation Act, 1845.
The Companies Clauses Act, 1863.

These two acts refer to companies incorporated by special Act of Parliament, except where their provisions are expressly repealed or varied by either public or private Acts.

The Railway Securities Act, 1866.
The Railway Companies Act, 1867.
The Railway Companies (Scotland) Act, 1867.
The Regulation of Railways Act, 1868.

The above acts, of course, as their name implies, refer to railway companies, and to certain tramway companies specially defined in the acts.

The Gas Works Clauses Act, 1847.
The Gas Works Clauses Act, 1871.
The Water Works Clauses Act, 1847.
The Metropolitan Water Act, 1852.
The Metropolitan Water Act, 1871.
The Life Assurance Companies Act, 1870.
The Building Societies Act, 1874.
The Friendly Societies Act, 1875.
The Friendly Societies Management Act, 1876.
The Industrial and Provident Societies Act, 1876.

The above refer exclusively to companies carrying on the business indicated in the titles of the act.

The auditor should also be acquainted with :—

"The Falsification of Accounts Act, 1875"

which points out the penalties attached to the alteration, mutilating or falsifying any books or papers, although I hope that no one present to-night will ever be brought under its penalties.

An auditor is also, of course, supposed to know the general principles of mercantile law as prescribed in the syllabus of the examination of the Institute.

Having made himself familiar with whichever of these documents applies to his audit, the auditor must then commence the investigation of the accounts intrusted to him, and in the prosecution of his audit he should be exceedingly systematic in all his steps.

An auditor has practically to guard himself against three classes of errors :—

Errors of omission.
Errors of commission.
Errors of principle.

To guard against errors of omission, is really the most difficult part of an auditor's work. When once an entry has been made in any of the books, it is to a certain extent a mechanical process to see that they are brought forward step by step until the revenue or profit and loss account and balance sheet is reached. But it is exceedingly difficult for an auditor to ascertain if an entry that ought to have been made in the books has been kept out. Many persons would contend that this is no part of an auditor's duty, which is simply confined to ascertaining that the accounts as presented either to the partners or shareholders of a company as the case may be, agree with the books of account, but this is taking a very low view of the auditors duties, and which I am bound to say, would meet with no favour from respectable practitioners. It is an auditor's duty to see that the record of the transactions of the business, whose accounts are under his investigation, show the actual result of the business, and should he have reason to suppose that these have not been properly recorded, it is his duty to attempt, by any means in his power, to ascertain whether his surmises are, or are not, correct, and it is here where an auditor has an opportunity of showing his skill, and where experience is of the greatest assistance to him.

As regards errors of comission, these are comparatively easy to detect, while as regards errors of principle, these as a rule are inquired into after the balancing of the books. For example, when the books have been balanced and the statements drawn, it is then the duty of the auditor to see that they are in accordance with the form prescribed either by law or by custom. In the case of a company, the auditor should ascertain that the authorised capital has not been exceeded, that the company has not exercised its powers of borrowing beyond those authorised, as cases have occurred where the company has made an over issue of debentures to the public, and an auditor would be very rightly blamed if this were not properly reported by him to the shareholders. An auditor should also ascertain that the funds of the company have not been invested in any securities forbidden by Act of Parliament or its own deed of settlement. In the case of a partnership, and specially where there is a sleeping partner who looks to the auditor to protect him, he should ascertain whether the drawings of the partners have exceeded the prescribed sums mentioned in the deed of partnership, whether their capital accounts are in accordance with the deed, and whether any special provisions referred to therein have been properly carried out. In the case of executors and trustees, the auditor should ascertain whether the legacies have been properly paid, whether the annuitants have been properly paid, and that the investments are those authorised by the will or in the absence of business of special directions, whether the investments are such as are specially prescribed for trustees by Act of Parliament, and generally that the directions contained in the will of the testator are carried out.

It is advisable on commencing an audit to have a list of the books in use, and if it be a business, the auditor should make himself acquainted with its nature, and the system upon which it is conducted. Having done this, he then commences the details of the audit, and here I come to a subject which it is absolutely impossible for me to go into particulars, as the books of every business are practically kept on the same system, but they all vary in detail.

The most complete form of audit is really that of a public company, and I will, therefore, confine my remarks as to details to the books of a company.

The same remarks are applicable with slight variation to those of a firm where the auditor is instructed to make a thorough audit by his clients, but it will not be necessary to go into so much detail where instructions are given only to make a partial audit.

Many private firms for example, are quite satisfied if the auditors take all their entries for granted, and merely require them to prepare therefrom a Profit and Loss Account and Balance Sheet. Frequently, the books do not balance, and the auditor is not even asked to examine them for the purpose of discovering the error.

In the case, however, of a thorough audit, the books should balance exactly, and in order to do this, it is frequently necessary for the auditor to call over the postings from the Cash Book, Day Book, Invoice Book and Journal to the Ledger for the purpose of discovering where the error lies.

In no case, however, is this necessary in the audit of a company's accounts, unless the auditor is employed independently by the directors to prepare the accounts, as he may require that the books be correctly balanced before they are placed in his hands. The articles of association usually prescribe that the accounts to be presented to the shareholders should be handed to the auditor, and then he has simply to confirm or reject them within a given number of days. In practice this is seldom done. As a rule the accounts are discussed with the auditor before being finally settled, and this is more convenient and more desirable in every way, as nothing can be more fatal to a company than to present its accounts which might be correct with a trifling exception to the shareholders, with a comment by the auditors that they are not perfectly correct.

As already stated, it is not the practice for auditors of a public company to call over the postings, their correctness are usually taken for granted, but the auditor must be entirely guided by his experience as to what he may take for granted, in fact anything he does take for granted is at his own peril.

The mechanical portion of an audit consists in examining the vouchers for payments stated to have been made by the Cash Book.

This, the most important point from an amateur auditor's point of view, is looked upon as the most childish operation, of the professional auditor's work, however this duty has to be done, and it should be performed carefully and conscientiously.

It is sometimes a little difficult to know what are, and what are not, genuine vouchers, and sometimes it is impossible for a company to produce a document as a voucher, but the payment may be satisfactorily vouched by the auditor in a different way. For example—If you know that the salary of a secretary is £300 a year, an auditor does not require a separate receipt for £25 monthly, in order to feel satisfied that the secretary has received his salary. If it is paid by cheque, the cheque can be produced, and if paid out of cash, there is sufficient proof in the absence of any document, even although the official may have left the service of the company before the auditor commenced his duties.

A list of missing vouchers should be made and handed to the secretary or accountants to the company, with a request that they should be found, followed up by an intimation if necessary, that the auditor will not be able to give an unqualified certificate until they are either found or duplicates obtained.

To guard against omissions on the receipt side of the cash book, is a matter of great difficulty. Fortunately accounts are seldom presented to auditors intentionally falsified in this respect, but should an auditor have reason to believe that the receipts have not been fully accounted for, he should try every means in his power to discover the extent of the fraud.

To give an instance of a fraud of this nature, I had to investigate the books of a firm for the purpose of ascertaining to what extent they had been robbed by their bookkeeper.

He commenced by taking a payment from one of the customers and not passing it to his credit in the cash book. This he afterwards did in several instances, consequently, these customers appeared as debtors in the books for amounts they had already paid. As time went on, the danger of discovery became greater, and in order to protect himself he took the monies of other customers and passed it to the credit of those customers from whom he had received money some months previously, leaving a fresh set of customers debtors. In the meantime he was gradually appropriating more moneys.

In order to record these transactions it was necessary for him to keep two sets of books.

When I first inspected the books I was much struck by the admirable manner in which they were kept, but the bookkeeper absconded in a hurry and left the duplicate set of books behind, which helped me in my investigation. Had this not been the case, there was absolutely no other means of finding out what moneys had been received, without applying to every customer of the firm, and it is exceedingly possible the accounts would have been audited and passed without finding out a fraud of this description.

Of course the first step to ascertaining if no items of receipt are omitted, would be to call for whatever subsidiary books might occur to the auditor as throwing light on the takings. For example, the counterfoils of Traveller's Receipt Books, Porter's Books, rough or Counter Receipt Books, &c., but a fraud of this nature is much more likely to occur in the books of an individual or small firm where only one or two clerks are kept, than in the case of a large firm, or of a public company, where the clerks are to a certain extent a check upon each other.

Having practically audited the cash book it should be reconciled with the bankers' pass book. It is not, of course, necessary to check one with the other in detail, as a rule, but, as I have said before, what might be unnecessary in twenty cases, might be, on the twenty first. It would be no answer for an auditor to a body of shareholders to say he had not thought it necessary to check any item in particular, the shareholders would have a perfect right to reply, "It is your duty to check everything."

It is, of course, entirely a matter of experience for an auditor to decide as to what extent he should check the various subsidiary books which culminate through the postings in the ledgers. As a rule, it is not usual to check the postings, or to compare entries from the original invoices and other documents, but if the auditor has the slightest doubt in his own mind that everything is not perfectly straightforward and correct, he should, at any rate, take some test cases, if he does not check the books through.

Having finished this portion of the audit, which is to a certain extent mechanical, he then deals with the results of the bookkeeper's entries in the shape of the accounts to be presented to his clients.

The usual accounts presented to a company are, a revenue or profit and loss account and balance sheet, or statement showing financial position at the date on which the books were closed. Some companies issue a cash account, either in conjunction with the revenue account or without it. A cash account does not form any part of the book-keeping proper. It is merely an abstract of the cash book, and is, therefore, a statistical book, showing the total receipts on one side and the total expenditure on the other side. As it does not in any way refer to the periods during which the liabilities were incurred or the receipts earned, it is not in any way a guide as to the financial results of the period embraced by the accounts. It is quite possible a loss may have been incurred during the period, although the balance in hand at the end of the account is in excess of that shown at the commencement, for the reason that the receipts may include a much greater amount of earnings of the previous period than was due at the close of the period, while the liabilities may be exactly the reverse, and be much heavier at the end of the period than they were at the commencement.

The certified accounts of a person in trade, or of a firm, are usually a profit and loss account and balance sheet, and, perhaps, the capital accounts of the partners, while the accounts presented to executors and trustees, in the case of a first audit, would include a statement showing the financial position of the testator at the date of his death, the dealings with the estate by the executors from the date of the death of the testator to the end of the period under audit, and the financial position of the estate at the end of this period. In future audits the two latter statements would only be necessary, although if there are several tenants for life, with special hypothecated securities for each one's use, it is usual to present a statement showing the financial position of each of these trusts.

The principles for examination of the revenue or profit and loss account of a company, individual or firm, are practically the same, the object being simply to ascertain that the whole of the revenue taken credit for has been properly earned during the period, and, secondly, that the whole of the expenses connected with earning it have been properly charged on the other side, including the full amount for depreciation of perishable property.

The revenue account, to be perfectly clear, should be divided into three parts; the first one showing the gross profits earned; the second one showing the net profit, being the amount which, in the case of a company, would be available for dividend, or, in the case of a firm, the balance available for distribution amongst the partners; while the third part should show how this net profit has been dealt with.

It is seldom, as a rule, that an auditor has to take any steps to find out that sufficient credit has been taken in the revenue account for earnings of the company—as a rule he has to guard against credit being taken for too much. For example, in the case of a trading company he should see that the last entries recording sales had *bona fide* taken place within the period, and that they did not really occur in the first two or three days of the succeeding period.

It is, of course, impossible for me to discuss in detail all the various forms of expenditure, but an auditor should, in every instance, take pains to ascertain that every charge belonging to the period under audit has been included in the revenue account, whether the same have been paid or not. The longer the audit takes place after the closing of the books the easier this becomes, as it, of course, can be ascertained by looking at the vouchers for the payments made after the close of the period, as to whether they should not be included in the indebtedness of the period under audit.

Where there is no profit, or the margin of profit shown by the accounts is only just sufficient to pay a small dividend, the auditor has frequently great difficulty in inducing the officials of the company to include outstandings on various pretences. This he must be exceedingly firm about, but it is, of course, not only allowable but proper to listen to arguments of this nature, and, provided the Articles of Association or Act of Parliament sanction it, he may allow a portion of the expenditure to be treated as an asset, and spread it over a number of years, charging only a proportion against the revenue account for the period. I may here mention that there is absolutely no authority for a company to spread the expenditure of any one year over succeeding years, unless expressly authorised by the Articles of Association. Where this clause has been omitted from the Articles, auditors are frequently asked to treat these items as assets, on the ground that it is the custom of all companies to do so, but custom is not sufficient, and auditors should point out to the directors the risk they run personally by declaring any dividend paid out of profits earned by treating accounts in this manner.

As far as the law at present stands, they would be answerable to a liquidator for any dividend thus distributed, on the ground of its having been paid out of the cap.:al of the company.

In all trading companies, the stock-in-trade forms a very important feature in the revenue account and balance sheet. It is not of course, part of the duty of an auditor to take the stock— that is always done by one of the officials of the company, but it is certainly part of an auditor's duty to inquire into the mode of taking stock, and ascertaining by examination of the officials and otherwise that it has been done in a proper manner, and, for his own protection, should require a certificate from a superior official of the company certifying to the value of the stock.

All stocks should be taken at cost price, never above it, and where the stock has been for some time on hand and has suffered from deterioration, or the market has depreciated since it was bought, a proportion ought to be written off for depreciation in this respect. Depreciation also should be written off every description of perishable security held by the company or firm.

Where property of this nature is of various descriptions the question of depreciation should be inquired into very carefully, of each class of property. For example, it would be considered by modern professional auditors, exceedingly unscientific to write off a round sum as a percentage on leases, buildings, machinery, tools and stock-in-trade. In the case of a lease, the sum must be arrived at by a proper table, and due regard must be had to the number of years it has to run. In the case of solid substantial buildings built on freehold land, a very small percentage would be sufficient. In the case of engines the percentage would be higher, but nothing like so great again as it would be on certain portions such as "Washers," or for workshop, tools, &c.

For the purpose of ascertaining the proper amount to be written off in the case of factories, machinery, &c., I recommend to your notice "The depreciation of Factories," by Mr. Ewing Matheson and "Factory Accounts," by Messrs. E. Garke and J. M. Fells.

Where any sum has been borrowed by the company, the interest payable on the loan must of course be charged against the revenue account before the net profit is ascertained, as its payment is not dependent upon the profits.

The company of course is at liberty to take credit for interest accrued up to the date of closing the books, although the sum may not be payable for some time, but, on the other hand, the expenditure must include accrued interest, including debenture and mortgage interest on all loans.

The revenue account is usually prepared from the trial balance, which term you are, of course, acquainted with ; and after all the items forming the revenue account have been eliminated the remainder forms the statement usually called for this reason, the balance sheet, or statement showing the financial position of the company audited. In auditing this account it should be the object of the auditor to ascertain that the liabilities have not been understated nor the assets over estimated.

Amongst the liabilities are put the capital of the Shareholders in the case of a company, or the capital of the partners in the case of a private firm ;the business being of course, indebted to them in their private capacities for the amount they have embarked in the enterprise.

When property has been mortgaged it should not, strictly speaking, appear in the balance sheet amongst the general assets. The proper way of stating it is for the sum borrowed to be placed amongst the liabilities with a statement that the lenders are fully secured by the particular property charged, the value of which should be stated and the balance being the amount which it is believed would be realised, only included in the assets. In practice this is very seldom done, and, where the company or firm is solvent, it is not of much consequence, but should it not be solvent it is then of the highest importance that the form recommended by me should be strictly adhered to, as otherwise the accounts are exceedingly misleading. For example, assuming the capital of a company is £30,000, the liabilities £90,000, and the ordinary free assets £30,000, also that it possesses freehold property worth £90,000. mortgaged for £60,000, the balance sheet on being prepared with the mortgages amongst the ordinary liabilities, and the property as a free asset would show a deficiency of only £60.000. This would appear to an unsecured creditor as if, on winding up, he would receive 20/ in the £. whereas, if the account be properly prepared, it will be seen that there is really only a dividend of 13s. 4d. in the £. for the unsecured creditors. This will be seen more readily from the following statement :—

Capital		£30,000	Assets unencumbered	£30,000
General Liabilities		90,000	Freehold Property.	90,000
Mortgages		60,000		
			Total Assets	120,000
			Balance Deficiency.	60,000
		£180,000		£180,000

Capital		£30,000	Assets unencumbered	£30,000
General Liabilities		90,000	Surplus after paying off Mortgages as per Contra	30,000
Mortgages	£60,000			
Freehold Property ..	90,000			
Surplus	£30,000		Total Assets	60,000
			Balance Deficiency.	60,000
		£120.000		£120,000

As I have already informed you, when discussing the Revenue Account, it is necessary that the expenses should include the amounts due at the date of closing the books, it follows necessarily, if this has been done correctly, that all the liabilities must be brought into the balance sheet and I need not therefore discuss these items separately.

In closing the balance sheet, the auditor should impress upon the directors the necessity of making perfectly clear to the shareholders the financial position of the company, and should not let there be any ambiguity as to that position. If the directors refuse to alter an account the auditor has always the power of remedying this by his report. For example, accounts are frequently presented to shareholders in which the last item on the asset side of the balance sheet is "balance." This of course to any person understanding accounts means the amount of the a deficiency in consequence of the liabilities of the company being that much in excess of the assets, while an uninitiated shareholder might think this means a balance to the good.

This method the auditor should decidedly object to, and if the directors will not add words showing there is a deficiency, he should make this clear in his report.

Either on the conclusion of an audit, or previous to its completion, it is usual for the auditor when the assets are represented by investments or property, to inspect the securities representing the same, to see that they are in the custody of the company and have not been improperly made use of. For this purpose he should be supplied with a full list of the property, and appoint a time for the inspection. In the case of banks and financial companies, the securities held are sometimes exceedingly numerous and quite impossible to be checked in one day. In these cases the auditor must take whatever steps he thinks desirable, to ensure that some of the securities are not presented to him twice, and for this purpose in some way or another, either by taking away with him the keys of the strong room or safe containing the securities, he must have the whole of them under his control, and they must remain so from the moment he commences the examination until he has concluded it.

If he has to check any securities of a company at the bank

or any place where they may be deposited out of the control of the company, he should by inquiry ascertain that they are not held by the persons in whose custody they are against any loan, and that they have no lien upon them.

Where large sums of money are in the hands of an official on the date of closing the books, it it is usual for the auditor to count them, but as this is sometimes resented by the official, it can be got over by his paying the whole of it into the bank on the evening of the previous day.

In examining the title deeds of property, unless the auditor is acquainted with documents of this description, he should for his own protection receive a certificate from the solicitor to the company, that they are in proper order, and not pledged to any mortgagee.

Having completed the audit, it is usual for the auditor to either confirm the accounts, or make a special report upon them. In many companies it is specially enacted in the articles of association that the auditors shall make a report, in which case it is obligatory for them to do so.

Although all articles of association are still drawn stating that the accounts are to be presented to the auditors, and returned by them within a specified time, either confirmed or reported upon, it is usual for the auditors, if they object to the form of accounts, to make their suggestions to the directors who generally acquisce, for it is pretty certain that an unfavorable report in the accounts of a company might be exceedingly disastrous, and would certainly affect the value of the shares in the money market.

With the exception of railway companies, no form of certificate is prescribed.

I should, myself, very much like it to be settled by the Institute of Chartered Accountants, what would constitute a thorough audit of every class of company, and for all auditor's certificates to be in this form:—"Audited in accordance with the form prescribed by the Institute of Chartered Accountants." After a certificate of this nature were appended to the accounts of a few of the leading companies, it would soon be the universal practice, and would give auditors an immense power in answering any objection raised by directors and officials, as to whether or not certain methods of conducting an audit, the examination of securities &c, were necessary.

At present, however, the form of certificate is left to the auditor, and supposing he is satisfied that the accounts are correct in every particular, I do not consider it of much consequence in what words his satisfaction is expressed. I, however, assert very firmly that an auditor should never, either to please the officials of a company, or to further his own interests, attempt to protect them or him by an ambiguous certificate. Unless an auditor indicates plainly in his certificate he is dissatisfied with the accounts his clients, have the right to expect things are correct in every particular. An auditor's signature after the single word "audited" is the strongest he can give, and implies that without a single reservation the accounts are correct in every particular, and that the securities have been found in perfect order.

At the conclusion of the lecture the CHAIRMAN said he felt sure a good discussion should ensue. The subject of auditing was of a very wide nature, and of the greatest importance to the members present. Auditing might also be described as one of their most ancient duties. He had seen some old records of the Grocers Company dated 1435, in which mention was made of a dinner for the auditors. SHAKESPEARE, too, used the term "audit" in "HENRY VIII," and in "SIMON OF ATHENS" speaks of "auditors."

In the "New English Dictionary" recently published, it seemed that a special kind of ale was brewed in Oxford, termed "audit" ale, but, probably, this ale was brewed for a "rent" audit. This evidently gave rise to BURON'S line, "But where is now the goodly audit ale."

The CHAIRMAN, in conclusion, said he was sure they were all very much indebted to Mr. PIXLEY for his very able paper.

Mr. W. HARRIS, A.C.A. also thought they were much indebted to Mr. PIXLEY for the lecture they had just heard, and the excellent attendance of members was an indication that Mr. PIXLEY'S remarks were appreciated. He trusted he was in good order in referring with pleasure to the presence, during some part of the evening, of Mr. WHINNEY, the President of the Institute, who had always manifested a warm interest in the Society, and a desire to help it. He regretted that before leaving them Mr. WHINNEY had not the opportunity of addressing them, but they trusted to be so favoured on another occasion. He was not sure whether he correctly understood the lecturer in one part of his lecture to say that the postings in books to be audited might be, as a matter of practice, or usually were, taken as correct and in order, if the books had been balanced. His own comparatively short experience had tended to give him the idea that no such thing ought to be assumed or was in practice assumed. If he remembered rightly a serious case of fraud had come before the City of London Court only a few months ago, which had been successfully effected through the neglect to check the postings, though the books were undoubtedly balanced, and it would readily occur to them, without details being given, how such fraud could be carried out with impunity if the postings were not checked. The suggestion that where property was mortgaged, the difference between the value of the property and the amount of the mortgage (assuming the latter to be less than the former) should be extended as the asset, and not extend as an asset the full amount of the property charged, and as a liability the full amount of the mortgage, was sometimes acted upon; but it appeared to him to serve no useful purpose, to be if anything inconvenient, and in any case to be a practice which was more suggestive of a bankrupt's statement of affairs than an ordinary balance sheet. Besides he could not see why, on the same principle, rent, rates and wages accrued due, and other preferential payments should not be deducted at the foot of the assets' side instead of being shown as ordinary liabilities. Still, speaking with all deference, he should be inclined to disagree with what was said about "limited" instructions as to the audit of private concerns, suggesting as he took it limited responsibility of the auditor. A private audit, in his view, agreed in many essential particulars with the audit of a joint stock company's account, and it always seemed to him altogether dangerous and unsafe for an auditor to suppose the balance sheet prepared by him was for the private use of the partners only. The auditor could never tell what use his balance sheet might be put to. The partners might use the balance sheet as the means of obtaining or continuing an overdraft from their bankers, or for the purpose of showing to creditors, or for many other purposes. In short it seemed impossible to tell what use might be made of statements so prepared, and what responsibility, morally or financially, or both, might fall on the auditor in consequence. It would of course be understood, that these remarks were made with the object of eliciting explanation, and to correct his own possibly mistaken views rather than anything else.

Mr. A. DANGERFIELD, A.C.A., said, that although Mr. Pixley's suggestion that a form of Auditors' Certificate should be adopted which should have the authority of the Institute of Chartered Accountants was not new, still it appeared one, that if carried out, would be of use to the whole profession.

Mr. EDWARD H. FLETCHER, A.C.A., said, they had listened that evening to a very valuable lecture from Mr. Pixley. He thought that it would have been a good thing if Mr. Pixley had dealt with some errors of omission that might generally be looked for. To take a typical instance, the omission of the item of rent. This could be satisfactorily checked by the copy of the rent roll, the examination of which should be made a regular part of the audit. In other matters similar checks might be adopted according to the circumstances of the case. Mr. Pixley had also referred to a case in which what was known as the "revolving system," of fraud had been adopted.

The CHAIRMAN thought the best means of preventing such, was to keep the cashier or person who entered up the cash book distinct from the person who posted from that book into the ledger.

Several other members took part in the discussion, and the meeting terminated with votes of thanks to Mr. Pixley for his able paper, and to the chairman, for his services in the chair.

THE ETHICS OF ACCOUNTANCY
(1888)

John Mather

What are an accountant's ethical responsibilities toward his clients, the public, and his fellow practitioners? This first published article on accounting ethics considers the etiquette of accounting practice--at that time, a wholly unwritten code of conduct.

MANCHESTER SOCIETY OF CHARTERED ACCOUNTANTS.

THE ETHICS OF ACCOUNTANCY.

By the PRESIDENT, MR. JOHN MATHER, F.C.A.

Address delivered at the Meeting of the Manchester Society of Chartered Accountants on Tuesday, 27th November, 1888.

Sometime ago a Birmingham accountant delivered an address, having for its topic the "Poetry of Accountancy," but I am not aware that anyone has yet taken up the subject of the "Ethics of Accountancy," though it is surely a topic which should offer a suggestive and inviting field for a disquisition on the part of anyone able and willing to deal with it in an exhaustive manner.

All I can venture to attempt in this address is, to offer you a few stray thoughts on this subject, which will not be entirely useless, if they provoke or encourage others to enlarge upon it hereafter. In any case it will be admitted that the discussion of such a subject must be in perfect harmony with what is described as the object of our Charter, viz, "to raise the status of the profession: the word *status* in this connection comprehending as I take it, our *moral* as well as social and intellectual character and influence in the community.

I find the dictionary definition of the word "Ethics" to be as follows: "The doctrines of morals or social manners, the "science of moral philosophy which teaches men their duty and "the reasons of it, a system of moral principles and rules for "regulating the actions and manners of men in society." I hope nobody will be alarmed at this formidable quotation. If I were to take it as a text, you might perhaps expect such a discourse as would lead one and another of my hearers to compose themselves for a quiet dose. But I shall rather treat it, as some preachers occasionally take the liberty of dealing with their text, regarding it as a mere starting point from which they are free to wander in any direction, so long as they can press into service any thought or illustration even remotely bearing upon their main topic.

We are sometimes told that "Law is the perfection of reason;" and though this charming theoretical description so often belies experience as to lead irreverent laymen to regard it as an ironical epigram, we may without any fear of derision, paraphrase it by saying that "Accountancy is the perfection of accounts," in other words the perfection of reason in the adjustment of accounts, and the perfection of truth in stating them. What is called the "glorious uncertainty of the Law"—illustrated not only in the varying interpretations of enactments, but often in the evidence of opposing experts in law suits—conveys an idea that rarely attaches to the figures, statements, or certificates of Chartered Accountants. And it is our hope and belief, that as we succeed in gradually raising the standard of the skill and the ethics of the profession, any such idea of chance or uncertainty will be still more foreign to its work in the future.

The playful proverb applied—most undeservedly of course—to lawyers' that "their first effort is to get *on*, their second to get *honor*, and their third to get *honest*," is of a kind that one never hears applied to the accountants' profession, though we cannot deny that in the past it has not been wholly free from conspicuous examples of black sheep."

I hope, since the granting of our Charter, the day has gone by when any accountant would, by an exorbitant method of charging for his work or by assisting in the process known as "wrecking" in order to make work, give any color to the imputation that used to be made occasionally that we were a kind of commercial vulture, which flourished most when carcases were plentiful, or whose gain meant other people's loss.

If asked to describe the accountant's mission in the world o[f] commerce, I should say it is "to right the wrong," and to kee[p] what is right from getting wrong. Some may say this is th[e] mission of all true men, or ought to be. But the fortunat[e] fact for accountants is that in the fulfilment of this missio[n] they earn their livelihood, some of them, it must be admitted rather a good one. The necessity, however, of bein[g] perpetually on the *qui vive* to right the wrong as a matter o[f] business is not without its difficulties and drawbacks. I[t] requires us to cultivate the spirit of criticism and distrust, no[t] to say the propensity for fault-finding to an almost abnorma[l] degree—at any rate to a degree which is not easy to combin[e] with uniform geniality of disposition. And some of us fin[d] that this spirit and propensity, so needful in our business, hav[e] a tendency unduly to develop themselves beyond that particula[r] sphere, so that it needs special self-restraint on our part, and perhaps some charity on the part of our friends, if we are to escape being likened to the man who pays too much attentio[n] to the "mote" in his brother's eye, and too little to the possible "beam" in his own.

While the law very properly assumes every man to b[e] innocent until the contrary is proved, in the practice o[f] Accountancy we are allowed to take nothing for granted, and however repugnant to our amiable feelings we have t[o] proceed upon the opposite assumption.

We lay no claim to infallibility, but any serious mistake i[n] our work ought to be considered all but unpardonable. Yo[u] will remember a statesman once described some act of the Government of the day by saying: "It was worse than a crime, it was a blunder." Whether or not we adopt the ethical notion involved in this remark, we must all wish tha[t] what was said of the late Mr. Crosbie—a member of one of the most eminent firms of accountants in London—might be tru[e] of us. His partner was heard to remark that during a[n] experience of 40 years he had never known him to make a mistake.

Some kinds of business, or the methods resorted to in conducting them, are confessedly hard to reconcile with any high standard of ethics. We contend, however, that no man is too good to be an accountant, and further that having regard to the nature of our duties, any man who should obtain a practice as such, if destitute of a high sense of honour or of conscientiousness, might fairly be described as a member of the "dangerous classes." How manifold are the instances in which confidence—I had almost said blind confidence—is reposed in us and our work. Not to speak of the cases in which parties, who know that their interests are mutually opposed, accept our statement of accounts as final, we are often placed in a position where any carelessness on our part—for example, in the apportionment of of capital and income, the method of treating interest calculations *pro* and *con*; the adjustment of conflicting interests in trust or partnership accounts, or otherwise—might lead to gross injustice being done to persons known or unknown, who will never challenge the accountant's work. A Scotch solicitor recently visited an accountant's office in Manchester to examine and take over the books and assets of a trust on behalf of the residuary legatees. After a brief inspection he was good enough to express his surprise and satisfaction that accounts extending over 17 years were so simple and clear from first to last. This was only a matter of course; but in opening these accounts there had been some nice points which the accountant had to settle for or against the reversionaries according to his own judgment and experience.

It is not very long since an accountant, with whom I am familiar, had the satisfaction of saving upwards of five hundred pounds to a trust estate which could ill afford to lose that sum, by pointing out the erroneous mode adopted in calculating the interest in a current account extending over many years. This statement which had been rendered in a perfectly *bonâ fide* spirit, would otherwise have remained unchallenged, in which event the accountant would have received no blame from any quarter but his own conscience. Such cases and others frequently occurring, remind us that we cannot overrate the moral responsibility attaching to our work, nor be too jealous for the honour of our profession in the method of doing it. "Remember, you are to take the place of the Vice-Chancellor in this affair," was the good-humoured remark with which, on one occasion, the late respected Mr. Sale (so well-known as a non-litigious lawyer) concluded his instructions in a certain case, where a dispute between two partners was to be settled—as it ultimately was—by the accountant's investigation and report.

While maintaining the best relations with the legal profession, which we may describe as "our august ally," we still claim that it is one of the highest functions of accountancy *to prevent litigation.*

When you think of the "envy, hatred, malice, and all uncharitableness," often associated with disputes at law—even in those cases where justice, and not merely the longest purse, is triumphant—it is a matter of profound satisfaction that by exhibiting the inexorable logic of figures, properly stated, we are the means of reducing the number of such disputes, and thereby assist our fellow-men to obey one of the practical injunctions of Christian ethics: "As much as lieth in you, live peaceably with all men."

If to prevent litigation while promoting equity is one of the highest functions of our profession, there is another, which in its bearing on social ethics is quite equal to it, viz., the *prevention of dishonesty*. I say *prevention* as distinct from *detection*. We all know how often defalcations are committed by men who had no dishonest intention when they took the first step on the dangerous incline. Under sudden temptation or emergency they "borrowed" their employer's money with the idea of repaying it long before the delinquency could be found out, because they had no fear of an auditor before their eyes. In such cases the very fact of an audit—even an imperfect one—would, by making the risk too great, have rendered the temptation non-existent, and thus have saved the servant from crime and the master from loss. Two striking incidents in my own early experience have made a life-long impression on my mind. As auditor for a concern which had branch establishments in two distant parts of the country for the sale of their goods, I suggested the propriety of a visit by the auditor for the purpose of checking the accounts of the agents. The latter were considered fully trustworthy by the managing director, who, nevertheless, approved of the idea, and advised the agents of the intended visit. The effect was magical, and I much regret to add that in one case it was tragical also. Within a few days after the intimation had been given, the clerk who acted as collector at one of the branches was found dead through having opened a vein in his arm; and enquiry disclosed the painful fact that he had collected moneys for which he had not accounted. In the other case, the agent came post-haste to see the managing director, and on his knees confessed to being unable to produce his cash balance. He begged forgiveness, and that the deficit might be treated as a loan, for which he offered some kind of security. The director was lenient, and arranged the matter in such wise as to give his agent (whom he had always regarded as an estimable man), a chance to recover himself. Circumstances proved that he was right. The man, being retained in his position, gradually discharged his liability, and for many years past has done well. The director having since died, I am perhaps the only person now in possession of the secret, which I need not say has been, and will be kept inviolate; and I never recall it without feeling thankful that in the ordinary discharge of professional duty, I was the unintentional means of preventing (just in time) what might have ended in moral disaster, and the ruin and disgrace of a family.

But there is another kind of dishonesty which is at least diminished by the existence of our profession. I refer to the dishonesty (for such I call it) of those who trade on credit—that is with other people's money—without keeping proper books of account. It is well known that this has been one of the germs of insolvency in many cases, and it is satisfactory to find that it is coming to be regarded as a much more serious offence than formerly. As an instance take the following paragraph which caught my eye recently in a financial journal.

"A bankrupt has had his order of discharge suspended for "3 months, because, although the principal books used in his "business were honestly kept, the subsidiary books were not "posted up, and the books had not been balanced at regular "intervals."

Lax Bookkeeping and lax morality, though not born relations, are often related by marriage, and they are both the natural offspring of slovenliness, and slipshodism, and the reckless rule of *laissez-faire*, against which the accountant swears eternal enmity. We have heard of those who love darkness rather than light, because their deeds are evil, whereas he who is of the truth is willing that his deeds should be made manifest, and exact bookkeeping is one means to this end. As "Nature abhors a vacuum," so the accountant abhors a discrepancy. He is ever wanting to put crooked things straight. He has no patience with anomalies or incongruities or anything which will not harmonise with what is understood as "the eternal fitness of things." The time is fast coming when the reckless trader, the defaulting bookkeeper, the fraudulent promoter, and the wilfully negligent director or trustee will all have the fear of the F.C.A. before their eyes, as a wholesome deterrent to themselves, and a protection to those who trust them.

Having thus glanced, though very imperfectly, at what I may call the objective side of the Ethics of Accountancy, let us turn to one or two points which relate more to the subjective side.

What is the duty of an accountant when he discovers unexpectedly that certain work which he has undertaken exceeds the remuneration he is to receive for it? This may arise through his having named a charge beforehand without fully realising the difficulties and delays which bad bookkeeping or other causes create for him, or through his having accepted an audit appointment at a fee which he finds inadequate to pay for a perfect audit. In such circumstances may the accountant "scamp" his work and say—"I will do as much as I am paid for and no more?" His own sense of duty and the possible risk to his clients will forbid anything of the kind. Whatever work he undertakes he must do it his best from first to last, whether the result be profitable to himself or not. Any other rule than this would lower the moral tone and dignity of the profession.

I may here quote the words of Mr. Fisher (President of the Birmingham Society and our genial host at the recent autumnal gathering.) In an address to the London Students' Society on "Bank Auditing," he says: "Do not let the amount of your "remuneration influence your work. If you find you are being "underpaid, make an application for a higher fee or give up "the audit. Never let it be said that you have done just as "much work as your fee covered; remember if you consider "your appointment as auditor good enough to accept, it must be "good enough to have at all costs your best energies, your best "abilities, and your best attention. In a word, you must realize "your duty and devote to your work brains, thought and skill."

It requires no small tact and discrimination to avoid on the one hand a habit of intermeddling or travelling beyond our legitimate province, and on the other an indifference to matters which, though they lie outside the strict limits of our duty, come within our cognisance as affecting our client's interests. But such tact and discrimination are to be cultivated as cardinal virtues by the accountant. As an illustration of the benefit of not confining our attention solely to the work we are paid for I may cite the following: A Manchester accountant who was auditing the accounts of a London company, found amongst the liabilities a heavy claim for income-tax. He felt convinced it was excessive, but being on the safe side it might have been allowed to pass so far as he was concerned. On questioning the secretary and book keeper, he found that they had sought unsuccessfully to dispute the claim with the tax-surveyor. The auditor took the matter in hand, prepared amended forms of the profit and loss accounts for three years, with explanations which satisfied the surveyor that the wrong balances had been taken by him; and the result was a reduction in the claim by a sum which was sufficient to cover the auditor's fees for several years. The small extra charge which the auditor felt justified in making for this extra service was, I need hardly say, cheerfully paid.

When an auditor finds himself left with almost entire discretion as to the limits of his audit (which is frequently the case) to what extent is he morally bound to include as part of the audit the detail checking of postings? If it be said that he may stop at the point where he is morally certain that everything is correct, I reply that in many cases we, and our employers also, are "morally certain" of this before we begin our work. Our duty is to be able to say that we have proved it to be so. Before we can say this it will usually be necessary for our clerks to do a large amount of detail checking, and I submit we are never justified in dispensing with this except in those cases where the internal organisation of the office and the arrangement of the books are such that no fraud or error which checking can discover will escape discovery.

Two other topics that may be said to belong to the Ethics of Accountancy were briefly discussed—too briefly from lack of time—at the recent Autumnal gathering of the Institute. One, the moral duty of an accountant, before he allows his name to appear as auditor upon a prospectus, to be satisfied not only of the *bonâ fides* but of the *prospects* of the Company in question. The other, accountant's certificates: their scope and the responsibility attaching to them. In regard to the first topic some attempt was made to fix the standard higher than was generally felt to be practicable. In most cases an accountant is no better able than other people to forecast the business prospects of an undertaking which, however sound, at the outset, may ultimately fail through mismanagement, change of fashion, invalidity of patents, or numberless unforeseen causes. His duty requires that in giving the sanction of his name to a prospectus, the auditor should have such knowledge of the promoters and directors, and of the history of the inception of the company as will satisfy him that there is nothing "shady" about its birth, that it is *bonâ fide* at all points, and that there is no *suppressio veri* by which any intelligent man might be deceived as to its merits. To expect more than this, or to assume that in accepting a position which binds us to protect the shareholders against false Balance Sheets, we are thereby recommending the investment from personal knowledge, of its merits, would be in the highest degree unreasonable. If such a standard were set up it would overshoot the mark, and lead the most scrupulous members of the profession to feel that they were shut out from most of these appointments.

The subject of accountants' certificates offers a wider field of discussion, and it revealed some slight difference of opinion amongst those who took part in the debate at the recent meeting I have referred to. There seems a general agreement that in certifying as to the position or profits of a business, for instance, which is proposed to be converted into a company, the accountant may not *prophecy* "unless he knows." In other words he must avoid the tempting region of fancy and stick to prosaic facts. But in the opinion of many he is fully justified in dealing with those facts in their bearing upon the future as well as upon the past, and in stating his belief—always providing it is based upon sufficient evidence—that the profit-earning capacity of the business may be increased by a certain increase of capital, or that a larger out-turn will diminish the cost of production in a certain ratio. Perhaps no hard and fast rule on this point can be laid down beyond this, that the accountant should pen every word of his certificate with as keen a sense of moral responsibility as if he knew that the intending investor would be guided by his statements alone, and he should never consent to the publication of his certificate with its qualifying clauses (if any) omitted. The temptation to oblige his clients by a compromise in this respect may sometimes be strong, but he must stand firm at all costs, in view of the risk involved by any laxity on his part.

I may here fitly quote a passage from a recent number of *The Accountant*; in its Obituary notice of one who might be fairly called the "Patriarch" of our profession—"Mr. QUILTER was a man of great decision and force of character, his sagacity, shrewdness, and independence, were patent to all with whom he was brought in contact. No report or certificate that he did not fully approve and believe to be accurate, would be signed by him, and many instances are known in which he lost business, by means of his strict and unbending conscientiousness. He was a type of what a public accountant should be, upright, straightforward, and perfectly destitute of any trace of professional jealousy in regard to his fellows. Taken all in all, it will be long before we shall look upon his like again." I hope not; in fact, I believe that the type to which Mr. QUILTER belonged is daily becoming a more common one in our ranks.

With regard to the conscientiousness and care required in an auditor, who attaches his certificate to a Company's Balance-Sheet, these qualities are no longer dependent solely upon his own sense of moral responsbility. Recent cases in the Courts have shown, that pains and penalties of no trifling kind—nay such as may mean simply ruin—hang over the head of the negligent auditor, even when his negligence is not what the Law terms "wilful." We do not complain of this increased responsibility, but it it is not too much to ask that it should be borne in mind when the audit fee is fixed, and further, that it should lead to some improvement in the mode of appointing company auditors, whereby such appointments may become in *practice*—as they are now often only in *theory*—independent of the control of directors.

As members of the Institute, it would be well if we were to make it our aim to secure for accountancy the title of "the incorruptible profession." As far as my observation goes, there is no business, or calling which has less to fear from such a sweeping enactment as that lately proposed by a well-known authority in the coal trade, who states that £800,000 a year is paid in the way of bribery, in connection with the gas industry of the United Kingdom, and urges that it be made "an offence, "punishable by penal servitude to ask for, offer, accept, give, "promise or suggest any bribe, tip or commission, as a con-"sideration for improper or undue influence in connection with "a business transaction." It is to be feared that more than one business at the present time is honeycombed with this cancerous disease, familiarly termed the "palm-oil" system. The accountant, in the course of his duties, will occasionally come across symptoms, which bring it within his province to show where the pruning-knife should be applied to this mischievous parasite, and serious incubus to healthy commerce, which grows by what it feeds upon, and which I regret to believe is even more prevalent on the Continent than in our own country.

I do not fear to recall one case (which I admit was a monstrous one) in our own profession, because I believe, as we must all devoutly hope, it was not only a rare, but of its kind a solitary case—the exception which proves the rule. I refer to one of the biggest firms in London, which collapsed by the sudden disappearance of its two principals, when the passing of the Bankruptcy Act 1883, required trustees to pay over to the Board of Trade any old-standing balances in their hands. I have heard that this firm's practice was largely built up by a process of supplying the wine-cellars and cigar-cupboards of chief clerks and officials who were in a position to influence business and appointments in their favour. If such a system had even began to take root in London, let us hope that this collapse has nipped it in the bud. We certainly rely upon the executive of the Institute, as our vigilance committee, to guard the profession against the first inroads of any such corruption, and we believe that every year will find us more secure from even the suspicion of it.

It would have been interesting and perhaps useful to discuss, as part of our present subject, what we may call the etiquette of the profession, that unwritten code which regulates the relations of accountants to each other as such. But I must content myself with a very few words on this topic. Although the spirit of competition and motives of self-interest can never be entirely excluded from any business or profession, I would venture to plead for a further development of that *esprit de corps*, and that courteous consideration for the feelings and interests of others which will lead us to think of our fellow-members as "brethren" rather than as "rivals." One of the distinct benefits which I think we may discern in connection with our Autumnal gatherings—where good fellowship and mutual acquaintance and esteem are promoted amongst those who were and would be otherwise strangers to each other—is the encouragement of this higher tone and standard of professional etiquette and dignity. We can point even in Manchester—where we are supposed to be rather rough and ready—to some worthy examples amongst our members, who would rather stand aside or even assist competitors to obtain business, than they would tread on their toes, or elbow them out, or join metaphorically in what football-players would call a "scrimmage." By following such examples I believe that, while gaining in the matter of dignity and respect, we shall not, in the long run, be losers in pocket. If we sum up the obligations imposed on us by professional etiquette in the motto: "Noblesse oblige," we shall not get far astray, for I take it, this motto, rightly interpreted, would lead us on much the same lines in business as that sublime and yet most practical rule of Christian ethics which teaches us "to do as we would be done by."

In closing what I fear I must call this somewhat rambling dissertation, I venture to hope that I have at least succeeded in proving that if the "Chartered Accountant" is not one of the most conscientious, and in fact, one of the best all-round men in the community, he *ought* to be so; and that the "Ethics" of his profession tend to make him so; that in his avocation there are few talents or good qualities which cannot find free scope and a congenial sphere; and that whereas at one time Accountancy was a sort of *omnium gatherum*, or refuge for anybody who had failed in other avocations, it now offers but little room or prospect for men of inferior ability, still less of inferior character. If, as we have reason to believe, the profession, though still in its youth, is coming to be regarded every year as of more utility and importance to the public, this must encourage each of us to do our little best to raise its standard of merit still higher, and to act in the spirit of the old Latin proverb. "*Qui cessat esse melior, cessat esse bonus.*' "Who ceases to be better, ceases to be good."

THE ETHICS OF ACCOUNTANCY
(1888)

Editorial from The Accountant

Elaborating on the issues raised by Mr. Mather's article.

The Accountant,

DECEMBER 29, 1888.

THE ETHICS OF ACCOUNTANCY.

THE address delivered by Mr. JOHN MATHER, F.C.A., to the Manchester Society of Chartered Accountants, and reported in our last, is a thoughtful and well-considered composition. It is rather unfortunate the discussion was not reported, as the views of some of those who spoke would have possessed great interest.

In raising the matters dealt with, tact and delicacy were exhibited, and a little introspection of the kind suggested by Mr. MATHER's remarks should not fail to be productive of good.

We hope, with Mr. MATHER, that the disastrous and suicidal policy of charging exorbitant fees and rates is ceasing; we are not so sanguine as to speak of it entirely in the past tense. The practice of grossly under-quoting for work already being performed by another accountant at barely remunerative rates, is also not wholly unknown.

As regards accountants who are said to have never made mistakes in their lives, we heard a sardonic critic once say that of such men one of two things, perhaps two, could be affirmed, they either took double the time they ought to have taken over their work, or the work they did could not have been very intricate. Of course we do not endorse this. We know some men who have justly made a reputation for literal accuracy, but it frequently happens that such men are the last men in the world to be entrusted to carry through awkward, contentious, and complicated questions of account; and to send such persons to stormy meetings of creditors or contributories, would be like putting old spinsters in charge of life boats.

As a general statement, it may be quite true that there is in the city in which the address was delivered, a good feeling of *esprit de corps* amongst the members of our profession. The saying that exceptions prove the rule is a charitable one, and we must take it as covering some offences in Manchester by accountants against their brethren, which we think ought to be publicly exposed.

Mr. MATHER might have given a line or two to another little social custom we have developed, that is, publicly praising in a most fulsome style the paper or speech of a member, and afterwards privately expressing disgust at it. We take a deep interest in this little amenity, and as may be expected, have peculiar sensations when, as actually happens, gentlemen get up at meetings and express opinions utterly and diametrically opposed to what are certainly known to be their true views. It seems a small failing; but to it can be traced more direct and serious evil to the profession, and the Institute, than flows from matters of greater apparent consequence.

INDEPENDENCE FOR AUDITORS
(1889)

Editorial from The Accountant

The refusal by an English firm of chartered accountants to sign the accounts of a Montana gold mine raises questions about the appointment, tenure, and security of auditors in the face of client pressures.

INDEPENDENCE FOR AUDITORS.

As the episode in connection with the accounts and annual meeting of the Sterling Gold Mines, Limited, has been referred to once or twice in our columns, the subjoined article from *The Statist* may not be without interest:—

The history of the Sterling Gold Mines (Montana) (Limited), whose annual meeting was referred to in a recent issue, raises many points of interest for those who are considering the proposed alterations in the law of Public Companies.

As the law now exists it is evident that the directors of a company can, if they so please, delay presenting any accounts to the shareholders for a period of two and a-quarter years from the date of its incorporation and issue of its prospectus. The prospectus of the Sterling Gold Mines (Montana) (Limited) was issued in October, 1886, and as the statutory meeting was held in January or February, 1887, the directors were able to postpone the next meeting of shareholders until the very last day of the year 1888.

Another lesson it teaches us is that holders of vendor's shares can at a meeting outvote those of the shareholders who have paid cash for their shares, and vendor's nominees can prevent an auditor who is trying to preserve the interests of the latter being heard on their behalf, and leave them at the mercy of the vendor and his clique.

It also shows that the directors can suppress a document affixed to the accounts to be presented to the shareholders, and issue with impunity what is, therefore, practically a mutilated statement.

Directors also are evidently able, where there is power given by the Articles of Association, to vary the agreement with the vendor to issue debentures to him in lieu of cash in case there is an insufficient number of shares applied for, notwithstanding statements in the prospectus that there will be ample working capital for carrying on the business, on the strength of which the company is formed, and thus by making him (the vendor) a mortgagee, placing the property entirely at his mercy.

To suggest a remedy is not always easy. The question of giving to or withholding from the vendor the power of voting requires the most careful consideration, as it is one of those to which there are pre-eminently two sides; but the result of Messrs. Chandler, Pixley and Co.'s refusal to sign the accounts of the Sterling Gold Mines (Montana) (Limited), clearly suggests some improvements in any new Companies' Act. The prospectus of a company should either state the minimum of capital on which the directors shall have power to allot, or in the event of the named minimum not being subscribed the applicants for shares shall be called together, and should themselves decide as to whether an allotment should take place.

Before any allotment takes place the applications for shares and the banker's pass book should be placed before the auditors named on the prospectus, who should give a certificate as to the number of shares applied for, and whether the application money has been lodged in the bank named on the prospectus.

At the statutory meeting a statement of results of business, either from the date of incorporation of the company or from the date on which a going business is taken over by a new company, should be laid before the shareholders, so that they may be able to decide as to whether the company shall be continued or immediately wound up. Had Messrs. Chandler, Pixley and Co. been asked to prepare a statement of the business done by the Sterling Gold Mines (Montana) (Limited), to be presented at the statutory meeting, the subscribers would have been astonished at the difference between the £14,400 per annum referred to on the slip attached to the prospectus and the value of the ore actually raised from the date of the incorporation of the company.

It is evident, moreover, that the hands of auditors require strengthening, and that they should be placed in a more independent position. The first auditors must of necessity be appointed either by the promoter or the directors. In the case of respectable firms there cannot be any possible objection to this. At subsequent meetings they are nominated by the shareholders; but notwithstanding this they are, in the majority of cases, really at the mercy of directors as to their re-appointment. If an auditor is troublesome, it is very easy for a board of directors to quietly have him shelved by arranging with one of their friends to propose the name of a *persona grata* at the meeting.

It appears to us that auditors once appointed should remain in office for an extended period, unless for some palpable misconduct, and the removal should be by an extraordinary meeting of the shareholders. Many people are, perhaps, unaware that under the Companies Act of 1862 it is not necessary to have auditors at all, but it has invariably been the practice for the Articles of Association to provide for their appointment, and modern custom has now practically settled that accounts shall be audited and issued to the shareholders with the certificate of the auditors affixed.

We asked in our last issue what was the professional etiquette of chartered accountants as regards each other. We do not, of course, really wish to discuss this question beyond stating that when a chartered accountant declines to sign the accounts and balance-sheets of a company, the directors ought to search the list of chartered accountants in vain before finding a single member who will for the sake of a fee, or a possible future audit, assist them in their struggle with existing auditors.

The additional difficulty Messrs. Chandler, Pixley and Co. had to contend with in the case referred to by the intervention of Messrs. J. B. Ball, Baker and Co., may be safely left to the Institute of Chartered Accountants. That body has lately shown that it is jealous of its good name, and the Institute has been gradually growing in favour since it received its Charter in 1880.

We believe that some people look upon the granting of this Charter as a monopoly, but reflecting business men are well aware that monopolies of this nature exist for the protection of the public, and as chartered accountants are for the future destined to play a leading part in commercial affairs, any attempt on their part to raise the standard of ability and honourable dealing should receive support.

TOUTING
(1889)

Editorial from *The Accountant*

Concerning the advertising of services by accountants.

The Accountant,

SEPTEMBER 28, 1889.

TOUTING.

We have had brought under our notice a publication, presumably issued weekly by a Yorkshire firm of Chartered Accountants, of which the following is a copy of the first page of the cover:—

Private and Confidential.

THE AUDIT ASSOCIATION

FOR THE IMPROVEMENT OF MERCANTILE BOOKKEEPING AND THE PROTECTION OF TRADE.

Gen. Managers, BLANK SON & CO., Chartered Accountants.
Head Offices:—1, Royal Arcade, Old St., Worstedtown.
Agents and Correspondents throughout the Kingdom.

WEEKLY LISTS OF CREDITORS,
Arranged according to Trades.

OBJECTS OF THE ASSOCIATION:

To promote proper Bookkeeping by Traders and thereby diminish the evils of Insolvencies.
To encourage the custom of periodical Audits by Professional Auditors.
To investigate on behalf of Creditors a doubtful Debtor's affairs before his estate is wasted.
To attend Meetings on behalf of Creditors and report thereon, and thus save the time of the Subscribers.
To obtain information for Subscribers of the Stability of their Customers.
To collect Debts for Subscribers.
To assist Subscribers in obtaining exemption or abatement of Income Tax in case of excessive assessment.

Subscribers should acquaint the Managers of any doubtful debtors and also communicate at once their first intimation of any failure.

TERMS ON APPLICATION.

The Friendly Societies Acts, and the Industrial and Provident Societies Act, 1876.
Mr. Ephraim Blank.—By Appointment of the Lords Commissioners of Her Majesty's Treasury
Public Auditor for England and Wales.

The other three pages of the cover are too lengthy to be reproduced. They set forth in eloquent terms the advantages which traders can gain through the "Association"—by paying of course. There is a matter-of-fact paragraph relating to the Institute, its formation, objects, and constitution, which, to our mind, rather identifies the Institute with the "Association" in a manner which may benefit the latter but scarcely the former. The inner portion of the publication consists of lists of principal creditors of debtors who have become bankrupt or effected private arrangements. These lists are printed in London, and we should judge they are supplied to, and distributed by, more than the particular firm whose name is before us. The publication, in fact, strongly savours of the Parish Magazine style, which, as most readers may know, consists of general literature supplied to Churches in all parts of the kingdom, each Church pasting a cover on the outside giving the births, marriages, and deaths during the month, and other local news. Whether the circulation of publications of this kind is an advertising offence, we should not like to say off-hand. The practice, at least, does not impress one as likely to be adopted by any member of the Institute who wished to earn and maintain a good standing in his profession. The state of accountancy in the whole of the West Riding of Yorkshire is generally, however, very peculiar. A very large proportion of the accountants commenced as rent and debt collectors, and to further their business usually started some sort of a trade "association," which was, or, as a rule, soon became, an association in name only. The taint contracted from such an origin, and from the semi-touting practices which it brought in its train, have not yet been wholly erradicated, though probably a good deal of circumspection is now exercised to keep such practices in the background as far as possible. Of course, as long as local accountancy is associated with debt collecting, as a regular practice, and with "status" enquiries, so long must it be content to see good accountancy work given to the accountants of distant towns who are accountants in the proper sense of the term.

THE FRONT PAGE OF A PROSPECTUS (1890)

Editorial from The Accountant

How is the investing public to be protected against fraudulent prospectuses endorsed by bankers and accountants?

The "Front Page" of a Prospectus.

IN commenting upon the Lord Chief Justice's remarks on Company Promotion, *The Times*, in its City Article, recently pointed out that a considerable amount of responsibility might aptly be imposed upon solicitors acting in connection with new companies, and *The Financial News* has also fully endorsed this sentiment, which, it must be admitted, is not without considerable weight. It was not to be supposed, however, that solicitors as a body would allow these comments to pass unchallenged; and, in a following issue of *The Times*, a long letter from Mr. JOHN S. PARKIN (who, however, is a barrister, not a solicitor) appears, which we here reproduce in full:—

> SIR,—In your City Article of to-day you again call attention to the observations which the Lord Chief Justice addressed to the incoming Lord Mayor of London in reference to the creation of public companies.
>
> You rightly call the observations weighty. They are the first suggestions publicly made that as great, or even greater, benefits can be derived from the

action of private individuals than from the action of the Legislature.

You suggest that solicitors should take a higher view of their duties in connexion with the formation of these companies, and, of course, as regards some solicitors this suggestion may be applicable. But I may point out that of all the officials connected with a new company solicitors are practically the only ones who take a high view of their duties towards the public.

On every prospectus may be seen the names of the banker, solicitor, auditor, and secretary of the new company. But of these four the only one who really examines into the *bona fides* of the intended company is the solicitor. But after all the duty of the solicitor is to attend to the legal aspect of the scheme and to see that there is nothing wrong legally. He is not a financier, but only a lawyer. The financial part of the business ought to be carefully looked into by the bankers and auditors, but how often do they do so? When anyone conversant with commercial matters sees the name of one of the respectable firms of solicitors on a prospectus he knows that the firm has gone carefully into the nature of the business, and that to the best of the firm's abilities they have satisfied themselves that there has been no fraud or irregularity in the formation of the company; and that, so far as legal matters are concerned, the promotion is an honest one. The name of the auditor is sometimes, though not so often as the name of the solicitor, a guarantee that he has examined into the financial aspects of the promotion and found them in order.

But the London bankers, with but one or two exceptions, allow their names to be advertised on a prospectus, and allow copies of the prospectus to be supplied to the public by their country branches, without making the slightest investigation into the correctness of the statements contained in the prospectus.

The bankers endeavour to excuse themselves for this neglect of duty by contending that their names on the prospectus only state a mere fact—viz., that in the future they will be the bankers of the company, and do not signify in the slightest degree that they guarantee the truth of the statements in the prospectus. Even if this contention were correct I do not see why bankers should not be asked to take the same high view of their duties as solicitors. But, as a matter of fact, people do invest in new companies merely because the names of their bankers are on the prospectus. I have myself stopped a man who had been many years in business in the City from applying for shares in a new company on the faith of an evidently fraudulent prospectus, relying solely on the fact that his banker's name was on the prospectus.

The bankers may think that the public place no reliance on their names, but certainly the shady promoter does not think so. He attaches considerable importance to having on his prospectus a bank with many country branches, and whilst the issue is going on watches with the keenest interest the returns from those branches.

It may not be necessary for the bankers, solicitors, and auditors to each make a separate investigation into the affairs of each proposed new company, but I think that at least the bankers and auditors should combine to form a joint committee, and should decline to allow their names to appear on any prospectus until the promoters had satisfied such committee of the *bona fides* of the new undertaking.

Such a committee could frame fresh rules from time to time as the ingenuity of promoters enabled them from time to time to circumvent the rules already laid down by the committee for the protection of the public.

The rules of such a committee would have an elasticity and power of meeting the wiles of the promoter which would be entirely absent from the stereotyped provisions of an Act of Parliament.

The bankers already have their institute, the auditors already have their society, so that there could be no difficulty in forming such a committee. It could at first take as its model the committee of the Stock Exchange, which already makes provision for the protection of its own members against the fraud of promoters; and it might be that in time, if the new committee did its duty, the Stock Exchange Committee would amalgamate with the bankers' committee, and so the promoters would only have to satisfy one committee as to the financial side of the scheme, and the lawyers as to the legal side of the scheme.

Yours truly,

JOHN S. PARKIN.

We venture to think that the two facts that ill be most obvious to our readers from a rusal of Mr. PARKIN's letter are, in the first ace, that it is an attempt to evade the direct ue raised by *The Times;* and in the second, at the counter suggestions contained therein e little short of childish.

With regard to the first point, our conmporary suggested that almost all the ccessful frauds that have ever yet been pertrated in connection with company matters ve been perpetrated with the assistance solicitors; and although, of course, it was t for one moment suggested that these licitors were in any way responsible for the uds, it was pointed out that it was—to say e least of it—undesirable that, for the sake of in, they should assist persons in earning a elihood by a means which, if not absolutely egal, was at all events more than questionle. We should have thought that this was a fficiently specific and a sufficiently serious atter to be approached from a like point of ew; but the only attempt that Mr. PARKIN akes to deal with it is his *ipse dixit* that "of all the officials connected with a new company, solicitors are practically the only ones who take a high view of their duties towards the public." In connection with this coment *The Times* states that if its correspondent d said that solicitors take a high view of their ties towards their clients, it would have reed with them; but it goes on to point out at, in regard to the formation of companies, solicitor's clients are not the public. These v remarks reproduce the precise situation so actly that further comment seems to be together unnecessary.

Passing on to the remainder of Mr. PARKIN's gument, however, which—so far as we understand it—amounts to nothing more than stating that, if solicitors are bad, accountants and bankers are worse, we may draw attention to the very considerable difference between the positions occupied by these three classes of persons. Inasmuch as it is desirable above all things to be practical, attention may in the first place be drawn to the very important distinction that, whereas solicitors invariably make a considerable profit out of the inception of a new company by way of costs, and whereas bankers (or, at all events, the bankers whose names are held in most request) invariably make a considerable charge for the use of their name, accountants are not in the habit of selling their names to company promoters for use upon a prospectus. An accountant's name upon a prospectus implies nothing more than that he will be prepared to audit the first accounts prepared by the directors of that company. Unfortunately, it does not even mean so much as that the directors shall be compelled to submit the accounts to the audit of the accountants named in the prospectus, and this is a point upon which the law ought to be altered without delay. But we are now dealing with the present and not with the future, and, as we said just now, all that is implied by the presence of an accountant's name upon a prospectus is that he is willing to audit the accounts of the company. We should very much like to ask Mr. PARKIN —or anyone else who may be sufficiently interested in the subject—how, in the name of common-sense, it can reasonably be suggested that, prior to allowing his name to be put forward in this capacity, any accountant can be expected to, at his own expense, make an exhaustive investigation into what Mr. PARKIN is pleased to called the "financial "aspect" of the venture. And—even supposing he is prepared to undertake this philanthropic work—what opportunities has he of acquiring the necessary information to enable him to form an opinion?

Leaving this point upon one side, however (and to a certain extent it is desirable to avoid attaching undue importance to it, because, of course, every accountant of repute would certainly desire to abstain from associating himself with rotten undertakings), let us take a more practical view of the subject, and ask what sort of investigation Mr. PARKIN would consider that an accountant ought to make into the "financial aspect" of, say, a mining company, before he allows his name to be associated with it upon the front page of a prospectus. It seems to us that, in practice, all that the accountant could do, is what any prudent member of the public would do before applying for shares, viz., inquire as to the respectability of those connected with the company, and also with the success which had attended their previous efforts in similar directions. But when this had been done, it is obvious that very little would have been accomplished; and it is important to bear in mind that the number of scandals in connection with mining and other similar companies is vastly above the average of other company undertakings.

In some cases, however, the auditor would have a better chance of gauging what the success of the company might be in the future, as, for instance, when it has been formed to acquire an existing undertaking, and he, as the accountant, had had the investigation of the previous accounts. But in a case of this description it may be pointed out that the arrangement invariably made between the accountant and those who instruct him is that he is to make certain investigation and report, and also to b the auditor of the company. Were he, aft making his investigation and reporting, t decline to be the auditor, he would probabl not be paid for his investigation, and anoth accountant would be employed instead. there is a suspicion that something is wron it is hardly to be supposed that any self-respec ing accountant will admit that he can serve th public better by *not* auditing the company accounts than by auditing them. It may b pointed out moreover that the real respons bility which the accountant does incur to th public (which, although, perhaps, at th moment there may be some difficulty in enfor ing it legally, will be admitted by all repu able accountants) is as to the accurac of the statements contained in his certificat If he takes a properly high view of his duties- as opposed to a strictly legal view—and stat the exact facts in the certificate, then we sa that he has done all that could possibly b implied by his allowing his name to b associated with the undertaking. It is, indee nothing short of absurd to suppose that th presence of a well-known accountant's nam upon any part of a company's prospectus is an warranty that the company will eventually b successful; and we may add that, if it were t be supposed to imply anything of the kind, th results in practice could be little short disastrous.

It would, however, be very interesting if M PARKIN will kindly tell us what useful purpos could be served by bankers and accountant forming a "joint committee" to make a inquiry upon the lines adopted by the Con mittee of the Stock Exchange. We assum that the latter inquiry referred to is that mad

, the Stock Exchange for the purpose of ntertaining an application for an official uotation. Those, however, who are acquainted ith the scope of this inquiry will bear us out our statement that the matters that are then one into by the Stock Exchange Committee late almost entirely to events subsequent to ne formation of the company and the issue of s prospectus, and it seems to us a little nreasonable to expect even bankers and ccountants to inquire into events that are bout to happen. But that, after all, is really hat Mr. PARKIN seems to expect them to do, z., to look into the whole undertaking at a age when it practically has not come into cistence, except in a purely nebulous form, nd to give the public a sort of guarantee as to s ability to be successful in the future. Such suggestion is, of course, absurd.

Apart, however, from the absolutely imprac- cal nature of any attempt being made in the rection indicated, it may be pointed out that othing but harm would come from the investing ublic being led to suppose that somebody had ade such inquiries on its behalf into the nancial standing of the undertaking and its obabilities of success, which, in point of fact, ight to be undertaken by each member of the ublic before investing in its shares. This that portion of the matter which must cessarily be left for each man to judge r himself. As respects the legal aspect, a ry different set of conditions obtains, and if licitors were to consider the clients ho pay their costs a little less and the ublic (out of whose pocket those costs are ally paid) a little more, unmixed benefit to e community would result. Anyhow, that ems to be the view which was put forward *The Times*, and which has been endorsed by *The Financial News*, with which we also most cordially agree. Certainly it is a proposition which is worth discussing on its merits, and this, as we have already pointed out, Mr. PARKIN has not yet done.

We trust, however, the matter will not be allowed to drop here, and that if there really is anything to be said from the point of view of company lawyers, someone else will step forward and state the case on their behalf.

The "Front Page" of a Prospectus.

II.

WITH further reference to this matter, which we discussed at some length in our last issue, we find that some little misconception appears to have arisen with regard to what can reasonably be expected from an accountant who has allowed his name to appear on a prospectus as the auditor of the company.

In this connection *The Financial News* states that the law is surely strong enough to ensure that an accountant shall get his fee for examining the books of an enterprise, even if he has refused to report on the terms desired by the promoter. That, of course, goes without saying; but we have yet to learn that it has ever been seriously suggested that any accountant was ever compelled to give a false or misleading certificate because otherwise he could not claim payment of fees due to him. Where a certificate is false or misleading there should be—and we believe that at the present moment there is—a sufficient remedy in the hands of all persons who may have been deceived. But that is not altogether the point which has to be considered. If an accountant is paid to make an investigation and report the result in the form of a certificate, he may with perfect reasonableness be required to report upon those particular matters concerning which his services were retained, and upon no others; and although the ultimate result may be such that the certificate becomes so colourless as to be practically of no value, that, it seems to us, is the misfortune of the promoter and not of t public, who by such certificates ought clear to be put upon their guard, or at least up inquiry. Where a certificate contains a m statement there is a remedy afforded by t law; but where, as is sometimes the case wi a defective certificate, the weakness is in t nature of an omission, we would ask those w are constantly girding at accountants in wh way the latter can prominently draw attenti in their reports to facts or conditions of affa which they have not been asked to certify.

Another somewhat remarkable statement p forward by our contemporary is *à propos* of remark which we made in a recent issue, th with regard to companies formed to take ov valueless properties, the result is that eith the public has gone into the undertaking wit out asking of what they consisted and wh was their value, or else they have been deceiv by false or misleading reports. Our conte porary adds, "It need hardly be said that t "principal reports on existing undertakin "taken over by companies are those of accou "tants." The remark is true enough in a ce tain sense, but anyone who will take t trouble to follow the facts will, we thi realise that the majority of undertakings whi fail because the property which they acquir was valueless, are not companies which ha been formed to take over "existing" business but have been formed to take over mines something equally speculative, in respect which the reports have been made by mini engineers or "mining experts." Undoubted these gentry are responsible for a very mu larger number of false and misleading repo than accountants. Indeed, we have no hesi tion in saying that the false reports that ha been issued by accountants in connection w company matters have been few and far between. In so far as exception can be taken to accountants' certificates, it usually must be on account of their extreme weakness and unconvincing nature, although in some few instances certainly the wording has been open to a double construction which might tend to mislead. Still, absolute misstatements of fact are all but unknown.

Our contemporary goes on to say that, "given a guarantee that solicitors, bankers and "accountants without exception shall act in "the strictest sense of professional honour, and "the swindling promoter will soon cease to "exist, or, at least, to fleece the public. His "success depends upon his command of "technical advice and assistance." To a very large extent this is true; and, as we pointed out in our last issue, without the assistance of the legal profession the promoter would hardly be able to escape the consequences in respect of the first of his promotions which passed into liquidation. But with regard to accountants the matter is upon another footing, inasmuch as the accountant is—even when acting under the instructions of the promoter—in no sense connected with the promotion as such. All that he has done is to make an investigation and report the result thereof in the form of a certificate, the ordinary arrangement being that he shall do this work for a certain fee, and afterwards allow his name to be used upon the prospectus as auditor. The reason for the latter condition is probably sufficiently obvious; but for the benefit of those who may not have taken the trouble to think the matter out, we may mention that in the event of the name of the firm of accountants acting as auditors differing from the name of the firm of accountants who certified the results, the undertaking would, in many cases, be seriously prejudiced. Consequently the promoter desires to safeguard from the outset the fact that he can rely upon the firm who are taking his money for the investigation to act as auditors when the company is eventually floated. At that time, even if the auditor were to ask the names of the directors, the promoter would, probably, be quite unable to afford him any information. Everything is then in an absolutely nebulous form, and it is absurd to expect that the promoter would consent to a stipulation that the prospectus which is subsequently issued should be approved by the accountant. The most that he would be prepared to do would be to say that if the accountant disliked the prospectus when it was issued, he might withdraw altogether from the business, but he would certainly reserve the right not to pay him for his investigation were he to do so.

That being the case, it may well be asked what possible benefit it would be to the public if an auditor were to retire at such a stage as this merely because he disliked the look of the prospectus or the names of some of the parties mentioned on the front page. To do so would be to invite these persons (whom, presumably, he does not trust too well) to nominate someone else as an auditor who would be prepared to take a more lenient view of their dealings, and this, it seems to us, could not possibly be in the interests of the public at large, or of those members of the public who might be induced to subscribe for shares on the faith of the prospectus.

The fact of the matter is that the auditor ought always to be regarded from every point of view as someone entirely outside the company or its promotion, who has gone into matters at the outset, expressed his view of the position of affairs in the terms of the certificate, and who is further prepared, when the directors have taken the whole matter over and run it for the prescribed time, to again come in and audit their transactions, and report to the shareholders whether or not they are all in order. To expect the accountant to prejudge the honesty of those who will be responsible for the promotion or the carrying on of the company, is to invite the auditor to be prejudiced. Although, if it *were* practicable for accountants to take this line, it might have the advantage that the presence of their name on a prospectus would, at all events, guarantee that they knew of nothing wrong, yet, on the other hand, it would inevitably mean that every accountant who audited accounts had already formed a definite opinion which seriously interfered with the independence of his subsequent judgment.

We quite appreciate that solicitors, who have arranged the precise form in which the promotion is to be carried out, and the precise terms of the articles of association (under which directors are entitled to make profits other than directors' fees, and a host of other provisions foreign to the Companies Acts as they stand at present), may reasonably be looked upon as more than mere professional machines, whose honour is involved in the success of the undertaking as a whole.

With regard to bankers, also, while they go through the form of making an exhaustive inquiry into the *bona fides* of companies, and charge a pretty stiff fee for the time occupied in so doing, it is only reasonable that the public should expect that the inquiry is something more than a farce—seeing, of course, that, in the long run, the fee has had to come out of their pocket. But, as we have already said, it seems to us that the auditor stands upon a different footing. The position that he occupies should be absolutely independent of all persons concerned with the company in any way whatever. So far as we can see, it is no more sensible to expect that he should be responsible for the honesty or probity of all persons connected with the company whose accounts he has undertaken to audit, than that the chief constable of any provincial town should be in any way held responsible for the crimes committed in his district. His responsibility is, of course, entirely limited to the detection of crime that has actually been committed. How would it be if no respectable policeman would go into Whitechapel because it was a bad neighbourhood?

But, beyond all this, we may point out that the real weakness in the arguments put forward in favour of auditors being held responsible for the success of the companies in connection with which their names appear, is that, were any such practice to become recognised, companies would still continue to be formed, some of which would continue to be unsuccessful. In the meantime, investors would become even less cautious than they are at the present time, and instead of learning—as they should learn, and as the object of any further legislation upon the subject should be to teach them to learn—to use their own judgment, and a little common sense, in connection with their investments, they would merely rely more and more upon the names appearing upon the front page of a prospectus as some guide to the success of the enterprise. The mere names upon a front page can, in the nature of things, never be any *guarantee* as to the success of the company; and the sooner this is fully appreciated by the public the better it will be for all parties concerned. At the present time, in many promotions a very large sum is paid for the names contained upon the front page, a fact which has been sufficiently disclosed recently within the memory of all our readers. It is, however, hardly saying too much to express the view that all such money is absolutely thrown away, in the sense that persons equally capable of managing the undertaking with as much success could readily have been obtained without any payment whatever; yet, while the public prefer to see fancy names upon a prospectus, those fancy names will, in the nature of things, continue to appear, and will command a price. That price will have to be paid, while it equally goes without saying that the people who pay the price will, in the long run, be the public.

What is required is that those who invest their money in joint stock enterprises should not look to the name of the company or the names of any of its directors or officials, but to the purpose for which the company has been formed. They should require to see sufficient information, and sufficiently reliable and explicit reports and certificates, to enable them each to form their own idea as to the probable success of the venture; and only when satisfied in these respects should they subscribe their capital. But this state of affairs is never likely to obtain while nine out of every ten applicants for shares care nothing about the success of the undertaking, but are merely concerned in the price of its shares within (say) the next three months after allotment. Therefore, as we have repeatedly stated, the main question which must be settled in advance of all others is as to what restrictions can be reasonably imposed upon the traffic in the shares of joint stock undertakings. When all illicit traffic and gambling in such shares has been stopped, there will be a reasonable prospect for those who are really desirous that joint stock companies should occupy the position in the world's commerce they ought to occupy, to consider how best that is to be obtained, for, until this fundamental point has been conceded and remedied, all prospect of improvement must, in the long run, prove absolutely futile.

AUDITS AND CERTIFICATES
(1891)

Frederick Whinney

An auditor's certificate "is the report of an expert, made up from certain matters, the accuracy of which he is able to ascertain, and certain other matters which he believes to be true."

The Chartered Accountants Students' Society of Edinburgh.

AUDITS AND CERTIFICATES.

BY MR. FREDERICK WHINNEY, F.C.A.

WE have recently been favoured by the Secretary of the above Society with a copy of that portion of the Transactions relating to the lecture given by Mr. Whinney, which we are now enabled to print as follows :—

MR. CHAIRMAN AND GENTLEMEN,—I do not think that any apology is necessary for me in bringing before you the important subject of Certificates given by Auditors. We all know that there has been a very great increase in the number of companies started lately—in fact, it has become almost a fashion now to carry on any large enterprise in the form of a Joint Stock Company, and there has also been a considerable amount of attention called to the question of Auditing lately. I do not know whether it has occupied your minds as it has ours in the South. We have had at our Autumn meeting, which took place at Newcastle, addresses delivered on Certificates. It is a subject which can be dealt with in several ways, and I propose to treat it somewhat differently to the way in which it was treated at Newcastle. You must please understand when I am dealing with Certificates given by Auditors, I do not intend for a single moment to come here and give you a lesson in Auditing. I am quite certain that Scotsmen are all born Accountants; at any rate, they are good Accountants themselves, and do not require much help from Englishmen, but I want to do this: I want to call your attention to what I may call a somewhat broad view of Auditing and Certificates, and to give you some material for thought. I need scarcely say I have thought a great deal over that which I have to say to you. Among other things, I thought whether it would be better to read you a written address or deliver a spoken one, and I came to the conclusion that it would be better for me and more interesting to you if I gave you an address from notes. I am somewhat fortified in that because I have been reading Lord Dufferin's address delivered at St. Andrew's University, and there he said there is no doubt in the world that a spoken address goes down very much better with an audience than a written one. It may not be such good reading afterwards, but I hope you will forget the shortcomings, and think over that which I will now say to you. I propose to tell you, or rather to explain to you, what an Audit is, how it comes about, what has been the legislation and litigation with reference to it, the mode of carrying it out, and the extent and effect of a Certificate given by an Auditor. There is quite enough in that, and I shall deal with it, as I told you, very broadly, and I hope to give you some food for meditation. You must please understand that anything I shall insist upon as law is the opinion of a layman who has had to look rather carefully at the law with which he has had to deal; and the first thing I say to you is, you should know something of the law, so that you will be able to apply your minds to it. I hold that the utmost an accountant can do, in connection with a study of the law, is to become an intelligent client, so that he can ask a question of his lawyer, and ask a right question at the right moment, and be tolerably certain of getting a right answer, because an intelligent client can appreciate the answer as to whether it is or is not, somewhere near the truth. The origin of Auditors goes back to Saxon times. The phrase arose from the meetings which were held, in which men rendered accounts to their "hundreds," who heard any objections to them. But for our present purpose I think we may say that the necessity for Auditors' Certificates, as we are going to deal with them, has arisen from the application of the Joint Stock Company principle. Directors of Joint Stock Companies are, of course, stewards of the funds of the company, and they have to render their accounts to their constituents, and these are examined and passed by their constituents. It is manifestly impossible, where there is an enormous proprietary, that they can be examined by everybody. It used to be done by two or three of the Shareholders deputed for that purpose, but it has been found to be inconvenient, to say the least of it, that it should be done in that fashion, and hence of late years it has been done by the Company appointing skilled Auditors, who may be looked upon, to a very large extent, as the delegates of the Shareholders. I ask you, if you please, to keep that in your minds, because it will crop up again in the extracts from the judgments which I shall have to read to you. Now the position of the Auditor and the material with which he has to deal become important. Questions have arisen in connection with this matter with which legislation has attempted to deal. It is no more than an attempt, and I think you will find that repeatedly the legislation is not consistent. Under the Companies Clauses Act 1845—I will give you the pith of the extracts—under the Companies Clauses Act 1845, which holds that in all Companies which obtain private Acts of Parliament, the duty of the Auditors is to examine the Accounts, and to make a special report thereon, or simply to confirm them, and their report or confirmation is to be read at the following meeting. The Accounts are to be made up with a distinct view of the Profit and Loss Account, and the directors are to prepare a scheme showing the profits of the Company and the proposed dividend. The Company are not to make any dividend whereby their Capital Stock will be in any degree reduced. This means they shall pay no dividend out of Capital.

In 1848 the City of London Sewers Act was passed. There provision is made that the Accounts are to be audited once a year, the vouchers are to be produced, and if the Accounts are found to be correct, then the Auditors are to sign them; but if the Auditors should find there is just cause to disapprove of any part of the Accounts, it shall be lawful for such Auditors to appeal to the Quarter Sessions. I want you to bear in mind that the Act of Parliament says that the Auditors may take exception to Accounts after having found there is just cause to disapprove of them.

The next thing I wish to introduce to your attention is the Companies Act of 1862. Table A is not compulsory. Companies are not obliged to adopt it. If they have Articles prepared, this Table A is not compulsory. If they prepare no Articles, then it is compulsory; but we all know that connected with every company there is sure to be a lawyer. Naturally the lawyer prepares Articles of Association, and it follows then that Table A is not made much use of. Table A says that the Auditors in their Reports shall state whether in their opinion the Balance Sheet is a full and fair Balance Sheet, containing the particulars required by the regulations of Table A, and properly drawn up so as to exhibit a true and correct view of the Company's affairs. You will find that phrase crop up again and again.

There is another class (if I may so call it) of legislation. The first example I give you is the Mersey Docks Act of 1867. Under it the Board of Trade has power to appoint a special Auditor to act alone, or with the elective Auditors, in the auditing of the Accounts, and all the Auditors may inquire into and certify as to the legality of all the transactions of the Board. Now this is not lightening the duties of the Auditor as compared with what we have seen.

The Railway Companies Act of 1867 is clear and specific as to the duties of the Auditor. There it is enacted that no dividend shall be declared by a Company until the Auditors have certified that the half-yearly Accounts proposed to be issued contain a full and true statement of the financial condition of the Company, and that the dividend proposed to be declared is *bona fide* due thereon, after charging the revenue of the half-year with all expenses that ought to be paid thereout in the judgment of the Auditors. That throws upon the Auditors the responsibility of saying whether all the items have been properly charged against Capital, and, in fact, whether anything has been charged to Capital which ought to be charged against Revenue. The Act further provides that if the directors differ from the judgment of the Auditors then the general meeting may decide.

There is next the Gas Companies Act of 1869. There the Auditor, if he finds the Accounts correct, is to certify them, but if he finds them incorrect in principle or detail, he is to require the company to correct the same, and until he is satisfied, no dividend is to be paid. The Metropolis Water Act of 1871: the Auditor is appointed by the Board of Trade. If he finds the Accounts correct he is to certify them, but if he finds the Accounts of the company incorrect in principle or in detail, he is to require the company to correct such accounts, and no dividend is to be declared until the accounts are certified by the Auditor. Strong power again. In Friendly Societies, in Industrial and Provident Societies, the Auditors are to examine and sign the accounts if they find them to be correct, duly vouched and in accordance with law. There you see the Auditors are made judges of the law. There again the necessity comes in for an Accountant or Auditor having some knowledge of law, at any rate being an intelligent client. In the Building

Societies Act the words are very peculiar. The Auditors are to "attest" the accounts. I do not quite know what that means. The Companies Act, 1879, by which the liability of shareholders in banks is limited, is a very important one so far as relates to the Certificate, and I think you will find that most banks where the Audit is performed by Accountants have something like the same kind of Certificate, and it is, generally speaking, in accordance with the Act. The Act says that the Auditors shall make a Report to the members of the company on the accounts examined by them, and on every Balance Sheet laid before the company in general meeting, during their tenure of office; and in every such Report they shall state whether in their opinion the Balance Sheet referred to in the Report is a full and fair Balance Sheet, properly drawn up so as to exhibit a true and correct view of the state of the company's affairs as shown by the books of the company. Perhaps that is one of the most important clauses with reference to Audit that has ever been passed by Parliament.

Some of you may have heard, I daresay, that the East and West India Docks came to grief some time ago. There was a fierce contest between them and the London and St. Katherine's Docks, and the result was that a joint committee was formed, which works the two docks. The provision is that there is to be one Auditor for each company, and, before they begin their Audit, they have to appoint a Chartered Accountant as Referee—a Referee upon any point upon which they may have any dispute. I have the distinguished honour of being that Referee, but, at present, I have never been called upon to act, so that it is a barren honour. The provisions of the Companies Clauses Act, 1845, are there applied as to the election, powers and duties of Auditors. The effect of that is that no dividend is to be paid without the accounts first being audited. The Lunacy Acts provide that their accounts shall be audited by an Accountant or other Auditor approved by the Lunacy Commissioners. They may prescribe the form in which the accounts may be kept. Perhaps the choicest specimen of form of Audit I have come across is one adopted by the Inspector-General in Bankruptcy, Mr. John Smith, a Member of your Institute. He contents himself in his Certificate with the word "Audited."

There is one other direction as to Audits to which I should like to call your attention. It arises under the Statutes made by the Commissioners appointed under the Universities Act, 1877. These Statutes have the force of an Act of Parliament. Under these Statutes all the Colleges have to render their accounts to the University, and, with the exception of one or two, to pay a certain tax upon the amount of their income. Therefore, it becomes necessary to see that their income is correctly ascertained. The provision as to Audit is this—that every College has to send to the Registrar of the University a Certificate, signed by the Auditor or Auditors appointed by the College, that the accounts of the College are duly kept in proper Books of Account, and that the Abstracts, Statements, and Balance Sheet are correct and contain a true account of the financial condition of the College. In case of refusal by any Auditor to sign the Certificate, he must give reasons for his refusal. There were, perhaps, special reasons why the Certificate should there show that the accounts are kept duly in proper Books of Account, because some of the books were very old-fashioned indeed, and were kept in a most extraordinary manner. Very ingenious some of them were, and not quite correct. Now, I think, they are all tolerably straightforward.

Well now, gentlemen, I do not know whether you have followed me while I have been reading these extracts. If you have, I think you will agree with me that the result of all these Acts of Parliament is that their provisions are not quite consistent with each other. Let me recapitulate. They are not consistent, at any rate, to this extent—that you can draw a clear moral from them all. There may be one which I shall introduce to your notice hereafter. In all companies which are formed under the Companies Clauses Act—all the companies which obtain a private Act of Parliament—and all Railway Accounts, I think I may say that the provision is clear that the Auditors are to certify that the Balance Sheet contains a full and true statement of the position of the company, and that the dividend which is being declared is being paid out of profits. Now, that is one class, and a very important class of Certificate. And that class of Certificate deals with some of the most important companies which are exercising their functions within the domains of the British Empire. But there is no power given to the Auditor to do that which he was required to do in the Mersey Docks, in the Friendly Societies, and in the Industrial Societies, in which the Auditors have to certify as to the legality of the transactions of the company.

Now, that is a very large inquiry for an Auditor to have to make—as to whether the transactions are legal; but I think you will see that an Auditor has to make this inquiry more or less in almost every company whose accounts he audits. In the metropolitan gas companies, where there is an Auditor appointed by the Board of Trade, the Auditors are required to state whether the accounts are correct in detail and principle. That has to be done by somebody who understands the accounts, and knows whether they are correct or not. The same inquiry has to be made under the Metropolitan Water Acts. As to banking companies, I have already read to you the Certificate, and with reference to that I can only say that whoever drew that clause drew it very carefully. Even the phrase to which a great deal of exception has been taken—that the Balance Sheet is full and fair, so as to exhibit a true and correct view of the company's affairs as shown by the books—which are the material words to which I wish to draw your attention—I think even in that, to which a great deal of exception has been taken the draftsman showed a great deal of wisdom.

Well, now, the fulfilment of the important duties of Auditor led to a great deal of discussion, more especially where companies were being wound up, and where there was great loss to the shareholders. That discussion has gone into the courts of law; and I want to invite your careful attention to what has taken place there. I am speaking now to gentlemen who either are or hope to be Auditors, and, therefore, that which I say will apply to all of them now or in the future—we have to apply the law so as to guide our proceedings with as much safety as possible. I wish to draw your attention to almost the first case where the question of the liability of Auditors was raised at all. It is a House of Lords case—the Agriculturist Company; a very peculiar Company. The decision was given something like, I think, fourteen or fifteen years ago, and the law was summed up by Mr. Buckley to be thus:—"The Auditors are agents of the shareholders so far as relates to the audit of the accounts, and for the purpose of the audit they will bind the shareholders." That, I believe, all the law lords agreed to. "But they are not the agents of the shareholders so as to conclude the shareholders by any knowledge which, in the course of the audit, they may have acquired of any unauthorised acts on the part of the directors." I believe there is not very much doubt about that—that is to say, I think it means this:—that the Auditors, by their audit, cannot absolve the directors from any wrong acts. They can grant them acquittance—the effect comes to that—when the shareholders adopt the Report they can give them a certificate which will be acquittance to that which they have done properly, but it will be no acquittance to anything they have done fraudulently, in breach of trust, or misstatement. The judgment then goes on to say: "It is no part of the duty of the Auditors to inquire into the validity of any transaction appearing in the accounts of the company." That part of the judgment is not agreed to by all the law lords, and I question very much indeed whether that part of it has not been given the go-by in other cases which have come before the English courts. The Auditors are the agents of the shareholders, and the passing of the accounts by the shareholders, founded upon the Report of the Auditors, is a discharge of the directors, unless they have done something which is fraudulent, or something in excess of their duty. If they have, the passing of the accounts by the shareholders will not bind the shareholders, even if the Auditors knew of the mal-administration by the directors.

Now, the question of the liability of Auditors has been directly brought before Mr. Justice Stirling in the Leeds Estates Company, and it is the most important case which has, I think, appeared. Now, the liability of Auditors will probably crop up most prominently in cases where the company is winding up. It is my experience, and I daresay the experience of a great many other gentlemen here, that when a winding-up takes place the shareholders begin to cry out very much about their losses, and they begin to find fault, and they say the directors have done this wrongly, and that wrongly, and the other thing wrongly, and that the Auditors very often certified that a great deal that was wrong was true.

In the Leeds Estates Company the Official Liquidator commenced an action against the directors and Auditor for dividends which had been improperly paid out of capital. Mark that word "improperly." Mr. Justice Stirling said, in his judgment, that the accounts which had been laid before the Shareholders did not properly represent the state of the company's affairs, and it was a breach of duty on the Auditor's part to certify them; and he made the Auditor liable for damages in respect of certain dividends paid during his period of office. I say certain dividends, because he absolved the Auditor from a portion, or rather he gave the Auditor the benefit of the Statute of Limitations. In the authorised report of the case, published in the Law Reports, Chancery Division, the head-note, which is to the following effect, contains material which ought to be taken to heart by every Accountant. The head-note says that it was the duty of the Auditor, in auditing the accounts of the company, not to confine himself to verifying the arithmetical accuracy of the Balance Sheet, but to enquire into its special accuracy, and to ascertain if it contained all the particulars specified in the Articles of Association, and was properly drawn up so as to contain a true and correct representation of the company's affairs. Now, because the Auditor had not done that, Mr. Justice Stirling made him responsible for, I think, four or five dividends. It is no answer to say that he only received ten guineas for his Audit. The proper rejoinder to that is, If you choose to take ten guineas for doing the work, that is no excuse if the work is done badly. With reference to this case, Mr. Buckley, who is one of the best authorities we have on Company Law, said, "The Auditor accepts the duty of making such investigation of, and such report upon, the company's affairs as the articles require of him. If he does not discharge this duty, and as the natural and immediate consequence of his breach of duty, acts are done (such as the payment of dividends out of Capital), which are a misapplication of the company's funds, the Auditor is liable in damages." But it appears his liability is for breach of duty, and not for breach of trust. Of course, if it is for breach of duty, then the Statute of Limitations will apply.

The decision in the Agriculturist case is not quite compatible with the decision in the Leeds Estates Company. In the Agriculturist case it was laid down that it is no part of the duty of the Auditor to inquire into the validity of any transactions, etc. It is clearly laid down by Mr. Justice Stirling, in language followed by Mr. Justice Kay in another company, that it is part of the duty of the Auditor to inquire into the transactions of the company, and to see that they are warranted by the Articles of Association. The two principles do not quite agree. So far as I can see, I think the right thing is to let the later view prevail, and to be very careful indeed to see that the accounts which you are Auditing are warranted by the Articles of Association. I think this case, the case of the Leeds Estates Company, fairly lays down this principle, that if Auditors are negligent they have to pay for it. If, from the result of their negligence and want of skill, dividends are paid improperly out of capital, then the Auditors are liable for the damage caused by their breach of duty. It is their duty to see that the accounts are true and correct.

Well now, I propose to run very shortly over what is usually done in Auditing. We are called in to Audit and report on the accounts of a company. One of the first things to be done, especially if it is a company to which you are called in for the first time, is to ask for the Articles of Association, and for the agreements upon which the company has been established, and see if the stipulations of the Articles of Association and the stipulations of those agreements have been properly complied with. For instance, if you see that the purchase price of property was £200,000, you ought to see that no more than £200,000 was paid for that property. If you passed the accounts showing that £300,000 had been paid, you would be held liable for negligence, and properly so, too. You, therefore, must see that the Articles of Association and those agreements have been complied with. Well, now, having seen that, you proceed to check your cash, get the vouchers and see that the cash is vouched, see whether the cash has been received and posted to the various accounts, check the postings of the Books, cash balances, vouchers, and securities, and verify the bills of exchange. These are things which can be done to a point: you can always ascertain these facts. Then you come to Stock-in-trade and plant. I am speaking now of manufacturing companies. Upon that I want to point out to you, and through you to the public, that you cannot ascertain for yourselves either the particulars of the stock-in-trade, or whether the prices fixed against it are right and proper. Of course, if you had a vast deal of time, you could take the stock-in-trade yourselves. I daresay there are many stocks-in-trade that Accountants would be puzzled to deal with; but I think you must take it that, as a matter of course, you are dependent upon the employees of the company for the accuracy of the stock-in-trade. The employees take the stock. It is brought to you with the original stock-books; you may check it as much as you please, but you yourselves cannot count the stock. In the first place, you are not in the premises when stock is taken, which is sometimes a very long operation. It must be obvious to everybody that you are dependent on the company's employees for that. As to the company's prices, no man can know what proper price to attach to the proper class of goods; the Auditor is dependent on the employees for the prices. I am going to put a limit on that, and the limit is this—that both with reference to the quantities and the price of the stock, the Auditor is bound to use his own skill and judgment. He is bound to look over the stock-list and compare it with the one of the previous stock-taking, and see if it differs very much, and find out what is the reason for the difference. And he is bound also to look at it, and see if there is anything whatever in the stock-list which is likely to be suspicious. The same thing applies to the prices; he is bound to see that the prices which are fixed to the stock, at the termination of the period which he is auditing, accord with the prices fixed at the previous audit; and that all just allowance has been made. If he does not do that, he will not get a proper Profit and Loss Account. But I want to impress upon you this—that we Auditors are dependent, very largely dependent, upon the honesty and fidelity of those who prepare the stock-list. And here will come in something which is not to be taught—that is, the faculty to judge whether the man or men who prepared the list have done so honestly or not. The faculty of judgment is one which can be acquired more or less rapidly by many men. It is a faculty which we Accountants are bound to acquire, or we certainly shall not succeed in our business.

Now, there is an Audit of a very important class of company which can be dealt with somewhat differently, and that is the Audit of the accounts of a bank. Now, there you can, unless the bank has numerous branches, verify certain things as facts. You can count the cash and see whether it corresponds with the amount of cash that ought to be in hand. You can verify the bank's investments; you may touch and handle them, or as is often done in England, you may get a Certificate from the Bank of England, which is frequently the custodian of the bank's investments, that they hold such securities, standing in such and such a name on such and such a date. You can count the other securities which the bank may hold; you may see whether the securities are correctly entered in the books. You may go through the Bills receivable, and, by yourselves or your clerks, verify the amount of these Bills receivable, and form an opinion whether they are all good or not. These are matters of opinion on which you must exercise some judgment, but you are to a very large extent dependent on the bank managers. In taking that opinion from the bank manager, you will not have used any judgment if you have failed to notice, for instance, that the bank manager has included in the amount of Bills held at a particular date, Bills which have been overdue two or three years. I have a case in my mind's eye at the present moment, where Bills of Exchange figured at the stoppage of the bank to the amount of £450,000. Out of that £450,000 no less than, I think, £230,000 or £240,000 had been overdue for periods running from six months up to two and three years. There was scarcely a sixpence expected from any one of them, and in respect of a good many Bills, the acceptors had become bankrupt. Still the Bills figured as assets. If you, as Auditor, passed Bills of that kind, I think you must expect to be whipped. I think the judge would say you were negligent, and that you were bound to go beyond the arithmetical accuracy of the figures. You must, in auditing the accounts of the bank, look to see whether the loans are, so far as you are able to judge, properly secured. You may also ask to see things at one Audit that you do not want to see on another occasion. In other words, you must exercise your skill and judgment. What is the result, as far as a Bank Audit is concerned? It really amounts to this, that there are certain things you can verify as matters of fact, that you may be as certain as it is morally possible to be that these things are true; but there are certain others which are purely and entirely matters upon which you rely on other people, but as to the truth and accuracy of which you must form your own opinion.

Well, now, what I have said with reference to banks, applies to a considerable extent to other companies. There you may verify certain matters; in certain others you must depend upon the opinion given you by employees. I have lately been consulted about a cab company which came to grief; indeed there have been two or three actions against the directors, and one against the Auditors for aving improperly certified a Balance Sheet. I cannot discuss the question whether the Certificate was a proper one, except to this extent:—The Auditor had brought to him a Certificate signed by a Veterinary Surgeon, who was constantly in the habit of seeing the horses, that there was a certain number of horses, which number tallied with the number shown in the books, and that the horses were worth £34 or £35 apiece. The manager ratified that valuation; it went before the directors, and they confirmed it. Well, now, I say that there is no question whatever as to the number of horses; it never was suggested that they had put in bogus horses, but it was suggested very strongly that the horses were not properly assessed in value.

How is an Auditor to know that? Just please consider what an Auditor can do with reference to a stock of horses—say the books show 500 horses. The Auditor would be no judge whatever of the value of the horses, and he could not tell whether they were worth £35 or £50 each. The result is that he is bound, he is forced, to depend upon the estimates and valuations made by others. At the same time he is bound to exercise his own skill and judgment to see whether these estimates are or are not reliable. Well, now, the conclusion to which I have come, with reference to a Certificate of an Auditor, is this—that it is the report of an expert, made up from certain matters, the accuracy of which he is able to ascertain, and certain other matters which he believes to be true. And the result is a combination of information which enables him to say that, in his opinion, the Balance Sheet which is laid before the shareholders contains a true and correct statement of the company's affairs. And I do not think, if you look at the matter fairly for a very long time, that you can come to a conclusion very different from that. The question has been a good deal considered whether it is possible to lay down a form of Certificate. I do not think it is possible to lay down any form of Certificate applicable to every company. I think you may lay down something which would be a basis; you may agree upon common ground as to the basis of the report. And I would suggest that the report should be based upon two statements. One is something which I have only seen in the Accounts of the University of Oxford—that you should certify that the Books and Accounts of the company have been duly kept in proper Books of Account. It has been said that the Accounts of a company are always properly kept. I do not think so. I have seen a great many companies—companies that have come to grief, that I have had to wind up, where the Accounts were by no means properly kept in proper Books of Account. I would rather press on you the propriety of considering and thinking out that suggestion, because we Auditors are frequently asked to finish the Balance Sheet and take out the balance, and write up the books. I always demur to that. It is the duty of the directors to prepare the Balance Sheet; it is the duty of the Auditors to audit it. As an Auditor I have no objection whatever to say whether I think a particular form of accounts is a good one. There is no objection to say that it might be amended, but I do object to have to make out the Balance Sheet and audit it at the same time. Well, I think it would be desirable, and I suggest it for the consideration of the older members of the profession, some of whom are here to-night, as to whether it is not desirable in all Certificates to set out that the accounts have been duly kept in proper Books of Account. Then, I think the other statement should be that the Balance Sheet, which has been compiled from the books, is, in our opinion, a full and fair Balance Sheet, properly drawn up so as to exhibit a true and correct view of the state of the company's affairs. I would omit that part of the Certificate as to Bank Audits, viz., "according to the books." I remember in one case of Auditing I put in these words, and shareholders wrote to ask, "What is the value of your Certificate? The books may be all wrong." My answer was, that I had taken care to see that the books were, in my opinion, right; and that I had done a great deal more than simply compare the Balance Sheet with the books.

I should like also, if it is possible, to disabuse the public mind as to what is the meaning of an Auditor's Certificate. I think the public, the shareholders, and those who are interested in companies, are very apt to suppose, if they get an Auditor's Certificate, that it means that everything is correct—that everything is exactly true as stated in the Balance Sheet. I think I have shown to you that that is not possible. I can give you another illustration. You state in the list of debts due to the company that a particular man owes £1,000; you state it as a fact; it is stated in the Balance Sheet as a fact; but it turns out that the secretary of the company has quietly pocketed the £1,000 three months before the Balance Sheet is issued; in fact, he has embezzled the money. It would be almost impossible to find it out immediately; but at the same time the Balance Sheet is absolutely false. Well, now, something occurred within my own knowledge during the last year, which shows the necessity of disabusing, not simply the public mind, but the official mind, of one idea that auditing means that the accounts are absolutely true. When the Companies' Winding-up Act, 1890, was brought into the House by the Board of Trade, it contained a very ugly clause, which was to this effect, "that if any person in any Prospectus, Balance Sheet, or notice, made any false statement which caused damage to any person, the Court in case of winding-up might make such person pay a sum of money by way of damages." A deputation went from the Institute of Chartered Accountants in England and Wales to see the President of the Board of Trade. I was spokesman, and pointed out that that statement would hit almost everybody; that it would prevent people becoming Directors or Auditors, or anything else in connection with a company. The answer I got was this, that if a man in business makes a false statement which causes damage to other people, then he must put up with the consequences. Well, as a business statement, I think this is pretty nearly true; but I ventured to point out that a Director was the agent of the Shareholders; that he had, under the Articles of Association, power to appoint secretaries managers, and others; and that leaving the clause as it was made him practically responsible for the fidelity, honesty, and skill of all the company's employees. I did not succeed in moving the President. I told him also, that in the case of a man carrying on business, he got all the profits, whereas directors only get their proportion of the share. I did not succeed in moving him one jot. Well, that clause was very much debated, very much debated indeed, and in the end it disappeared, and it is not in the Act now; but if it had been, what would have been the position of any Auditor who signed the Balance Sheet of any company which subsequently failed? I think he would have signed many false statements; he would have been found responsible in damages, and that to an enormous extent. That just shows that it is not simply the ordinary public which has an erroneous notion as to the effect of an Auditor's Certificate, but that that notion has been shared, and very very largely, by a great many people. Well, now, that passage was struck out, but I have to read you a few words which a very good authority has written down in reference to false statements—Mr. Buckley. He says: "Truth, as pointed out in Derry against Peek, is, in the mouth of any man, a thing not absolute, but relative to the belief of the speaker. Now, that a statement should be absolutely true in fact is, in the vast majority of cases, beyond the reach of human capacity." And you will find that so if you go and think it out. "In many, perhaps most, cases, that which you are pleased to call true, is only that to which human knowledge has for the time being attained, and even in matters which are capable of being stated more or less nearly with exactitude, the statement is to a large extent only approximate." And the more you think of it, the more true you will find these remarks to be. Well, now, I have ventured to point out to you something like a form of Certificate. I ask you to consider it; to think it out. It is an important matter. Deal with it in all its bearings, and possibly we shall find gradually that a form of certificate is hammered out somewhat on the lines that I have submitted to you. And one word more in reference to Chartered Accountants Students' Societies. I have had something to do with them. I have addressed them on two or three occasions, and the idea dawned upon me lately that Chartered Accountants Students' Societies are likely to fill a want which has been felt, and they are likely to be, not merely schools for educating Chartered Accountants' Students, but for educating older members of the profession. I do not think I am very far wrong in saying that, up to the present time, pretty nearly all practising Accountants have formed principles and methods of action for themselves, which principles and methods of action have only been corrected after having been brought into collision with other Accountants. There are plenty of things upon which there may be great variety of opinion. But, although we may differ as to the form of Certificate, we shall all, I am sure, concur in this, that the more an Auditor's Certificate is understood, the greater is likely to be the call for our services as experts; and that the position of an Auditor is one of true trust and confidence, and that we must carry out our duties with skill and integrity, and so add to the respect and confidence already gained by our profession.

INVESTIGATIONS: THEIR OBJECT AND EXTENT (1893)

Lawrence R. Dicksee

The best remembered nineteenth century accountant looks at accountant's responsibility for investigations--special audits undertaken for a particular purpose. He explains (1) how they differ from ordinary audits, (2) how the accountant should define and delimit an investigation, and (3) how he should conduct it, especially when asked to certify the correctness of reported or prospective income.

Leeds and District Chartered Accountants Students' Association.

INVESTIGATIONS:

THEIR OBJECT AND EXTENT.

By Mr. Lawrence R. Dicksee, F.C.A.

At a meeting held on February 16th, 1893, Mr. Lawrence R. Dicksee, F.C.A., delivered the following lecture:—

Mr. Chairman and Gentlemen—When your late honorary secretary, Mr. H. Senior Smith, B.A., honoured me with an invitation to come here and address you to-night, he was good enough to give me *carte blanche* as to the choice of my subject: and, after a little hesitation, I decided upon that of "Investigations," partly on account of its extreme importance to members of our profession, and partly because it is a subject to which I have devoted a good deal of attention during the past few months. When, however, I came to go more fully into the question, I was somewhat dismayed to find how often the question has been already dealt with by far abler men than myself; and—had it been open to me—I would gladly have sought an opportunity of addressing you upon some less hackneyed subject. An engagement once made, however, is not to be lightly broken; moreover, your late honorary secretary had told me that —so far, at least, as Leeds was concerned—the ground that I had proposed opening up would be altogether new. I therefore judged that it would be best for me to keep to my original subject; and, if the suggestions I make to you to-night should not strike you as being altogether original, I must ask you to remember it is one of the fortunate circumstances of our profession that, so long as we are sound, we are not usually called to task on account of any want of originality.

An investigation—so far as our present purposes are concerned—may be described as "A special audit, undertaken for a particular purpose." The particular purposes for which an investigation is usually made are as follows:

I. Upon the sale of an undertaking:
   - (*a*) To a public company.
   - (*b*) To a private purchaser, or purchasers.
   - (*c*) To a continuing partner, or partners, by a retiring partner, or partners.

II. For the purpose of obtaining special information as to the position of an undertaking.
   - (*d*) On behalf of a Committee of Investigation appointed by shareholders.
   - (*e*) On behalf of a present or prospective creditor.
   - (*f*) With a view to the discovery of suspected fraud.

It is our purpose to-night to consider the extent to which it is desirable that Investigations should be carried, with a view to attaining the particular objects that have led to their inception; but the time now at our disposal will not allow us to consider the whole of our subject in detail. I will confine my attention to-night to Investigations with a view to sale, postponing the question of Special Investigations until a more favourable opportunity.

When making an investigation of any kind, it must not be forgotten that those relying upon our report will naturally, and indeed reasonably, take it for granted that, so long as they adequately explained their object in seeking our assistance, it is for us, as experts, to decide both as to the nature and the extent of the examination itself; and, in the event of it being subsequently discovered that an investigation had failed to achieve its intended object, I think it would be for the accountant to show that such failure did not arise from any cause which could have been prevented by a more complete, or a more exhaustive, examination. Cases are not unknown in which a faulty investigation has been attempted to be shielded under the plea that special instructions had been given by the client, and that such instructions had been duly carried out; it being argued that where the client has given special instructions as to the course to be pursued, the accountant must be exonerated from any mishap arising from the defectiveness of those instructions. This doctrine appears to me to be a most dangerous one. There can, I think, be no doubt that whatever instructions the accountant may have received were intended rather as a description of the object to be effected than as a definite requirement as to the means by which that object was to be attained. It goes without saying that the best authority as to the means to be employed must be the accountant himself (who receives his instructions by virtue of his being an expert in the matters requiring investigation), and I therefore think that—however desirable it may be that he should receive, and even welcome, suggestions as to the *modus operandi* of his work—an accountant cannot submit his professional discretion to the dictation of his clients without sacrifice of self-respect and grave danger to his clients' interests. I think that due consideration will suffice to show that the accountant who undertakes the responsibility of an investigation must not seek to shield himself from the implied responsibility of proceeding upon that investigation on the lines which his professional experience convinces him are the proper ones.

Before proceeding to consider our subject in further detail it would appear desirable to clear up a point which has the greatest importance upon the whole question, and upon which a considerable difference of opinion appears to exist. I allude to the position of the accountant who has certified as to profits, which, in consequence of the falsification of the accounts investigated, have subsequently proved to have been over-stated. So far as I have been able to ascertain, there appears to be no decision directly bearing upon this point; but a case which came before Lord Kyllachy at the Court of Session in Edinburgh, some six months ago, is of considerable interest. The case was that of the *Edinburgh United Breweries, Lim., &c.* v. *James A. Molleson* (*Nicholson's Trustee*), *&c.*, and the question then at issue was as to whether the circumstance that the profits disclosed by the books of the Palace Brewery, Edinburgh, were in excess of the amount actually made was (in the absence of fraud on the part of the vendors) a sufficient ground for the cancellation of the purchase, or for damages. It will be seen that this case has only an indirect bearing upon the point which we are now considering; indeed, the interest which it possesses for our purpose is dependent rather upon the nature of the evidence than upon the point actually at issue. It was contended on the one side that books submitted for examination by accountants were to be taken as warranted free from falsification; while, on the other hand, it was argued that it was not the custom for any such warranty to be implied, and that a proper investigation of the accounts should have disclosed the fact that the profits had been, more or less, overstated. In giving his judgment, his Lordship stated that it appeared to him that the question was as to whether it was a condition of the contract of sale, expressed or implied, that the books of the brewery were to contain no errors, or, at least, no errors that were not easily to be discovered, and he confessed his inability to discover any reason for so holding. He could find no standard according to which the purchaser's examination of the books was to be conducted, and he was, therefore, unable to hold that the plaintiffs were entitled to reopen the contract, and now raise the question as to whether a condition as to the amount of profits had been fulfilled. The chief point in this decision which really interests us in our present enquiry is the finding that there does not exist in a contract for sale, based upon a statement of profits, an implied condition that such statement is correct. Exception must of course be taken in the case of a fraudulent mis-statement, for naturally such contracts would be voidable upon proof of fraud. The question remains, however, that if the vendors have acted *bonâ fide* there is no redress for the purchasers if they have given too large a price for an undertaking in consequence of an incorrect statement of profits by the vendors (provided the purchasers have had an opportunity of verifying such statement), or in consequence of a statement of profits that has been falsified —it may be by some employé of the vendors, unknown to them. It would therefore appear that, in such a case, an investigation that failed to reveal the actual condition of affairs would have failed to achieve its most important object.

I do not propose to discuss the legal position and responsibilities of an Investigating Accountant under such circumstances. Neither do I intend to criticise the Investigation that was made in this particular instance, but I think that we may find much that is deserving of our attention in the various opinions that were expressed by the expert witnesses who appeared in this case.

Mr. Wm. H. King, A.C.A., appears to consider that there is a difference between checking books and investigating profits, and I gather that it is his opinion that an investigation of profits, even if properly conducted, would not always reveal an actual mis-statement thereof.

Mr. T. P. Laird, C.A., gave it as his opinion that in making such investigations he did not consider it any part of his duty to go through all the books and vouchers as in the case of a regular audit.

Mr. James Alex. Robertson, C.A., stated that in investigating the profits of a business with reference to a sale, his experience was that an accountant was not expected to check the books and entries for the purpose of tracking falsifications. There was a marked difference between an audit and an investigation with a view to profits. The falsifications in this case could not have been discovered without a comparison of the postings in one set of books into another, and he held that was no part of the duty of an accountant turned on to investigate profits. Personally he always inserted the words "Assuming the accuracy of the books" in his certificates.

Mr. Frederick William Carter, C.A., expressed himself as being of the same opinion as Mr. Robertson.

Mr. Wm. Graham (of the firm of Nicholson, Graham and Graham, solicitors) expressed his opinion that accountants, when instructed to investigate into the profits of a company, were not expected to go into such details as would have been necessary to discover the falsifications in this particular case.

Mr. Alexander Young, F.C.A. (Messrs. Turquand, Young, Weise, Bishop, & Clarke), said that it was not the custom, in such cases, to examine the books in detail: accountants considered that they were entitled to assume the genuineness of the books. On the other hand,

Mr. James A. Molleson, C.A., thought that a proper examination would have discovered the falsifications; he considered that an accountant pursuing an investigation that would be useful would wish to *analyse* the accounts, and if this had been done the frauds would have been discovered.

Mr. RICHARD BROWN, C.A., also considered that the falsifications should have been discovered; he considered that an examination of the individual (trade) accounts was necessary to form a correct idea of the nature of a business, and had this been done the frauds would have been discovered.

Mr. DAVID SIMPSON CARSON, C.A., expressed himself as being of the same opinion as Mr. Brown.

As a matter of fact, this mass of expert evidence is, in reality, less contradictory than it appears to be at first sight. It was generally admitted that an exhaustive examination is not usual in those cases, and it was not denied by anyone that the falsifications might very readily have been discovered, had the investigation been a little more minute.

I was in Edinburgh a few weeks since, and had an opportunity of exchanging a few words with Mr. Brown upon this case. He appeared to share my opinion that an investigation which fails to detect fraud cannot well be considered to be altogether satisfactory; and, further, that the protection of our clients from fraud is at least as desirable in an investigation as in an audit.

You will doubtless have read the leading article that appeared upon this subject in *The Accountant* on the 30th July, 1892: I think that this article sums up the whole circumstances of the case in an able and impartial manner. In speaking of the object of these examinations, the writer says: "What the public seem to want is, not the nearest approach to facts that can be obtained in so many days or weeks, but the nearest approach to facts that is humanly possible." I think this will be found to accurately express the views of the average layman.

We may now return to the consideration of the objects with which an investigation upon the sale of an undertaking is usually instituted. It will be obvious that such investigations may be made either upon behalf of the vendors or the purchasers, or on behalf of both. In the case of a dissolution of partnership there would appear to be no particular objection to an accountant acting for both parties, but in all other cases I think it desirable that the accountant should act upon one side only. This is probably a question upon which a difference of opinion may occur; but I think that the accountant who attempts to act fairly towards both parties to a sale will usually find that he has secured the thanks of neither party.

Whatever difference of opinion there may be with regard to a private firm, there can, I think, be but little difference in case of a public company. It seems to me beyond question that the accountant who professes to make his examination on behalf of a proposed company should hold himself entirely independent of the vendors. For this reason I am inclined to think that the regular auditor of the vendor's accounts is not a suitable person to make an investigation on behalf of the proposed company, and I do not think that this opinion need imply any imputation whatever as to the impartiality of the members of our profession. What I maintain is that, when an undertaking is purchased by a company, and subscriptions are sought from the public on the faith of an accountant's certificate, it is in the highest degree desirable that, whatever may happen in the future, there should be no sort of suspicion that the accountant's certificate (upon the faith of which the public have subscribed) was not altogether impartial. Moreover, it would seem that upon such an occasion much benefit might result from the introduction of a professional expert who would come upon the scene with an absolutely open mind; for we all know that there is a tendency for the best of us to run into grooves, and it is conceivable that an accountant whose mind was absolutely unencumbered with any previous acquaintance with the circumstances of the case might see things in a different light from that in which they had appeared to the regular auditor.

For the purpose of pursuing our enquiry in further detail, I propose to narrow our field down to the question of investigations made on behalf of a projected company; and I think that our most convenient method of dealing with our subject will be to contrast the methods to be adopted in such an investigation with those ordinarily employed in a regular audit.

From a theoretical point of view there need, of course, be no difference of method; for both audits and investigations aim at a complete disclosure of the facts. In practice, however, it is usual to restrict our enquiry, so far as is possible without imperilling the efficiency of our examination; and it is because the objects of an audit are not altogether the same as those of an investigation that the method adopted in each case—*i.e.*, the abbreviated, practical method—varies somewhat.

A regular audit professes to discover the true position of affairs. An investigation as to profits, made on behalf of a proposed company, professes to discover the position of affairs so far as they affect the particular object in view. In some respects the narrower field of an investigation will permit us to reduce the scope of our examination; but, on the other hand, there would appear to be many points upon which a greater strictness of enquiry was necessary. Thus, supposing we are acting upon behalf of the purchasers of an undertaking, we may, I think, take it for granted that the accounts submitted to us by the vendors do not underestimate the profitable nature of the business, or the strength of its financial position. Consequently, it does not seem necessary that we should enquire with the same exhaustiveness that we should use in the case of an audit into the completeness with which every source of income has been duly accounted for, neither does it appear necessary for us to consider the validity of the various items of expenditure charged in the accounts, nor to check such expenditure minutely with the vouchers. On the other hand, if we were acting on behalf of the vendors, it would clearly be desirable that both these points should receive our careful attention, but in that case the investigation would not differ greatly from the complete audit; for it is obvious that we could not authorise the submission of accounts to the proposed purchasers until we were satisfied that such accounts were true in all respects.

Yet another difference between investigations and audits will not fail to strike the observer. An ordinary audit must always aim at the discovery of fraud; but an investigation as to profits would not appear to involve any such inquiry, except (for I think we must make this exception) in so far as the assets or profits might have been fraudulently over-stated for the purpose of concealing defalcations.

I need hardly remind you that there are, broadly speaking, two ways in which books may be falsified for the purpose of concealing fraud. The first method is by falsifying the Balance Sheet, either overstating assets or understating liabilities to cover the amount stolen; the second method is by falsifying the Revenue Account, by understating income or overstating expenses, so that the profit shown by the books may be reduced to the profit which was actually netted by the proprietors, after deducting the amount misappropriated by the defaulting official. If the first method has been adopted, the purchasers will not necessarily be prejudiced, for the profits shewn by the books will have been the profits actually made; while the assets which appear in the books at an unduly inflated price will usually be guaranteed as to value by the vendors, or else vouched for by the certificate of an independent valuer. In practice, however, it is not unusual for the investigating accountant to assume responsibility for the accuracy of the schedule of the book debts taken over by the proposed company, and in such cases, it will, of course, be necessary for him to carefully enquire into their correctness.

Under the second method it would appear that the purchasers would actually gain by the defalcations of an official of the vendors, for the actual profits earned would be in excess of those shown by the books, while the latter would form the basis upon which the purchase price for Goodwill was calculated; and, as the Balance Sheet would correctly record the financial position, there would obviously be no injustice done to the purchasers if these figures were taken as a basis for valuation. I am therefore of opinion that the investigating accountant acting on behalf of a proposed company need not trouble to go exhaustively into the question of the *bona fides* of the various expenses debited, his great object being to make sure that the expenses are completely recorded in the books submitted to him. On the other hand, he will require to look carefully into the *bona fides* of many transactions, which the auditor would naturally pass either unquestioned, or at all events, after due representation of the circumstances to his clients. The difficulty of the investigating accountant's position arises from the fact that his real clients (*i.e.* those in whose interests he is acting) are an unknown, and, at that time, non-existent body. It is, therefore, obviously impossible for him to consult them in any way during the course of his investigation, and his only means of acquainting them with the result of his enquiry will be by means of his certificate.

In making an investigation as to profits, therefore, the accountant must be careful never to lose sight of the object for which his investigation is being made. That object may be said to be

(*a*) To ascertain whether the business of the vendors is worth purchasing.

(*b*) To ascertain whether such business is worth the price asked for it by the vendors.

I do not say that the accountant is asked to express a definite opinion upon either of these points, for it is obviously the business of each intending shareholder to answer these questions to his own satisfaction before applying for shares, but what I wish to impress upon you is that the accountant's certificate forms almost the sole basis upon which the shareholder can judge of the prospects of the proposed company, and it is my contention that it should be the accountant's aim to so conduct his investigation, and so frame his certificate, that the materials necessary for a correct judgment may be placed before the public.

There is yet another point which the accountant must not fail to bear in mind. Inasmuch as he will be liable to make good at any future date the statements that he has certified, he should not fail to make the most copious notes of all that transpires during the course of his investigation. These notes should not be confined to actual figures and calculations: whatever explanations he may have received in reply to his enquiries should be committed to writing, so that they may be available if required. If this be not attended to, and legal proceedings are subsequently instituted requiring the accountant to substantiate his report, his position would not be an enviable one, for he would probably have to go over at least a portion of the ground a second time, and perhaps some of the evidence he had utilized would be no longer available.

It is generally held that it is no part of the accountant's duty to prescribe the term of years over which his enquiry should extend. I see no sufficient reason for objecting to this proposition, but I should like to remind you of the importance of expressly stating in your certificate the period that has been covered by your investigation; and, further, I consider it absolutely essential that the enquiry should be brought up to date. It may be found convenient to report only upon the results of completed years, but the odd months elapsing between the date of the last Balance Sheet and the date of our investigation must not escape notice, and if they show any material falling-off, the fact must not escape our attention. I may add here that it is very desirable that the accountant's certificate should separately state the profits of each year covered by the investigation.

Before actually commencing an investigation I consider it very desirable to make most careful enquiries as to the position and character both of the promoters and the proprietors of the undertaking. A man is always apt to be known by the company he keeps, and we can none of us afford to be mixed up with persons of more or less doubtful reputation. Moreover, if a man bears a really bad character, we may safely take it as being at least probable that the Company in which he is concerned is not likely to prove a very good investment to the public; and, for my own part, I do not think that an accountant is ever likely to do himself much good by mixing himself up with unprofitable companies.

The next point that claims attention is the general system upon which the books have been kept. And, in this connection, I may mention that—inasmuch as it is very desirable that the accountant should secure the co-operation of the employees of the establishment—it is a mistake for him to abuse the system of accounts which he finds in use, in the presence of the bookkeeper. Any such want of tact upon our part is almost certain to put the bookkeeper's back up, and then, instead of information flowing to us smoothly, it has to be dragged out by a course of cross-examination that involves a heavy expenditure of both time and temper.

If the books have been regularly audited by a Chartered Accountant, I think it a good plan to seek an interview with him, and endeavour to gather the precise extent of his examination, and also his general opinion upon the matter. I believe that this course is somewhat unusual; but I cannot see in what way it is objectionable, while I can conceive cases in which it might be a most valuable course to adopt. For instance, if a thorough audit has been made at regular intervals by a competent and trustworthy accountant, we might, I think, feel fairly safe upon most matters of mere arithmetical accuracy, and confine our attention more exclusively to questions of principle and to values. On the other hand, if there has been no regular audit, and *à fortiori* if the books have not even been regularly balanced, it seems as though we could not, with safety, neglect an absolutely exhaustive enquiry into all the facts.

I am not unmindful of the objections that have been raised to this position; the most important—in my estimation—being the objection that such a complete examination would occupy a much longer time than is ordinarily available for the purpose. I would, however, respectfully submit that it is our duty to make an effective investigation—not the most effective investigation practicable in the limited time placed at our disposal—and I maintain that we should so conduct our affairs that we need not shrink from accepting the fullest responsibility as to the extent of our investigations.

Another general point to which I should like to draw attention is the danger of looking only to the Profit and Loss Account for information as to profits. Cases are not unknown, where the assets are taken over at an agreed valuation, in which the investigating accountant has confined his attention entirely to the Revenue Account, without concerning himself with the sufficiency or otherwise of the amounts written off for depreciation and bad debts; the result being that the certified profits "as shown by the books" were greatly in excess of the profits actually earned. The accountant who aims at something more than pocketing his fees and keeping his skin whole will not rest satisfied with that sort of investigation.

Let us now suppose that the accountant is about to commence an investigation into the profits of a manufacturing or trading concern during the past three years, with a view to its being purchased by a joint stock company; the land, buildings, plant, and stock-in-trade being specially valued for that purpose by an independent valuer. We will further suppose that the accounts have been continuously audited by a firm of Chartered Accountants, who are satisfied as to their correctness. The question now comes in, What special points will the investigating accountant require to examine which do not arise in the ordinary course of a regular audit?

Taking first the Revenue Accounts for each of the three years, he will compare these with each other, and see whether or no they indicate a fairly steady or consistent condition of affairs; whether the turn-over is fairly constant; and whether increasing; at a standstill; or diminishing; whether the percentage of gross profit is fairly constant, and such as is usually earned in such undertakings, and whether the percentages of expenses and net profit to gross turnover are reasonably steady. A marked reduction of expenses during the last year must be viewed with the greatest suspicion, for such reduction, if excessive and not *bonâ fide*, may have a very serious effect upon the future prospects of the undertaking.

So far as is reasonably practicable, the accountant must examine the *bonâ fides* of all sales, especially those recorded during the last few months. The prices of at least a portion should be compared with current rates, and any remarkable increase in the amount of sales or in the number of new accounts opened should be regarded with suspicion. All entries "on approval" must be disallowed, and where sales are post-dated it seems essential to make sure that they have actually gone out of stock. The entries for the next few weeks after the closing of the books should be carefully scanned, and if they show an exceptionally large number of returns, and an exceptionally small number of sales, we must draw our own conclusions as to the *bonâ fides* of such entries. In dealing with the question of consignments, we must remember that the goods have probably been invoiced up at selling prices, while the unsold balance can only be allowed for in the accounts at cost price. Another point which must not be lost sight of is the question of travellers' commission: care must be taken to charge up commission upon all sales that are included in the accounts. Due allowance must also be made for all outstanding discounts; and empties which are returnable, but not yet returned, cannot safely be taken credit for at the full price charged.

With regard to the purchases, the problem is similar to the sales, but somewhat simpler, because we can usually get hold of the creditors' statements. It is, however, very necessary to be on one's guard against the omission of post-dated invoices when the goods have actually gone into stock.

I do not know whether here, in Leeds, you are very much troubled with post-dated invoices; but in some trades they are very prevalent, and must not be lost sight of.

Where reliable Stock Accounts and Cost Accounts have been kept, there exists a very valuable corroboration of the contents of the Trading Account; but, where these cannot be obtained, we must do our best with the material available.

It is especially important that the various stocktakings should be conducted upon similar lines, *i.e.*, they should be based upon the same scale of prices, due allowance being made for the depreciation of articles no longer in fashion, or in small pieces.

If the various stock-lists have been prepared upon different prices, they must be recast upon a uniform method, as any such difference may very materially alter the profits shown by the accounts. The valuation of the stock-in-trade made by the valuer should be compared with the vendor's stock-list, and if there is any material difference between the two, we must not fail to examine the effect of such difference upon the accounts. Thus, supposing we arrive at the conclusion that, throughout the past three years, the stock has been consistently overvalued, say 15 per cent., and supposing the stock is £10,000 heavier at the present time than it was three years ago, then during those three years the net profits will have been overstated £1,500, or say £500 a year, which is a material difference when one comes to pay eight or ten years' purchase for a Goodwill.

When the Stock consists of such articles as cotton, iron, grain, lead, etc., which have a definite but unstable market value, the question of the legitimacy of profits arising from such alterations in value as may have occurred is a consideration of no slight importance. I confess that this is a point upon which I would rather not express too decided a view at the present time, but I give it you as my opinion that (1) no profit should be taken credit for upon the rise in value of unsold stock, although Revenue must be debited with the contingent loss arising from any fall; (2) no profit should be included as part of the trading or manufacturing profits that has arisen out of a "gamble" pure and simple, but that gambling losses cannot safely be ignored; (3) where any material portion of the profits has arisen from favourable fluctuations of value—as opposed to true commercial profits—it is very desirable that the two sources of profit should be distinguished in the accountant's report.

If there are any further items to the credit of the profit and loss account, we shall require to see that the profit has been actually netted, and that it is fairly incidental to the business of the undertaking. Even then, however, a purely exceptional source of profit (*e.g.*, the fact that an important exhibition had been held in that particular industry, or an altogether exceptional contract executed) should always be specially noted in the report.

Another point of no slight importance may be mentioned here, although it does not immediately arise from the preceding considerations. Where the undertaking is of such a nature that it cannot be advantageously carried on except in the present premises, I think the accountant should satisfy himself that those premises will be conveyed to the company for a reasonable term. No sensible man would buy the goodwill of an hotel unless he could get a long lease, if not the freehold, of the hotel premises; while the goodwill of a music hall held on a yearly tenancy would not usually be considered a good investment. If the lease to be granted to the company is at an increased rental, we must on no account forget to mention the fact.

Turning now to the expenses debited to Profit and Loss Account, we should require to satisfy ourselves that every legitimate expense was actually included. The ordinary current expenses present no especial difficulty: if we have the accounts for the past three years we can get at them fairly well, while a study of the accounts since the date of the last Balance Sheet will probably disclose any outstanding liabilities that have been improperly omitted. I have already called attention to the danger of a *malâ fide* ruinous curtailment of expenses, so there is no occasion for me to again dwell upon that point.

There remain now the questions of Bad Debts, Repairs and Renewals, and Depreciation. For the purpose of dealing with these points we must refer to the Balance Sheets, as well as the Profit and Loss Accounts; and, inasmuch as we are no longer in the realm of cut-and-dried facts, we must use the greatest amount of circumspection in arriving at our ultimate opinion.

In dealing with bad debts, the circumstance that we are dealing with three years' accounts will help us to a certain extent, for it will enable us to strike an average, and we can compare that average with what our experience teaches us to be the average usually obtaining with similar classes of undertakings. Again, the book debts of the first year, at least, are almost certain to be either collected or else written off before the end of the third year, and we can compare the percentage of the first year's actual bad debts upon its sales with the average amount written off. Such a comparison is of necessity only tentative, but it is useful so far as it goes. Then we can carefully examine the last schedule of book debts: the chances are that we shall know a very appreciable proportion of the names there set down, and if we find that the schedule contains names that some of our other clients look upon as bad, or doubtful, we must draw our conclusions accordingly, to the best of our judgment. In any case, and under all circumstances, we shall require to satisfy ourselves that a sufficient provision for bad and doubtful debts has been debited to profit and loss.

With regard to the question of depreciation our position is perhaps a little more difficult. Speaking generally, if the values set forth in the balance sheet submitted to us exceed the amount of the valuer's estimate, we may add such difference to the amount of the depreciation debited to profit and loss during the three years under review. The method is not infallible, however, for the valuation at the commencement of the period may have been too high—in which case we shall be charging an undue amount against the profits of the three years—or it may have been too low—in which case we shall not have charged enough. There are however, normal rates of depreciation which we may use to verify our results, and our previous experience, combined with a sound judgment, will probably keep us from going very far wrong. Repairs should in all cases be charged up to revenue, but actual renewals need not be, provided ample allowance has been made for depreciation.

If part of the assets taken over consists of shares in other companies, care must be taken to see that these are included in the accounts at their proper value. Where shares (perhaps unquoted shares) have been received in payment of book debts, especial attention is necessary, as the trading results are directly affected. Under no circumstances should revenue be credited with more than the normal value of the work done until the shares have been actually sold, and if the profits realized on such shares form any appreciable portion of the total profits we should mention the fact in our report.

Where patents form part of the proposed purchase, and where such patents have not been submitted to a specialist for valuation, I think the accountant should make it his business to see that the inventions purchased are actually protected. In a recent case, I found that a so-called patent that had been purchased by the original proprietors of the undertaking in perfect good faith was not really patented at all.

We shall by this time have arrived at an opinion as to the amount of profits ordinarily earned by the undertaking we are investigating, but I do not think that our work quite ends here. As Mr. J. A. Molleson expressed it, when giving evidence in the case I have already quoted, "an accountant pursuing an investigation that would be useful would wish to analyse the accounts." I am quite of Mr. Molleson's opinion: not only do I consider such a course most desirable as a safeguard against fraud, (where a regular and satisfactory audit does not practically remove this contingency from the sphere of possibilities), but also, I think it extremely valuable for the purpose indicated by Mr. Richard Brown, in the same case, of revealing the general nature of the business under review.

The accountant will now have collected sufficient data to enable him to form a general impression of the business under review. He will have had ample opportunity to study the general mode upon which the business is conducted; and he will have formed his own opinion of the *personnel* of the management; he will have ascertained the amount of capital required to conduct the business upon its present lines, and have formed his own opinion as to the scope it offers for an increased capital (if such a thing be contemplated); he will have ascertained how far the continued success of the undertaking depends upon: (*a*) successful competition; (*b*) the continuance of a monopoly, and (*c*) the caprice of public demand, and have formed his own opinion concerning their continuance. In a word, he will have formed his own opinion of the probable success of the venture. The point we have now to consider is how far, if at all, his personal opinion upon these points should influence his report.

If it be conceded that the object of the accountant's investigation is to supply the place of an independent examination by each proposed shareholder (as the object of a professional audit is to supersede and supply the place of a personal examination by each proprietor), I think we must admit that these opinions are entitled to some expression. Yet I think the expression of personal opinions used should be cautious and not dogmatical, and that it should be very clearly separated—where expressed at all—from our professional opinion as experts in matters of account, and further, that it should never degenerate into either estimates or prophecies. It is, however, very difficult to lay down any general rules upon this point; but, so long as the question is considered upon its merits in each particular case, we shall probably not get far wrong.

The question may very possibly be raised that the accountant who pursues the course I have advocated is not likely to enjoy a very extensive investigating practice. I think that this conclusion offers an injustice to company promoters as a class. The profession of a company promoter is a very mixed one, doubtless, but I think the black sheep—although naturally the most notorious—are decidedly in the minority, and I am convinced that there are very many promoters who would thoroughly appreciate a greater strictness in our investigations, which could not fail to help to restore the somewhat rudely shaken confidence of the public in joint stock enterprise as an advantageous mode of investment.

Be this as it may, however, our first duty is not to the professional promoter but to our own profession. Let us therefore unite in employing our best energies and our keenest resources in the pursuit of our calling, in that manner which may best serve to protect the public from foolishness and fraud. By so doing we shall surely add, not only to our own personal reputation, but also to the good name of the profession to which we belong, and to the happiness and safety of the community.

THE TRUE MEANING OF AN AUDIT CERTIFICATE (1894)

J.S. Harmood-Banner

The search continued for a verbal formula which would tell the reader of annual reports unmistakably what the auditor had done and what reliance could be placed on the financial statements as a result of his work.

THE TRUE MEANING OF AN AUDIT CERTIFICATE.

(By Mr. J. S. Harmood-Banner, F.C.A.)

I do not propose to offer any apology for the introduction of so simple a subject as that on which I purpose making a few remarks, except in so far as I may be found to infringe on the address of the President, or anticipate any portion of the subject dealt with by my honourable friend who is to follow me.

My effort will be so to narrow the argument on one single aspect of the wide question of audit, so to limit the point of my remarks, that I will not interfere with the discussion of any wider view of the whole matter.

I am bound to say that I consider the point of my discourse most important in connection with the duty of an Auditor, especially at the present time, and that is—that the framing and wording of an Auditor's Certificate must be so concise and complete, or so fully worded and explicatory, that it may be in consonance, not only with the general sense in which it might be received or construed, but in consonance also with the duties of the office to which an Auditor is appointed; so that it may be liable to no misconstruction, either by men who are well versed in matters of business and general affairs, or by men who are now so frequently investors in industrial concerns, the members of the general public who, having little knowledge of business, but great aptitude to follow the lead of others, are apt to cursorily glance at the meaning of any commercial document, and to accept without due examination the outside appearance of a general set of terms.

Now, it appears to me that there are two aspects in which an Audit Certificate ought to be considered, viz.: *i.e.*, the true meaning of an audit certificate in both the legal and the moral aspects. As regards the former, the legal aspect, I purpose to leave it where it at present stands, and to assume that there is no negligence in the work of audit precedent to the giving of a Certificate or no possible misrepresentation in the form or nature of a Certificate, but that everything has been done so as to keep within the four corners of the present very serious regulations concerning our connection as Auditors with Limited Liability Companies, and to be free from the extended legal responsibilities which the action of the Board of Trade, in my opinion, unjustly endeavours to thrust upon the profession. But the moral aspect arises where the legal aspect ends, and to this point particularly I venture to draw your attention. In view of our legal responsibilities it has become absolutely necessary to carefully consider the use of the words with which we frame our certificate, and to insert such limitations, and so to guard our expression, that we are in no way (provided we have done our preliminary duty in a careful and exact audit of the documents and accounts before us) brought within the meshes of the law. The question is, Do these reservations and exceptions in any way, or to what extent, detract from the value of an Auditor's Certificate, in giving to his clients the correct and proper view of the position of accounts, or is it possible that they may be misunderstood, so as to give an absolute value to that which is of qualified significance, and if so, what is the best method to adopt in order to bring about that full disclosure, that full understanding of facts, which it is both our duty and interest to obtain?

Now a Certificate may be at times worded in two ways, so as to detract from the value of the fact that it is called and entitled an Audit Certificate—firstly by a limitation as to the intent of the certificate, and secondly by adopting a phrase to express the completion of the work, which in no sense can be taken to imply a finished audit.

For instance, as an illustration of the first point, the ordinary certificate relating to the accounts of Railway Companies runs as follows:—

"AUDITORS' CERTIFICATE.

"We hereby certify that the foregoing Accounts and Balance Sheet contain a full and true statement of the financial condition of this Company, and that the dividends proposed to be declared on the several Stocks and Shares are *bonâ fide* due thereon, after charging the revenue of the half-year with all expenses which ought, in our judgment, to be paid thereout."

Whilst there are certain certificates which have these words added—"To the best of our knowledge and belief." Thus:—

"AUDITORS' CERTIFICATE.

"We hereby certify that we have examined the Accounts for the half-year ending 30th June 1894, and that, to the best of our knowledge and belief, they contain a full and true statement of the financial condition of the Company, and that the dividends proposed to be declared on the Preference and Ordinary Stocks of the Company are *bonâ fide* due thereon, after charging the Revenue of the half-year with all expenses which ought in our judgment to be paid thereout."

The addition of the words "To the best of our knowledge and belief" is a limitation in point.

I have no doubt it may be desirable to add the words referred to, and undoubtedly they are a protection against legal liability for error, yet whilst, as a rule, they would pass unnoticed by a member of the general public, they are an unexplained addition to a hitherto simple form.

If there is any good reason for adopting the additional phrase, it would, in my opinion, in order to fully explain the true meaning of the Certificate, be desirable to set out the reasons in wider and plainer terms.

There is another, the old formula—"Audited and found correct," which has been used with qualifications, and sometimes runs—"Audited and found correct, E. & O. E.," to which the same remark applies.

Then as regards my second point, the following wordings at the foot of accounts form an illustration of how, whilst the public might say that they believe in a certain public company, because it is audited by the eminent firm of A. B. & C., the report of the Auditors, using the word "report" instead of the word "certificate," indicates no final and definitely formed opinion which can be considered of service, as indicating a duly audited and certified account.

The wordings are, for instance—

"AUDITORS' CERTIFICATE.

"Audited and approved."

and

"AUDITORS' CERTIFICATE.

"We have examined the above Profit and Loss Account and Balance Sheet, which are in conformity with the Books kept in London and the Accounts received from abroad."

There is surely something omitted here, and no satisfaction can result from the perusal of such indefinite documents.

Now the position I desire to take up is as follows: That whereas an Audit Certificate is presumed to be founded on scientific enquiry, and is therefore to be considered a fair and full statement of facts; whereas in many cases the complexities and ramifications of modern business, both at home and abroad, render it impossible for a complete Certificate of Audit to be given without some qualification or limitation; whereas, in addition, the responsibilities imposed upon Auditors render it incumbent on them to make such qualification or limitation in the phrases used as will prevent undue legal responsibility being imposed upon them; whereas such phrases have been and are being employed, which, while truly setting out the extent and nature of the Audit, and also tending to release Auditors from undue responsibility, yet do not sufficiently show to the general public the extent and nature of such limitations, so as to make them fully acquainted with the circumstances under which the limitations are given; and whereas a misunderstanding as to the true meaning of such limitation is apt to make shareholders misconceive their true position, and to involve imputations of moral responsibility on Auditors which is not desirable, and to create a feeling of diffidence and discontent with the work which is entrusted to them, therefore it is desirable, in order that there may be no doubt as to the true meaning of an Audit Certificate, that in all cases in which a limitation or qualification is used, that it should not be limited to a short set of phrases likely to be misunderstood, but should be set out in full and sufficient detail, so as to avoid any possible misconception, and to make perfectly clear to the general public the full sense of the terms in which the Audit Certificate is given.

In shorter words, my view is that the qualifications in most cases hitherto given have been of too short and perfunctory a character to be fully understood by the public, and that a more detailed wording, when there is any departure necessary from the old-fashioned simple forms, should be used.

The following Audit Certificates, principally of Banking or Financial Institutions, will give some idea of my general meaning:

First—There are the simple forms—

(*a*) "Audited and found correct."

(*b*) "We have examined the Books and Accounts of the Company, in accordance with the provisions contained in the Companies Act 1879, and hereby certify that in our opinion the above is a full and fair Balance Sheet, properly drawn up, so as to exhibit a true and correct view of the state of the Company's affairs."

(*c*) "We have audited the foregoing Balance Sheet and Profit and Loss Account. They are, in our opinion, full and fair accounts, properly drawn up, so as to exhibit a true and correct view of the Company's affairs."

(*d*) "We have examined the Securities representing the Investments of the Company, and those given against Loans and Calls at short date; we have also reviewed the Cash Balances and the Bills Discounted, and have found them in order. We have agreed the foregoing Accounts with the books of the Company, and certify to their correctness."

(e) "We have examined the foregoing Balance Sheet and Profit and Loss Account, and have compared them in detail with the books at the Head Office, and with the certified returns from each Branch, and we are of opinion that they are properly drawn up, so as to exhibit a true and accurate view of the state of the Bank's affairs.

"We further beg to repeat that we have ascertained the correctness of the Cash Balances, and of the money lent at call and short date, as entered in the above Balance Sheet, and have inspected the Securities held against the same, as well as the Securities representing the Investments of the Branch, and have found them in order."

These are unqualified Certificates, and of unquestionable value.

Then there are the following, which have a qualification, principally of the words "as shown by the books," or the equivalent, and probably it would in many cases pass without notice to what an extent such a limitation might apply. In the words of "The Book and the Ring"—

"Art may tell a truth
Obliquely, do the thing shall breed the thought,
Nor wrong the thought missing the mediate word."

(f) "We hereby certify that we have examined the books at the Head Office of the Bank, and the returns from the Branches, and the London Office, also checked the Cash and examined the Securities; and we beg to report that the Reserves and Investments of the Bank are correctly stated and vouched, and that the preceding Abstract General Balance Sheet corresponds with the Books of the Bank."

(g) "We beg to report that we have examined the above Balance Sheet, and that in our opinion, it is a full and fair Balance Sheet, properly drawn up so as to exhibit a true and correct view of the state of the Company's affairs, as shown by the Books of the Company."

(h) "We have examined the Books and Accounts of the Company, also the Bills of Exchange and Securities held by the Bank, and find the above Balance Sheet and Profit and Loss Account correctly drawn up in accordance therewith."

(i) "We have examined the above Balance Sheet with the Books of the Head Office, and the certified Returns of the several Branches, and we are of opinion that the Balance Sheet is a full and fair Balance Sheet, properly drawn up so as to exhibit a true and correct view of the state of the Company's affairs, as shown by the Books and Returns aforesaid."

(j) "Examined with the Books, Vouchers, and Securities in London, and with the certified Returns made by the several Branches, and found correct."

(k) "We have examined the foregoing Accounts, and find they are in due conformity with the Books and Vouchers of the Company. Further, we have satisfied ourselves of the correctness of the items of Cash at Bankers, and of the Securities and Bills of Exchange at hand, according to the Books on the 31st December 1892."

(l) "We certify that we have satisfied ourselves as to the correctness of the Cash Balances, and the Bills of Exchange, and we have verified the correctness of the Money at Call and Short Notice, Government Securities, and other Investments.

"We have also examined the Balance Sheet with the Books at the Head Office, and with the certified Returns from the Branches, and we have to report that in our opinion such Balance Sheet is full and fair, and properly drawn up so as to exhibit a true and correct view of the state of the Company's affairs, as shown by the Books."

There are three Certificates of more detailed wording, which are worthy of being read.

(m) "We have examined the above Balance Sheet in detail with the Books of the Bank, and we certify it to be correct.

"We have counted the cash at the Head Office and Branches, and have minutely examined the Bills of Exchange at hand; and further, we have inspected the Securities for the Investments of the Bank, and also those held for Advances and Loans, and have found them all to be in accordance with the Books of the Bank.

"In accordance with the Articles of Association of the Company, we certify that in our opinion the above is a full and fair Balance Sheet, and contains the particulars required by the regulations of the Company, and exhibits a true and correct view of the state of the Company's affairs."

(n) "We have examined the above Accounts, and find that they have been correctly kept, and that they are in due accordance as regards details:—

1st.—With the Books and Accounts of the Head Office.

2nd.—With the Duplicate Books of the several Branches, kept at Head Office.

3rd.—With the Books of the Branches visited by us.

"We have also examined the Securities representing the Bank's Investments, and we have ascertained the correctness of the amount of cash in hand and at Bankers. Further, we have inspected the Bills of Exchange, the Title Deeds of the Bank Property, and the Securities deposited by customers against Overdrafts, and find them to be in due accordance with the Books and Vouchers of the Bank. No interest has been taken to profit on sundry advances on Real and other Securities, on ultimate realization of which a loss may be expected."

(o) "We have examined the foregoing Balance Sheet and Profit and Loss Account with the Books at the Head Office and Branches, and, in our opinion, they exhibit a true and correct view of the state of the Company's affairs.

"We have counted the cash at the Head Office, and have had produced to us the Certificates of the Agents verifying the correctness of the cash at their respective Branches. The Balances at Bankers are confirmed by statements received from them.

"The Securities representing the Bank's Investments and those held against Loans have been produced to us, or otherwise accounted for, and we are satisfied that they fully represent the amount appearing in the Balance Sheet under these heads.

"The Bills Discounted, and the Securities held against a portion of the advances on Current Accounts, &c., have also been examined by us."

"In our opinion, the whole of the Assets in the Balance Sheet are fairly stated, and, subject to the ordinary contingencies of business, may be considered good."

These give point to my desire for a more detailed wording, after any departure from an unqualified or absolute form, for they are most complete and satisfactory.

There is one form of Audit Certificate which, however, requires, in my opinion, special attention in order to give full light to its real meaning. I allude to the form, in its varied expression, relating to the Accounts of Companies trading in foreign countries, of which I will read a few Certificates.

"We have audited the above Profit and Loss Account and Balance Sheet with the Books and Vouchers in London, and the Returns from abroad, and certify them to be correctly stated."

"We have examined the above Accounts with the Books and Vouchers in London, and with the Returns from abroad, as certified by the Manager, and subject to such Reserve for Depreciation as may be necessary, we find the same correct."

"We have examined the above Accounts with the Books and Vouchers of the Company kept in London, and with the Certified Accounts from abroad, and, in our opinion, they correctly represent the position of the Company on the 31st December last."

"We have examined the above Balance Sheet with the Books and Vouchers in London, and with the Accounts received from abroad, and find the same correct."

I think it will be admitted that, as a general rule, in Companies trading in foreign countries, where the Audit Certificates are as above mentioned, the work upon which the Audit Certificate is founded is based (1st) upon a correct incorporation of the Balance Sheet and Profit and Loss Statements sent home from abroad, in the accounts submitted to English shareholders; (2nd) upon the adjustment of exchange, if necessary; (3rd) upon the checking of the Books relating to the transfer and register of shares, and to the usually few and small transactions of the Head Office in this country; and (4th) upon a general examination of any points of Depreciation, Valuation of Stocks, Bank Balances, &c., which may specially come under notice; and I venture to think that a reference to the Fees voted to the Auditors in Companies of this nature is not amiss, when we find that sums not exceeding £50 to £100 are paid as Audit Fees in cases where the capital exceeds six figures, and is even at times in excess of seven figures.

Now the question arises, not as regards the legal responsibility, where the fact is duly stated in reference to the work done prior to the Audit Certificate, but as regards any moral responsibility which, rightly or otherwise, may be attached to Auditors for Certificates given, however limited in extent, where the work done mainly relates to the incorporation of statements sent from abroad, and yet where the public accepts the Accounts as a correct representation of fact, though, as regards the general work of the Company upon which the Balance Sheet and Profit and Loss Statement of the Company are founded, no examination of detail whatever has been made, or is possible.

For instance, Balance Sheet and Profit and Loss Statements are produced, properly certified by the Foreign Authorities, to be incorporated in the General Statement, and contain a mass of dealings abroad by Directors or Managers, payments made, contracts entered into, ships chartered, purchases completed, sales effected, &c. There has been no outside check or audit to see that these transactions are either properly vouched, or are in accordance with the Articles of Association, and there has been no supervision to prevent them being unauthorised dealings by either the Directors or officials of the Company, nor under present circumstances is there any possibility of such check or supervision.

Are the Certificates now given sufficient to lead the public to an appreciation of these facts, or to attaching a true meaning to the words used in the sense that they fully understand the facts on which the Certificate is based. The answer must be in the negative, and looking at the increased number of cases connected with trading in Foreign Countries under the Limited Liability Act, it is undoubtedly desirable that in the Audit Certificate a more full and complete statement be made as to the work which has been done, and also as to the work which has been omitted to be done in consequence of it not being within the power of the Auditor to do it, in order that the public may understand the nature of what is presented to them, and if they think fit of requiring a fuller system of examination, and also of paying a bigger price for it.

It is possible to show the Directors of Foreign Companies, for instance, how to act more in accord with the interest of English shareholders. There should be some control and say over the foreign examination of Accounts, either by authorising the Auditors to direct such a system as they may think fit for the purpose of checking transactions abroad, or by making regulations as regards the appointment of Foreign Auditors, with whom the English Auditors, on behalf of shareholders, and quite apart from Directors, can be placed in active and intimate contact.

There is also the system of Duplicate Books and Vouchers, by which a fairly complete Audit can be effected, and it is not difficult to adopt.

If Directors cannot be influenced to do more than submit the returns sent home from abroad, in the shape which, as a rule, they now present, it is essential to note the omission, and to know that the public clearly understand it. There can be no audit irresponsibility, moral if not legal, and no set of terms, however correct, if not clear and well defined, can free the profession from imputations of moral blame for omissions of explanation of facts if hereafter deemed necessary to elucidating a Statement of Accounts.

It is unnecessary to trace out further instances or classes of Companies where the dependence on such matters as the existence of Stocks, the extent of Capital Expenditure or Depreciation, form the main element in the results of a Balance Sheet, and where the necessary qualification is set out in short but perhaps not easily understood words. In an article in a Scotch newspaper written after I had selected the text of this article, I read a letter pointing out that the Certificates of Auditors were now so full of exceptions that in the opinion of the writer it was doubtful whether it was worth while to pay an Audit fee for such documents; but I do not think it would be possible for such language as this to be used if the wording of Certificates were so full and complete that shareholders would understand without a shadow of doubt where and how the omissions from absolute perfection arose. They would be able either to appraise the Certificate of Audit at its true value, or, which is the better course, be prepared to enforce upon their directors the points on which any remissness or shortcomings arose, and what is to the interests of our profession, be prepared to pay a proper fee for the work expected and ordered to be performed.

In the words of "The Tempest"—

> "Hence bashful cunning,
> And prompt me plain and holy innocence."

It is not too exalted an idea, I think, to treat our work as one of true Art, as well as Science, and as a work of true Art it must speak in an absolutely truthful way to show its true meaning. There must be no padding or deficiency. If the severely correct forms of old are not sufficient for our modern materials, we must use no false or one-sided system; but we must elaborate, decorate, and build up our facts until they offer for the understanding of all except the wilfully blind a correct and artistic presentment of words which will carry knowledge and conviction of both the inward and outward conditions.

Mr. T. A. WELTON, F.C.A. (London), proposed a vote of thanks to Mr. Banner for his very excellent address. Mr. Welton said the paper contained so much matter that it required on their part consideration and reflection, and he thought it would be impossible to deal with it offhand. He was sure they would feel that it would be better to consider the paper at leisure, when they had seen it in print, than to attempt to discuss it at once. At the same time, in order that he might say something before sitting down, he would like to offer a few opinions of his own bearing upon the subject matter. One was, that there was a possibility of some kind of legislation affecting the form of audit certificates, and he would like to submit for the consideration of the meeting, though not for immediate decision, the proposition that any legislation as to accountants' certificates, to be useful, must include provision as to the forms of Balance Sheets. He thought if they had legislation as to the forms of Balance Sheets, it would immensely simplify the question of auditors' certificates, and that the Legislature, in dealing with the one subject, would be compelled to consider the difficulties of the other. He had already on another occasion referred to the desirability of having a Royal Commission to consider this question—not a Board of Trade Commission, but a Royal Commission consisting of impartial persons, composed in part of men interested in commerce, as well as the two professions best able to deal with the matter. Out of such a Commission he thought it would not be difficult to obtain a good many forms of Balance Sheets applicable to particular businesses. Instead of binding down by any Procrustian limit to 20 or 50 forms, the door should be left open to any other form which any directors might propound, only such a form should be allowed after consideration by a Committee constituted by law. That Committee he should like to see composed of a gentleman appointed by this Institute, one appointed by the Incorporated Law Society, one by the Board of Trade, one by the Bank of England, and one by the London Chamber of Commerce. He believed such a Committee would be able to deal with any proposition as to forms of Balance Sheets intelligently, and if any two out of the five members dissented, the form could be disallowed. The second proposition he would like to throw down was this—that, whilst prepared to welcome legislation, by means of which delinquent members of the profession might be removed from the published roll, he should be unwilling to allow such a strong remedy save in a case where a solicitor would be similarly treated. He was aware there were persons in the world who went so far as to say that where a clear mistake or omission happened in an audit, they would at once deprive that auditor of the power of practising in the future, without any trial other than the ascertainment of the mere fact that there had been a mistake or omission. That was not the way solicitors were treated, or the judges of the land dealt with, whenever they made such a mistake. The third point he would like to make was this—it was his contention that, in considering all questions affecting professional practice, the first place should be given to the ascertainment of what was right and just and advantageous to the community, and the second place as to what the law was. When they had determined what was right to be done, they should consider carefully whether the state of the law hindered them from acting in that way, and they should keep as near to the right way as they safely might. The prime consideration was, what was good for the community, what was good for the enterprise and energy of the country—and there ought not to be any ridiculous trammels thrown in their way. He believed, therefore, that with such a commission, appointed as he had indicated to investigate the questions, there would be excellent results, and that a paper like that of Mr. Banner would come in extremely useful, as part of the material for the consideration of such a tribunal. With these remarks he would move that their cordial thanks be given to Mr. Banner for his extremely enlightened and useful paper. (Applause.)

Mr. C. R. TREVOR, F.C.A. (Manchester) seconded the vote of thanks, and considered that Mr. Banner had put before them a very excellent and important paper. It was a subject of great importance, requiring considerable thought; and they were very much indebted to Mr. Banner for the various lights in which he had placed it before them. On the matter of the Audit Certificate, he thought it was very important that, in many cases, what had been done should be distinctly stated. For instance, in the case of a bank audit the auditors should explain what they undertook to do, and what they had accomplished. One could hardly be expected at that moment to enter upon a discussion of the points that Mr. Banner had submitted to them. They were worthy of very grave consideration, especially the latter part of the address, which referred to the difficulty of dealing with accounts which were prepared in foreign countries, and which came over to this country without any proper audit. That was a matter deserving very great consideration, and much more perhaps than had hitherto been given to it. He had always felt it to be a very great difficulty to an auditor in England, viz., that of having to pass accounts sent over from other countries, without having a specific audit of any kind whatever. He hoped that was a subject on which they might be able to gain more light, in order to guide them on the difficult points which arose in connection with the matter. He very heartily seconded the vote of thanks to Mr. Banner. (Applause.)

Mr. C. BEEVERS, F.C.A. (Leeds) said he understood from Mr. Welton that there was to be no discussion on the subject of the paper. If so, there was no use inviting any remarks, because without discussion the result would be worthless. Did he understand that there was to be no discussion.

THE PRESIDENT replied that what he understood Mr. Welton to mean was, they could not go into any prolonged discussion that day on the paper. At the same time they would be glad to hear the views of any gentleman present. (Applause.)

MR. BEEVERS thought that they so seldom had an important subject like that introduced by Mr. Banner before them, that it was a pity it should be allowed to pass without comment. He for his part took quite an opposite view from Mr. Banner's, and if they went away without expressing their opinion on the subject the outside public might naturally come to the conclusion that they were all of one mind. He did not agree with Mr. Banner that they should give very elaborate and detailed certificates. He believed that would be a great mistake. He considered that if they were not to be trusted to have made their examination thoroughly and honestly, and to give such a certificate as they felt would conscientiously represent what they had done, they would place themselves in a very false position indeed. Who asked a doctor, when he had given his prescription to his patient, what the stuff put down on paper consisted of? (Laughter.) The patient took the doctor's prescription and he swallowed it. He thought therefore that they ought not to be called upon to give detailed statements in their certificates to Balance Sheets. He opined that it was an utter impossibility to do it, and he defied anyone to give a certificate which would cover the whole of the ground they had gone over, be it in banking, in merchandise, or anything else. He had no regard for the public, but only for the shareholders in such matters.

Mr. W. H. Fox, F.C.A. (London) remarked that, while not agreeing entirely with what the last speaker had said, because the more detailed the certificate was the better, at the same time there were one or two points in the lecture itself deserving of comment. He understood Mr. Banner to say that any qualified certificate was undesirable. In that case the lecturer assumed that every Balance Sheet put before him was properly prepared. That, however, they knew was not the case. Sometimes they were of opinion, as auditors, that points should be qualified in the certificate. The lecturer, of course, referred to the qualified certificates in which the words "according to the books" appeared. It seemed to him it was almost unnecessary to add the words, but there could be no harm in doing so. Mr. Welton, in his remarks, had referred to the question of an Act of Parliament, by which all Balance Sheets should be made the same. Was it possible to provide any Act which would treat the case of every particular audit they might have in hand? He thought it was utterly impossible. He did not think that the Commission suggested was necessary, and he believed, at the end of that Commission's labours, they would be no nearer to a solution of the various points arising in their professional practice. He understood that the lecturer had referred more especially to Bank Accounts. (A voice: "No.") He understood that the Bank of England had appointed an inspector in London from the ranks of their own profession to carry on a daily audit. Mr. Welton had referred to the form of accounts, but the form of accounts had been settled in Table A. He believed that very few people followed that form, but a form had been laid down which could be copied by people making up companies' accounts.

Mr. Adam Murray, F.C.A. (Manchester) thought the subject of Mr. Banner's paper was one of such importance, and dealt so much with the very responsible position which auditors occupied, that it was very desirable they should have a full discussion of it that day. (Applause.) It was a subject which must have given many of them anxiety in the past, to feel sure that they were discharging their duty in a satisfactory manner. While Mr. Banner was reading his paper it had occurred to him, when they heard of those lengthy certificates, whether it would not be well to consider if it were possible to simplify such certificates. (Hear, hear.) Thus, in the case of banks, without saying that the cash had been counted, the bills had been examined, and also the certificates and investments, it had occurred to him that these things might be taken as a matter of course, and such that would be included in any audit of the accounts of a bank. (Applause.) Further, that when the name of an accountant was attached to the Balance Sheet, without any words at all, it would mean that the accounts had been audited as far as it was possible to audit them. (Hear, hear.) It was not desirable to go minutely into details of ordinary work and examination that had proved satisfactory, but rather, if they felt dissatisfied, to draw attention to important points which ought to come before the shareholders. In considering those points, of course they had to be very careful in seeing that they did not enter at all upon the question of management. Mr. Banner, he believed, had referred to the certificates of audit in railway accounts. Now, in railway accounts they audited as far as they could, but there were some things that had to be taken for granted. For instance, they gave their certificate on the faith of the certificates of the superintendent and locomotive and rolling stock superintendents. They knew that in railway accounts renewals were dealt with in a variety of ways—in some cases by having duplicates to take the place of those that were worn out; in other cases, again, a certain number of carriages and locomotives were added every year; but they could scarcely go into the question of renewals beyond the certificates of the officials aforesaid, and if they brought that question before the railway managers they would not agree upon a uniform system of dealing with renewals. They had had meetings with railway managers but they had found it impossible to agree upon a uniform system of providing for renewals. What they as accountants would like would be to see that the Revenue Accounts of railway companies were charged with a uniform amount for renewals, that the life of rolling stock should be ascertained, and a proper provision should be made by carrying to the Renewal Account, as was done in the case of some railways, and that the outlay, which in one year or one half-year might be £50,000, and in another £100,000, should be charged against the provision which had been made. Then something had been said about the words "According to the books." Now, in one view it was desirable that those words should be continued, as in the case of the statutory certificate for banks by the Act of 1879. They knew that in some bank Balance Sheets the gross profit was shown upon the liability side, without the deduction of the expenditure for the half-year, the expenditure for the half-year being on the other side of the Balance Sheet under expenses. Now, he asked, was it possible that that Balance Sheet was "according to the books," when they knew that the books of the bank would be closed at the end of the period, and the expenses would be written off the Profit and Loss Account. Notwithstanding that, certificates were sometimes given that the Balance Sheet was "according to the books," when they knew very well such was not the case. So that there could be no possible excuse for showing the gross profit on the one side, and the expenses on the other. If it was wanted to show the expenses at all they should put the gross profit, carry it short, and deduct expenses. In one London bank the gross profits were actually shown, and the expenses were not shown at all under the head of assets. (Laughter.) They were not shown separately, and were therefore included in the item of current accounts or some other account. (Renewed laughter.) That was a very unsatisfactory state of things, and it had gone on, he should think, for 20 years within his knowledge, in the case of two banks in London and two banks in Manchester. The accounts of the two banks in Manchester had been put right; one of those in London had also been put right, but the other one remained faulty to this day. (Laughter.) Therefore it was very needful to retain those words, and that the Balance Sheet should be "according to the books." With those remarks he had pleasure in supporting the vote of thanks. (Applause.)

Mr. Gerard van de Linde, F.C.A. (London), remarked that Mr. Banner had referred to one form of certificate which he confessed he had never heard of before. He thought Mr. Banner had said—"Examined and found correct, E. & O. E." That formula was one which affected him somewhat, because on two occasions he had been privileged to address assemblies of merchants' clerks and others, and on one of those occasions he pointed out how perfectly checked were the books of merchants. Speaking from the experience of 17 years, he said that during that time he had seen account-sales going out with these letters—"E. & O. E." but never once could he remember in all those years that a single error or omission had been rectified. He had therefore called the attention of his fellow students to the fact that while he strongly deprecated the words "errors and omissions excepted" appearing in their certificate, they should always bear in mind there was the danger of errors and omissions occurring. He said on that occasion, if he remembered rightly, that as far as human efforts could go they should do their duty, and he therefore hoped they would not follow the merchants of London and Liverpool in adopting those words, "errors and omissions excepted." It might give the public a very wrong impression indeed if they certified to a thing they were not sure of themselves. With regard to merchants the phrase had got so stereotyped that it was an accepted form, but he hoped that in no case would the Institute of Chartered Accountants tolerate such words. He was sure he would have the sympathy of Mr. Banner, that he would not like it to appear in any certificates with which he was connected, either directly or indirectly. He had just mentioned it because having so often used the words, "errors and omissions excepted" in talking to the students, he would not wish them to think that he was one of those advocates who would like it to appear in their certificates, which ought to be as clear and precise as possible. At the same time he thought that what Mr. Banner had set forth that day was worthy of their very serious consideration, and that their very great thanks were due to him. The paper was one which supplied much food for reflection, and they ought to study it in print, so as to be better able to digest and deal with it. (Applause.)

Mr. W. F. Moore, F.C.A. (Preston) thought a satisfactory certificate was "Audited and found correct," and that in many cases a lengthy report on the Balance Sheet must do harm to the shareholders of the company. If a lengthy report were given, there might be the impression that something had been left out. The directors were responsible for the Balance Sheet, and not the auditors. If directors did not present a proper report, it was the duty of the auditors to point it out. As to the formula "E. & O. E.," being used in an audit, he never heard of such a certificate. (Laughter.)

Mr. Howard Smith, F.C.A. (Birmingham) said he would be sorry to prolong the discussion, but it was a matter which every accountant had already thought out to a great extent, so that he could hardly agree with Mr. Welton that they were not prepared at a few minutes' notice to say something about it. The particular point he wished to emphasize was that, in so far as they could not get a complete and absolute certificate, it appeared to him that what they might insert was with reference to what they had not done, and not been able to do, rather than to enumerate the various checks they had put on the accounts. He did not think it was necessary that the auditor should always enumerate all the processes he had gone through in checking the account. It appeared to him that what should be stated was that part where the evidence was not complete. They all knew there were cases where companies had transactions abroad, where the stock and assets were valued, and where the only evidence as to value came from the officials of the company. In such cases it was necessary to say that they had received reports as to the value of the stock from the managing director or whoever it might be. It appeared to him that was the kind of qualification that might be inserted in certificates. Without such, if a man signed a certificate saying the accounts had been audited and found correct—accounts containing items which were not satisfactory—he laid himself open to blame hereafter for having passed items without sufficient evidence. At the meeting the shareholders might have further explanations as to whether the question of the value should be taken, or whether they might adopt another course. At any rate the auditor should state precisely what he had done, and his contention was that in giving a certificate, which for his own part he rather preferred to call a report on the accounts, he should make it as true as he possibly could. He believed the best thing would be to enumerate the work which had been done, but an auditor should specify in respect to those accounts where the evidence had been to a certain extent incomplete.

Mr. J. W. Davidson, F.C.A. (Liverpool) said that certain remarks appeared to have been made on the assumption that everybody was satisfied with auditors' certificates as they had hitherto existed. He believed that they all of them knew, more or less, that was not the case. There had been criticism, both from the press and from the Bench, showing that neither the judges, the press, nor the public were quite satisfied with auditors and their certificates. He understood Mr. Banner's contention to be simply this, that when they gave a certificate it should be given in the form that could be understood by the public; and that, if they could not give a complete certificate they should indicate in what way it was not complete. He could hardly conceive there was any gentleman present who would deny that very reasonable proposition. What they had to consider, therefore, was in what way they could improve their certificates in order to obtain more confidence than they already possessed from the public and from the press. There was one very practical point which Mr. Banner had hardly touched upon. Of course, he could not touch upon everything, and yet it was one of the practical difficulties which they all felt in giving their certificates. It was a difficulty which appeared more or less in all accounts—not only in large accounts, such as the accounts of banks and railways, but in small manufacturing concerns—and it was this. It was quite common for accountants, when they audited the accounts of any kind of mercantile or manufacturing concern, where the stock was of a very varied character, to protect themselves against giving a certificate that the stock was of that value. There was no doubt that they could use many and valuable checks to see that the shareholders and the public were not egregiously misled, but there were accounts where a very serious difficulty presented itself. He would give such an illustration in the case of accounts of a steamship or a shipping company. Here they had accounts presented to them in which ships or steamships were shown in the accounts as the property of the company, representing the amount they had cost to the company, or representing the amount they had cost with an inadequate depreciation taken off. Now directors, shareholders, and all of them knew, and the Stock Exchange knew, that the property did not exist to the value set down in the accounts. Now, what were they to do in this case? A similar difficulty presented itself in the case of a large manufacturing concern, where the property was to a large extent machinery, and matters connected with machinery. There, if they were not careful enough to take off a sufficient depreciation, the account presented values to the public that they knew perfectly well did not exist. To what extent should the auditor come in and say, "I do not know what that machinery or that ship would fetch in the market, if it had to be sold as a going concern; I am quite sure that it is not of that value, and if I allow these accounts to pass, and present them to the public with my certificate, I may not mislead all, or the majority, but I may mislead a minority." That appeared to him to be the great difficulty in connection with these reports. They could, as a rule, make themselves quite sure as to whether the books had been properly kept, and whether they had been honestly kept. They could also make sure whether the more simple assets, such as cash and tools and so forth, were all right. They could make sure whether a fair attempt had been made to divide the income from capital, and the income expenditure from capital expenditure; but the difficult matter was whether they were to step in and say to the Directors, "you are presenting an account that is manifestly wrong, and we shall require that the assets are written down to some such value as they are worth in the market were they to be sold." (Applause.)

Mr. R. L. Impey, F.C.A. (Birmingham), had just one remark to make, not so much on the subject of the paper, as upon something which had been said by a member present. It was an extremely brief remark he had to make, but he did not feel that they should agree with what had been said by the gentleman who did not care for the opinion of the public. He was unable to distinguish between the public who were shareholders to-day and those who would be shareholders to-morrow. (Hear, hear.)

Mr. John Mather, F.C.A. (Manchester), said they had had much discussion that day, and on previous occasions, in regard to the words, "as shown by the books," and also the words "in our opinion," but he had not heard any reference made to the bearing which those words had upon each other. It struck him that they were a double qualification, and that they should not appear both in the same certificate. If they were to say that, in their opinion, things that were equal to the same thing were equal to each other it might be thought a little absurd, and it did appear a little absurd that a statement of facts should be treated as a matter of opinion. Because, if a Balance Sheet was a correct statement of the company's affairs as shown by the books, whether the books were right or wrong, it was a matter of fact and not of opinion. Therefore, when they felt it necessary, and were led as they were led in the case of a bank, to use the qualifying words, "as shown by the books," simply because it was an impossibility to check every transaction of a bank, when they used that phrase they did not need to use the other qualifying phrase, "in our opinion the Balance Sheet is correct as shown by the books." He simply suggested that while it might be a matter of consideration on the merits of each case, as to which of those phrases they should use, it was not desirable to use both on the same certificate.

The President said he did not propose to prolong the discussion, because he felt he could not do justice to the many suggestions which had been made by the different members who had spoken. He gathered, however, from Mr. Banner's paper that the main feature he wished to enforce was that, where they were in difficulty or doubt they should make their certificates sufficiently clear to make certain that no one was misled by them. Whether the certificate should be long or short, whether it should say absolutely what had been done, or simply, as some speaker had indicated, what they had not done, must depend very much on the judgment and discretion of the individual members. He had already referred to this delicate subject in his address, and he would repeat that no Chartered Accountant was justified in attaching his name to a Balance Sheet unless it conveyed to the shareholders, and even to the public, a just and responsible view of the true position of affairs. (Applause.) Beyond that he would not presume to go that day; probably hereafter they might have some discussion as to what Mr. Welton had foreshadowed, and they might come to some general agreement. He doubted very much whether it was possible to agree on any particular form, and if they were to attempt to establish a different form for each different set of accounts, he doubted whether, as Mr. Banner's forms covered half the alphabet, the remaining half of the alphabet would cover the other forms which would be required. He was sure, however, they were all agreed in thanking Mr. Banner very cordially for the trouble he had taken in preparing his valuable paper. (Cheers.)

The motion was put, and carried by the meeting.

Mr. Banner then returned thanks for the hearty manner in which the resolution had been received, and for the discussion which had taken place upon his paper.

SOME NOTES ON THE RESPONSIBILITIES OF CHARTERED ACCOUNTANTS WITH REGARD TO THEIR CERTIFICATES (1897)

R. Whitehill

The auditor's responsibility for certifying historical and prospective financial statements; various forms of certificate, and what they represent in terms of audit examinations; the purposes of certification, the legal liabilities it imposes, and possible sources of trouble arising from the audit examination itself.

Birmingham Chartered Accountant Students' Society.

Some Notes on the Responsibilities of Chartered Accountants with regard to their Certificates.

By Mr. R. Whitehill, F.C.A.

At a meeting of this Society held on Tuesday, November 17th 1896, the following paper was read by Mr. R. Whitehill, F.C.A., Mr. W. Randle, F.C.A., presiding:—

In dealing with the subject of my short lecture, I do not expect to be able to put before you much that has not been previously presented to you in some shape or form. The subject is one which covers a great extent of ground, and in a sort of hurried raking over it, I will only hope that I may chance to produce to you some facts and opinions in a light which will enable you to realise, and in some degree to appreciate, them better, perhaps, than you may have been able to do before.

The measure of responsibility of accountants in relation to their certificates can, unfortunately, only with certainty be gauged by reference to what has been authoritatively laid down with regard to it in the Courts of law. I say unfortunately because, so far as students are concerned, what in the ordinary course can be learned by them from legal decisions generally applicable to the duties they will be called upon, in their every-day professional life, to perform, is so infinitesimal that they are likely to be kept in a continuous state of doubtfulness until experience shall have done its work.

My subject would appear to divide itself naturally under two main heads, namely:—(1) Certificates, and (2) Responsibility with regard to certificates.

A certificate in its simplest form may be described as a written declaration of some fact or facts. Accountants' certificates are usually written declarations made upon accounts which accountants are called upon to examine into and verify. They are as important in relation to what they may be made to omit to disclose, as they are in relation to what they are made to purport to reveal. What, clearly, they are required to make known is truth; what to omit, falsity. The qualification given to a certificate in which truth is set forth and falsity excluded, is the qualification of honesty—a qualification which a Chartered Accountant is in honour bound to strive to make applicable to every certificate to which he puts his hand.

The two chief classes of accountants' certificates are, certificates used for the purpose of conveying to members of the public information concerning the profits of businesses offered for sale as businesses to be carried on by trading companies under the law relating to companies limited by shares, which, for present purposes, I will call prospectus certificates, and certificates, which I will call certificates of verification, used for the purpose of making known to proprietors the opinions of experts upon the correctness and truth-revealing nature of a collection of figures, made at a given time, and representing transactions for a stated period, and matters in connection with the carrying on of a trading or other concern.

The following, without any particular regard to the selection of words, are forms of certificates of the kinds I have mentioned, and which are believed to make known the truth, and to omit that which might rightly be regarded as false:—

Prospectus Certificate.—Pursuant to the instructions of   , I have examined the books and accounts relating to the business carried on by   , and I hereby certify that the net profits thereof, for the period of   years ended   189 , amount to the sum of £   , the profits for the respective years being as under:—

In arriving at these figures due and proper provision has, to the best of my knowledge and belief, been made in respect of wear and tear or depreciation of buildings, plant, machinery, and the like, and in respect of expenses of all kinds other than proprietary management and interest on capital and loans.

Certificate of Verification.—I have examined the details of the foregoing statement, and I hereby certify that in my opinion it is a full and fair statement properly drawn up so as to exhibit a true and correct view of the state of the company's affairs to which it relates.

I have indicated that knowledge of certainty concerning accountants' responsibilities in particular cases is ascertainable only by reference to judicial decisions. Such knowledge must, of course, as a rule be relied on implicitly. What else is ascertainable cannot, I am afraid, be relied upon with other than the reliance to be placed upon matters of opinion.

The responsibility attaching to the accountant who is a party to the publication of a prospectus certificate is a very heavy one, and one which, in my opinion, should not be assumed without the exercise of the greatest possible care. The assumption of the responsibility renders the accountant liable, in fairness, to be called upon to prove, as an expert, the truth of what he certifies, and that, to the best of his knowledge and belief, such truth is the whole truth; it renders him liable to be called upon to refute objections which may fairly be made to his reasons for arriving at his belief as to the information given, and may necessitate his rendering material satisfaction in regard thereto should his reasons be other than fair and proper.

The chances of a certificate for publication in a prospectus, made and given without the exercise of due and proper care and regard in relation to its contents, being called into question depends, as a rule, upon the success or failure of the business to which it has reference. The knowledge of this is the cause I believe, of many risks being accepted which otherwise would not for a moment be entertained. The risks involve the omission from a certificate of relative facts known or readily ascertainable by the exercise of such skill or expertness as a trained accountant is known or expected to have acquired. Among the omissions I have in my mind are (1) the omission to make known, in the case of a long established manufacturing concern, the results of its trading for more than a period of a few selected months; (2) the omission to state that the profits declared have been ascertained to be net profits, after providing for depreciation and expenses of all kinds; and (3) the omission to indicate that in calculating the amount of the profits (so called) set forth in the certificate, the sum brought into account in respect of the increase in the stock-in-trade is representative of an estimate having no reliable foundation in fact, and that, therefore, any conclusion drawn from the certificate as to the correctness of the amount stated as profit may be wrong.

With regard to the first of these there has been no decision by the Courts, so far as I know, from which it can be unmistakably gathered that it is a matter of legal necessity, and not of prudence only, to put before intending subscribers to the capital of a company the means to enable them to form a correct conclusion as to the true value of the business whose property or assets they are invited to purchase.

It has been laid down in the House of Lords, however, that "persons who purchase property and then create a "company to purchase from them the property they "possess stand in a fiduciary position towards that company, and must faithfully state to the company the facts "which apply to the property and would influence the "company in deciding on the reasonableness of acquiring "it."

Instances have come under notice during the present year in which one trained accountant has declared that he has ascertained the profits made in a business during a period of three months, and indicated that, on the amount ascertained being multiplied by four, the sum arrived at represented the profit to be relied upon as being the profit for a year; and in which another trained accountant has certified that the sales for a year, a considerable part of which was unexpired, "would represent about £ ," and that the profit earned on such assumed amount of sales "would "amount to about £ ."

In a batch of a dozen prospectuses, which I took out haphazard from a drawer in my office, I sought, in the certificates, the proper indication of the quality of the profits certified, and I found it given in six cases only. There is one word, well known by all accountants, by which that indication is given, and that is the word "net." It is open to question whether, when that word is employed, it is necessary to go further and make reference to the fact that due and proper provision has been made for depreciation and certain other expenses. The reference, when made, however, cannot but afford satisfaction. In more than one certificate I had before me, the accountant, apparently having in his mind his omission to give an indication of the unreliability of the value put upon the stock-in-trade, and knowing that more often than not the chief factors in ascertaining true profit are the figures of stock at the beginning and end of the period covered, has deemed it necessary to declare, to those to whom his certificate is addressed for the purposes of publication, that the value of the stock at the end of the period is such and such an amount, that the value has been estimated by the vendors of the business, and that the vendors guarantee the amount of the estimate.

Let us inquire for a moment as to the use to be made of accountants' certificates of the class I am speaking of, and let us see what the omissions I have referred to may, and in some instances will, in the end result in. Commercial experience teaches that, in fairly and equitably assessing the value of the goodwill of a business of several years' standing, the amount of net profits earned may be said to necessarily be the basis of assessment, and that regard must be had, not to the profits of one year only, but, necessarily, to the profits of a number of years in succession.

Directors of public companies are presumably men of experience. If not men of experience, they are men on whose knowledge, judgment, and probity, shareholders are rightly entitled to trust and rely. An accountant, in delivering his certificate to the directors of a new company, formed to deal with the property or assets of a long-established business, knows that it is required for the purpose of assisting its readers to form a judgment of the past or prospective value (or both) of the business to which it refers. Customary requirements, relating to the purchase of a business, dictate to the purchasers that the amount of the purchase money is not to be more than the equivalent of the sum on which the profits realised or realisable are sufficient to pay a reasonably certain or regular percentage of profit or dividend.

I have indicated the strict purpose for which the accountant's certificate is requisite, and I have also indicated that the purpose may be that of directors or that of possible shareholders. It will not now, I think, be difficult for you to imagine the position of those who make and publish, or who are responsibly connected with making and publishing, a certificate which may be known to set forth the so-called profits of a period of trading designedly selected, the amount of which is arrived at without regard to recognised requirements, and after dealing, in particular, with figures representing the value of stock which is not known to have any substantial foundation in fact. I do not, however, purpose to call upon your powers of imagination as to the position laid bare; but, in drawing this branch of my subject to a close, I would suggest your keeping impressed upon your mind the following:—That though to-day the degree of uncertainty relating to the responsibilities of accountants and others, with regard to the information disclosed or omitted to be disclosed in a prospectus, is a matter of opinion, to-morrow it may be otherwise. The director who has been a party to knowingly or carelessly basing the value of a business for sale to the public on grounds which custom may prove to be glaringly inadequate, will, when he is made to suffer, draw in, for a share of the punishment, the accountant who lent him professional aid in doing his proven misdeeds. It is, I think, always safest to assume that the existing law, when appealed to, will redress substantial injustice.

Under circumstances of doubt an appeal to the law is

always liable to be made. The arm of the law is strong. Until about eighteen months ago no accountant had been made to suffer as, in the case of the *London and General Bank*, a member of our profession was made to suffer for lack of judgment and courage such as was in that case proven in connection with the making and issuing of a certificate to the shareholders. A year and a-half hence some accountant may be made similarly to suffer for lack of judgment or courage, or what may be proved to be something worse, in connection with the making and issuing of a prospectus certificate. Then, in such event, those accountants who have been unaware of the extent of their responsibilities, or indifferent to their weight, will take care to have specific evidence of instructions as to the nature of the investigations they are required to make, their purpose, and the period they are to cover. They will take care to ascertain that the profits certified are the net profits: and they will, in connection with stock-in-trade, when adjusting or examining the figures for the purpose of ascertaining true profit, see, as far as practicable, that the stock at the end of a period is valued on the same lines as that at the beginning of the period; or, failing that, will make such tests as they can apply—and most, if not all, Chartered Accountants I believe know well what they are—to satisfy themselves as to the actual existence of the stocks, and as to the substantial accuracy of the value placed upon them, whether the value be arrived at in detail or by estimating in lump.

In turning away from the somewhat unsavoury matter of prospectus certificates to the probably more important, if not less difficult, questions bearing upon the responsibilities of accountants in connection with certificates of verification, I shall, no doubt, direct you into some thorny paths which, but for your desire to become acquainted with every in and out of them, you might probably wish me to avoid. The responsibilities in connection with the verification of statements of liabilities and assets, or Balance Sheets, include those in relation to checking of details, non-disclosure or partial disclosure of facts, fraud, depreciation of wasting and other assets, stocks, exceptional losses, profits available for dividend, and the payment of dividends out of moneys not derived from profits arising from the carrying on of the business.

No effective responsibility will attach to an accountant in connection with his certificate for failure to check details except in the case of the details being proved to be materially wrong.

With regard to non-disclosure or partial disclosure of facts, the question of responsibility is dependent upon the materiality of the facts hidden. To omit to report the non-disclosure of a debt due from a director, say, for moneys borrowed from his company, would under ordinary circumstances be neglectful. The borrowing of the money by the director is probably rightly regarded as an impropriety. But let us assume that, directly after the date of the Balance Sheet, and before the date of the accountant's certificate, the amount had been returned to the company, and it will then be felt that the responsibililty connected with the non-disclosure is a light and inconsequential one; a partial disclosure would be including the amount in the Balance Sheet in the item, say, of sundry debtors and calling the item "sundry debtors including cash on loan." To omit to report the non-disclosure, in a Balance Sheet, of the full amount of the liabilities of a company is neglectful. The penalty for the neglect is dependent upon the damage done to any person who has been misled by the certificate.

The responsibility of the accountant in connection with fraud on the part of a company's servant, associates itself with the stating of each and all of the liabilities and assets on the Balance Sheet. There is no doubt whatever that the certification, as correct, of a Balance Sheet containing statements which are wrong—wrong as a consequence of undiscovered fraud—may be taken generally to impose a degree of responsibility upon the certifying accountant for which he may be called upon to pay the penalty when the fraud is revealed. Accountants are not insurers against fraud, and it is not difficult, of course, to contract out of responsibility, except, perhaps, that in respect of pure and simple neglect. Where the highest regard for responsibility obtains, there always will the best results accrue.

Regarding depreciation of permanent assets, it is not yet, I believe, established by law that any regular periodical writing down is compulsory. The responsibility of the certifying accountant relating to it consists in seeing that the course pursued, with reference to the values at which such assets are entered in the Balance Sheet, is fully and fairly indicated to the shareholders. I distinguish in the case of buildings, machinery, and the like, between depreciation—so-called—and a deduction covering actual or visible deterioration or a state of want of repair, and I will make clear the distinction further on. Leases of different kinds, concessions, and other assets, which, from their nature require frequent renewal, involve treatment, for the purposes of the Balance Sheet, which, if erroneously applied to any material extent, renders the accountant responsible should he fail to draw to it due and requisite attention. To give you an idea of the distinctions which may be drawn, I will instance the possession by a company of a lease of a stores which has a term of years to run, and in respect of which consideration money has been paid. The requirement of the premises is casual. No amount of profits made in connection with it should be finally passed which has not been made subject to a charge in respect of the sum of money paid. I will instance also the case of a company which has been formed expressly to work a colliery. It is known that in a given period the coal will be worked out. Coal is won at a profit. It is not necessary before stating the profit to make a deduction in respect of the ground worked out in getting the coal. An instance of another sort is that relating to cupolas, annealing-ovens, and the like plant of a kind which is subject to a somewhat rapid consumption by reason of the great heat at which it is worked. The profits derived by a company using such plant should, besides being debited with the cost of repairs, be debited with an amount deduced, for the purpose of so debiting them, from the ascertained cost and length of endurance of the plant referred to.

Exceptional losses and exceptional expenditure may cause

the certifying accountant considerable trouble. The belief is entertained that it is legitimate to treat the amount of an exceptional loss, incurred in connection with the trading of one particular year, as apportionable over the trading of a number of subsequent years. A Balance Sheet containing an item of the kind treated in this way cannot rightly be passed by an accountant without comment if he would avoid responsibility. Take the case of a specially large bad debt as an example. It is contracted during a certain financial year and the loss is absolute. What is there to justify any part of such a loss at any time appearing as an asset? I know of nothing. Take, further, the case of a trading company having a number of depôts in various parts of the world. An additional depôt is established during a financial year, and considerable expenditure is incurred before the doing of any profitable business is possible. In the Balance Sheet, at the end of the year, the whole of the expenditure may be passed by the certifying accountant as a good asset without incurring risk. In a subsequent year it is ascertained that, owing to unforeseen circumstances, business cannot be successfully carried on at this particular depôt, and that a very large loss has at once to be faced. The exclusion of this loss, from the Trading Account of the year, would be an error which the accountant would be bound to point out. It is not properly permissible for credit to be taken, on one hand, in respect of profits on depôts, until losses on depôts have been dealt with on the other. The effect of taking credit for profits, before dealing with losses, could be held to be that assets were unduly swollen in order that the balance of profit shown by the Balance Sheet might be made to represent a sum sufficient for purposes of dividend.

Of the accountant's responsibilities in connection with stocks, much has of late been heard. Considerable doubt is entertained as to the extent of the risk incurred in passing the figure of stock without having ascertained that it is substantially correct. The value of stock should, in strictness, always be ascertainable from an account showing the balance of expenditure, during a year, in respect of materials purchased which have not been consumed, and the labour and expenses specifically applicable thereto, and incurred in connection therewith. The counting, measuring, and weighing-up of the stock at the end of the financial period, constitute the check upon the balance appearing in such account. An account of the kind was indicated by the Judge, who, in the *Kingston Cotton Mills* case, gave it as his opinion—though on appeal the opinion, for certain reasons which I will refer to later, was set at nought—that an auditor, in not detecting ascertainable errors in the figures representing the value of stock appearing in a Balance Sheet, is guilty of neglect and responsible in damages. In the absence of an account of this sort, regard is had, as the only existing alternative, to the written sheets or book of particulars relating to the taking of the stock, and, if any suspicion is entertained as to the correctness or integrity of such particulars, a process of examination and inquiry is gone through by which the certifying accountant satisfies himself whether his suspicion is groundless or otherwise. Although it is outside the scope of this lecture to enter into particulars of the accountant's methods of testing figures of stock, it will not, I think, be out of place, having regard to the great importance of the item of stock in a Balance Sheet and Profit and Loss Account, to remind you of some of the essentials of the process I refer to, such as the scrutinising of weights and quantities, the comparing of prices with those of the previous stocktaking, the checking of extensions and additions, and, where the exercise of care on the part of those responsible for the figures is not, on the face of them, apparent, requiring the production of the notes made at the time of stocktaking by the tellers of the stock, and by means of question and answer, relative to the course which had been pursued to secure accuracy in pricing, &c., obtaining the information upon which the accountant partly bases the opinion he is required to express, as to the view of the position of a company exhibited by its Balance Sheet.

The question of the extent of the accountant's responsibility in connection with stock, hovers, at present, around the degree of suspicion by which he may feel himself bound to be actuated in pursuing his examination. "If there is "nothing to excite suspicion," said one of the Court of Appeal Judges in the *Kingston Cotton Mills* case, when reversing the decision of the Court below, "less care may "*properly* be considered reasonable than could be so "considered *if* suspicion was or *ought* to have been aroused." The importance of the bearing of the actuation of suspicion upon an accountant's work and responsibility, cannot, I think, be over estimated. A statement is submitted to an accountant to be examined and certified. He takes it up in a state of belief or disbelief as to its correctness or incorrectness, its integrity or otherwise. If in a state of belief, his examination may be casual, perfunctory, or perhaps careless; if in a state of disbelief or suspicion, it will extend to every figure reasonably to be regarded as being likely to misrepresent. Actuated by suspicion, the trained experience, knowledge, and skill of the accountant are called into operation. These are the qualifications he professes to possess—the qualifications he is rightly expected and paid to exercise. Neglect at any time, or under any circumstances, fairly or reasonably to exercise them cannot but be followed, as a rule, by responsibility for its consequences. Imagine the following:—

I am a veterinary surgeon; you are a client. I have certified as sound a horse provisionally purchased by you. On receipt of my certificate you have paid a considerable sum of money for the horse—one of the conditions of the contract with the seller being that on the horse being certified by me as sound the money should pass and the transaction be complete. A week elapses, and you call upon me and report inherent and other defects in the horse, the knowledge of which operates so as to discount the greater part of its alleged value. You complain of my apparent neglect, and I in simple truth remark: "I did not suspect there would be "anything the matter with the animal which I could not "detect on the surface; I thought it was all right, and the "seller's groom, who was by when I made my examination, "never indicated anything wrong to me; in fact, his indi-

"cations were all the other way, and I took it for granted, "without giving myself the now apparently necessary "trouble to ascertain, that nothing, so far as it was possible "for me to judge, was wrong. Had it occurred to me, at the "time I was looking at the horse, that I might be doing you an "injury by taking so much for granted, I would have exer- "cised my skill in applying such tests as I know—tests which "would have revealed the defects you now report."

Would you in such circumstances seek redress from the professional man whom you had engaged to safeguard your interests? And, if so, would the Court refuse to grant it on the ground that nothing arose during the examination to excite suspicion?

The matter of responsibility of the accountant in connection with the certification of figures relating to profits available for dividend, and the payment of dividends out of moneys not derived from profits arising from the carrying on of the business of a company, is one of the last matters upon which I shall comment. In the Balance Sheet of a limited company there is usually to be found an item described "Profit and Loss Account—profit brought forward "from last account as made up to 18 , and "profit earned since that date £ ." This is the item which sets forth the amount of the profit available for dividend, and on which the whole of the certifying accountant's responsibility may be said to hang. I will not enter into all the considerations involved in the question as to what is profit available for dividend; but, in order that you may have a knowledge and appreciation of what constitutes the certifying accountant's main difficulty in determining it so as to avoid being held responsible in damages, it will be necessary for me to make some remarks in connection therewith. Profits available for dividend are represented by the cash and other resources of a company which have accrued over and above fixed capital as the result of carrying on its business during a stated period. Their existence is provable by an account or by accounts in which amounts in respect of all actual, or what may rightly be regarded as the equivalent of all actual, accretions may be credited, and in which are debited amounts in respect of every description of cost incurred, and, except in cases where it is recognised that a company's capital may be unrepresented by intrinsic assets at the end of a term of years, in respect of the value of every asset or part thereof absorbed in, or in connection with, producing the total of such accretions. I may say that, in proving the existence of such profits, it is allowable in some cases that account need not be taken of losses shown by earlier accounts, or of assets whose value has become diminished or non-existent for reasons probably outside the regular course of the business, or beyond the ordinary power or control of directors.

While I may chance to let in a glimmer of light on the matter, it is not my intention to trouble you with opinions which are held as to the existence of profits available for dividend being more reliably proved by the so-called single account system, which necessitates periodical valuations of assets, or the so-called double account system, which necessitates the classification of each purchase made or asset acquired into fixed or circulating assets, or into capital, or revenue charges; for, although it is true that results exhibited by an account of the one kind may be made to differ from results shown by an account of the other kind, it is equally true that accounts made up on both systems may be made to show practically identical results. To exemplify this, take the case of a land and buildings company, whose fixed capital normally consists of the funds with which it operates exclusively in buying, selling, and otherwise dealing with land and buildings, and of what I will call the instrument necessary to enable it conveniently to perform its operations—say its clerical and managerial establishment. It elects to keep its accounts on the double account system. The records in pounds, shillings, and pence of its transactions are kept with scrupulous care, and in respect of each completed transaction there is an allocation of the receipts and payments to capital and revenue, to principal and income. At a given date a balance sheet is prepared. In it, in respect of completed transactions, are credited the profits on such transactions, represented by money in the bank or invested, or there are credited the amounts *bonâ fide* owing in respect of the same—the amounts including therein the capital or principal expenditure or advances, made to secure the profit, as well as the profit itself. In it there are also credited the actual amounts taken from the treasury representing principal or capital, or capital expenditure or advances made with a view to securing profit. On the fixed capital, or its equivalent, as shown by a previous account (if any) being debited, and a balance being struck, there would be exhibited, if the credits are in excess of the debits, the amount of the profit available for dividend, subject only to the answer in good faith to be given to the following question: "Will the amounts stated to be owing "be received?" Now take the case of a similar company which, in addition to buying, selling, and otherwise dealing with land and buildings, holds itself out, without restraint, as a building company, and regularly engages in extensive building operations. This company elects to keep its accounts on the single account system. The power of election may, perhaps, be exercised unwisely, but the company, being at the time unfettered with regard to forms or systems of accounts, may do as it pleases. In keeping its pounds, shillings, and pence records, no express distinction is made in the receipts and payments as between capital and revenue, or principal and income. The annual or other account is made up. On the question arising as to how the results of the trading are to be ascertained, taking stock of the assets on hand suggests itself, and valuations are ordered. Valuations, you are aware, are made according to circumstances or instructions. In some cases regard is had only to cost; in others, to the selling prices of the day; and in others again, regard is had to what the commodities valued will conjecturally realise as a part of a prosperous going concern. On the debit side of the account is entered the capital fund, and, on the other side, amounts representing the cash on hand and the debts owing, as in the previous case; amounts representing a valuation of the building plant and stock on hand; and amounts representing the conjectural value of the capital or principal expenditure, or advances made with a view to securing profit, such value being arrived at from an examination or survey of the commodities stated covered by such expenditure or advances. The balance is struck, and, if the credits exceed the debits, the amount shown is declared as profit. What is really shown is a balance which may include the profit on completed transactions, if any has been earned, and which includes the amounts by which the capital or principal expenditure, or advances made with a view to securing profit (representing the money taken from the capital fund), may have been written up in the process of valuation. The adjustment of this balance so as to show, as in the case first instanced, profits available for dividend, is admittedly a costly and troublesome operation; but you will have gathered how it may be done, and it will be apparent to you, I think, that, according as directors may make choice in ascertaining facts, with or without judgment and discrimination, or with eyes open or partially closed, so, unless the certifying accountant intervenes in such a way as to prevent it, are shareholders asked to accept, and do accept, as real and divisible profit that which is only potential or assumed or conjectural profit. Those of you who have any present intentions of following up further this particular part of the subject of my lecture will do well to study the exceedingly concisely written and most instructive little book entitled "How are profits for the year to be "ascertained, or What is the capital of a company within "the meaning of the prohibition that dividends may not be "paid out of capital?" published by Mr. Bernard Dale, an experienced London lawyer who has made himself a master of all apparently that the law has laid down appertaining to company capital, profits, and dividends. Mr. Dale's book was published because of what he describes as the supposed uncertainty of the law as to what are profits of a company within the meaning of the rule, now firmly established at law, that companies may not pay dividends out of capital; and he gives it as one of his objects to show that the law is not in the state of confusion in which it is so frequently represented to be. At the end of his book he sets forth a statement of the law as it then stood, thrown into the form of a series of propositions.

These propositions include the following, which I will make no apology for reading:—

In the case of an entire venture the profits are to be determined by means of a Balance Sheet to be prepared on its conclusion, in which the assets, whether used as fixed or circulating capital during its continuance, will be stated at their then value, and in which the paid-up capital will be included amongst the debts and liabilities. Any excess in value of the assets over the amount of the debts and liabilities, including paid-up capital, will be profit, and any deficit, loss.

In the case of a venture where there is a provision in the regulations for an annual division of profits, any increase or decrease of the selling or market value of assets used as fixed capital should be disregarded in arriving at the year's profits.

If a loss of capital arises from the loss of an asset used as fixed capital otherwise than from wear and tear or waste in the service of the current year, such loss, in the absenc of any provision to the contrary in the regulations, nee not be taken into account in arriving at the profits for th year.

In the case of a venture where there is a provision in th regulations for the annual division of profits, loss of capit in a previous year need not be made good out of the re ceipts of the succeeding year before declaring a dividen for that year.

To be noted are the names of, and references to, the case quoted in support of these propositions. They are a follow:—

Verner v. General and Commercial Trust, Lim. (*Time* Law Reports, 7 March 1894).

Salisbury v. Metropolitan Railway Co., 22 L.T. 839.

In re Oxford Benefit Building Society, L.R. 35 Ch.D., p 502.

Davison v. Gillies, L.R. 16 Ch.D. 347.

Rishton v. Grissell, L.R. 5 Eq., p. 326.

Lee v. Neuchâtel Asphalte Co., L.R. 41 Ch.D., p. 14.

Dent v. London Tramways Co., 16 Ch.D. 344.

The responsibility of the certifying accountant in regar to the matters I have just referred to is now, I think, fairl recognisable. If he certifies that, in his opinion, the accour setting forth the liabilities, assets, and profits is full an fair, and exhibits a true and correct view of the state affairs, it is rightly to be assumed that he has satisfied hin self, by the reasonable and careful exercise of his knowledg and scrutinising powers, that the stating of the account, i its relation to the points I have been mentioning, has bee fully, fairly, truly, and correctly done. If he has given hi certificate without having so exercised his knowledge an powers, he is liable in damages in case the account shoul ultimately be proved to be wrong, and the measure of dire damage is the amount in dividends, based upon this accoun which has been paid away out of funds not derived fro profits arising from the business of the company. If th means of satisfying himself have not been resorte to, or have not been at his immediate disposal becaus they did not exist in such a form as to enab him at the time to form a judgment—and this would b the case where the books of account did not record th items of income and expenditure in such a manner as t render it readily practicable to draw up from the figure appearing a correct Balance Sheet and Profit and Loss Ac count—he has but to clearly indicate this in his certificat and his responsibility is at an end.

I have now brought you out of the thorny paths I referre to a little while ago, and I have probably tried the patienc of some of you in the effort. In drawing my statements t a conclusion, I will endeavour finally to impress you wit this: That the importance attaching to questions relatin to the responsibilities of Chartered Accountants with regar to their certificates is such that the necessity for givin careful and even anxious consideration to its demands wil be ever existent in your professional life. You will remembe that a certificate should create a correct impression; tha intending investors have a right to expect the certificates c Chartered Accountants to state profits as net profits withou any ambiguity, and unaccompanied by any statement which might obscure the actual position; that to render a certificate of real value the certificate should show over a period of years whether the profits have increased or decreased; that a statement setting forth the results of an investigation confined to the transactions of a few months does not enable an idea to be formed as to the actual value of the business concerned; that a Chartered Accountant is in duty bound to see that the terms of his certificate are not unduly stretched; that his figures should not be made to represent what it is supposed might occur; and that, though no legal responsibility is incurred by making statements referring to estimates as to probabilities in relation to profits, the practice is regarded as reprehensible and as one of a kind which every Chartered Accountant should avoid having imputed to him. You will remember that, as an accountant, having a licence, so to speak, to practise under a Charter obtained from the Queen, you will be pledged to strict rules of conduct, and to so keep up the character of the profession of your choice as to secure for the community the qualifications and sense of responsibility it may rightly expect to find. You will not draw too fine a distinction between your legal and moral responsibility, and never allow the measure of the former to be the measure which will guide you in the discharge of your duty; you will not forget the golden rule of the accountant to take nothing for granted, nor that, though you have nothing to do with a company's policy or impolicy, you have everything to do with your own. It is not a very difficult thing to do, to so fence with your own best reasoning as to allow yourself to come temporarily—perhaps only momentarily, but yet improperly—to the belief that wrong is right; you know, though it is delusive, that to make white look green you have only to put on a pair of green spectacles. You, conduct, if you would be free from harm, must at all times be reasonable and proper, whether it is personal to yourself or whether it be in relation to your professional duty. It has been laid down in regard to your work that you must bring to bear, upon what you have to perform, such skill, care, and caution, as a reasonably competent, careful, and cautious expert would use; that if there is anything calculated to excite your suspicion, when you are examining accounts, you must probe it to the bottom, though what that anything is, which is to excite it, is not laid down, but is left with you to decide. You will study not how best to avoid the trouble of doing your duty in regard to your work, but how best to do it; not how best not to make statements which you know you ought to make, but how best to make them, remembering to be cautious and not forgetting that in publishing a certificate you have not only the interests of shareholders to consider, but the directors and their interests, and the general credit with the public of the company with whose affairs you are concerned. Doubts will arise in your mind, but if they are real doubts, not conjured up doubts, which reasonably, naturally, and honestly present themselves, you will deal with hem without difficulty, and your decisions, I doubt not, will in the majority of cases—for you cannot always be right—be on the side of what is proper, on the side of what is reasonable, on the side of what is fair.

THE LIMITS WHICH A CHARTERED ACCOUNTANT SHOULD PLACE ON HIS DUTIES AND RESPONSIBILITIES AS AN AUDITOR (1897)

B.S. Harvey

The routine work of an audit--checking for errors and omissions--is less important than a careful analysis of accounts, for this qualitative evaluation provides the main basis for an auditor's opinion.

Chartered Accountants Students' Society of London.

PRIZE ESSAY.—By Mr. B. S. Harvey, B.A.

The Limits which a Chartered Accountant should place on his Duties and Responsibilities as an Auditor.

The Committee of this Society, during the Autumn Session, offered a first prize of £4 4s. and a second prize of £2 2s. for the best essays on the above subject.

The eight papers received were submitted to the President of the Society, Mr. E. Waterhouse, B.A., F.C.A., and three selected by him were also submitted to Mr. J. G. Griffiths, F.C.A.

The essay of Mr. B. S. Harvey, B.A. (articled to Mr. Gérard van de Linde, F.C.A.), was placed first, and that of Mr. J. H. Moritz (articled to Mr. L. Hardy, A.C.A.) was placed second, and they were awarded the prizes.

The following is the text of Mr. Harvey's essay, which was read at a meeting of the Society held on Wednesday, the 16th day of December 1896, Mr. Frank N. Keen, A.C.A., presiding:—

Theoretically, there should be no occasion for the subject of this essay; practically, the subject is one of the most vital interest to the profession. The duties and responsibilities of an auditor are a matter, one would imagine, for law, not for opinion, and the limits of such duties should not be elastic nor able to be modified by circumstances, but rigid and unalterable. But law is the outcome of litigation, and litigation is dependent upon time. The profession is yet young, and the decisions of the Judges with regard to auditors are few and far between; even such decisions as there are, are indefinite, as to an auditor's duties, perhaps, more than as to his responsibilities.

But, contrary to what might be expected, the public have little to gain from any legal definition. The burden the auditor now takes upon him would be likely to be lightened rather than made heavier by legislation; uncontrolled, the conscientious auditor—and I imagine the majority are such—would magnify, rather than minimise, his labour, in order to be upon the safe side. But once allow the law to step in, and his position is altered. He knows exactly what is required of him, and he does that, and no more. It is, however, highly improbable that such a state of things will come to pass. No two audits are alike, and what is necessary in one may be superfluous in the other; it is next to impossible to imagine that law could be made either regulating audits *en bloc*, or still more so controlling them individually.

Generally speaking, then, I take it that the duties and responsibilities of an auditor are a matter for his individual opinion, and I think it will not be denied that this is at present, at any rate, an essentially weak point about auditing, and one which has the additional difficulty attached to it of being very difficult to remedy. The tendency of time is to add both to the auditor's duties and responsibilities; in previous years accountants did not think of checking accounts as much as is done now, and were in many cases content to append their name to a Balance Sheet, if they were satisfied that it agreed with the books. Now, such is not the case. Entries in books of primary record are vouched or traced through to their original sources; the value of large assets, such as stock, is inspected by means of percentages, or of debtors by a careful examination of the thousands of details of which it is composed. In a word, the duties of auditors are on the increase—but the fees are not.

It might be imagined that the limit of the auditor's duties and responsibilities was with his certificate, but such is not quite the fact. He may, if he choose, so word the certificate that it shall appear to have a saving clause in the case of work he has left undone, but it is very uncertain if such clause would exempt him from the responsibility of that work. Or, again, in the audits of railways, banks and life assurance companies, the wording of the certificate itself is fixed. The auditor has to certify that "the Balance

"Sheet is a full and fair one, properly drawn up so as to exhibit a true and correct statement of the company's "affairs as shown by the books." Here, indeed, the law lays down a limit, as it were, but the limit is so vague as to be next to useless. Also, in the audits of building and friendly societies the work is more or less defined by the Acts by which they are governed. In the case of private firms the work done by the auditor, and his responsibilities, rest entirely with the partners. The auditor's only duties then are to make sure that the partners understand how far he examines the books, and to affix his name to a certificate that is not too comprehensive, in view of the work done.

The articles of association of a company, or, in the case of those who have none, Table A of the Companies Act 1862, is another example of the means by which the auditor is governed; and in this connection it should be said that the auditor has no power to interfere with the work of the directors, apart from the memorandum and articles of association. If the latter are deviated from in any way that affects him or his certificate, he may lay the affair before the shareholders, either at the company's general meeting or by a special report to each individually. Mr. Justice Vaughan Williams, in the case of the *London and General Bank*, says that, with regard to the form of the certificate and of the Balance Sheet, the duty of auditors must be more or less defined by the articles of association of the particular company.

Auditors are usually supposed to have to direct their attention to three classes of errors, namely:—

(1) Errors of commission.
(2) Errors of omission.
(3) Errors of principle.

By far the most important of the three is the last. The first, or errors of commission, include technical or clerkly mistakes. The second may apply to such an error as, for example, neglecting to write off depreciation; the third, to such an one as charging revenue items to capital, or *vice versâ*.

The danger, undoubtedly, that lies nearest the auditor, more especially in respect of large audits, is of letting the main point at issue slip by unnoticed in his anxiety to perform properly all the very necessary routine work that goes to make up the sum total of the audit. The errors of commission and omission may be noted, but the errors of principle may be allowed to pass unnoticed. Even in the matter of routine work, which forms, so far as time goes, the bulk of the audit, a wise auditor will do well to separate what is vital from what, like Shakespeare's cat, is "harmless "and necessary." *Ne sutor ultra crepidam;* even the conscientious auditor need not cast *every* page of the Postage Book. There, at least, is one limit of his duties and responsibilities.

I propose now to deal with one or two of the most important points in connection with auditing, as it is obviously impossible even to mention all; and, even with these, one can only hint at the more salient features of the difficulties the auditor has in regard to them.

First, then, as to the depreciation of assets—a question which abounds with difficulties for the auditor. The general principle of this must always be a systematic reduction out of profits to something below the actual value of the asset. In companies whose profits fluctuate—who are one year able to pay a dividend and the next not—difficulties will arise for the auditor who desires the writing down to be systematic. The shareholders will not object to depreciation as long as they receive a substantial dividend; but if, as may be the case, the amount necessary to adequately depreciate the asset means that they are deprived of a dividend they otherwise would have had, they will be apt to declare such depreciation unnecessary. But, as has been said, depreciation must be systematic, and the bad years must bear their proportion of it as well as the good. As a matter of fact, in bad years the need of proper depreciation is greater, for the assets, in the event of liquidation, are nearer then to being realised. Hence they should all the more be stated at their proper value.

Apart from this, however, the application of this principle may be often very difficult. The actual legal decisions may conflict with the prudent management of the company—witness the case of *Lee v. The Neuchatel Asphalte Co.* Or, again, writing down plant, though not actually enjoined by law, is desirable and may be even essential in practice.

In the case of trust companies, while the articles may expressly relieve the directors from stating the value or estimated value of the securities at the date of the Balance Sheet, yet the latter may show an immense excess owing to the investments in it being taken at cost price. The auditor in this case should take care to become acquainted with the *value* as well as the *cost* of the securities. The difference may, in many cases, be only the result of a temporary fluctuation of the market, and the investment may, in such cases, not need depreciation; but where there are actually ascertained losses it is the duty of the auditor to see that they are met in one of two ways, either by

(1) Writing down out of profits,
(2) Formation of reserve funds,

which latter should be invested in gilt-edged securities.

It is in this direction that the auditor should exert his influence, and to this that he should draw attention in his report, though he may confine himself to stating the fact of the deprecation, while omitting the actual extent thereof.

Secondly, with regard to debtors. I imagine none will deny that it is the duty of the auditor to check these individually from the Sales Ledgers. He will also, as far as possible, notify those that are bad or long outstanding. A good check in total upon these may be had, if the system admits of it, by the adoption of an account "Debtors" in the Private Ledger, to the debit of which account the total of all Sales Day Books, Journal debits, etc., are carried; and to its credit, all cash received, bills receivable, Journal credits, returns of sales, etc. The balance on this account will then represent the sum of the balances in the Sales Ledgers.

Another important consideration in the case of debtors is to see that sufficient reserve is made for discounts.

There are some firms of accountants, I believe, who adopt

the plan of verifying the debts by an actual notification to the debtors individually of the amount of their debt on a given date, requesting them to let them know if such amount is incorrect. Such a precaution ensures the clerical accuracy of the books and guards against the introduction of fictitious debtors in the Sales Ledger.

Turning now to the question of Stores Accounts, we find them a most important consideration in the accounts of companies—railway, water, gas, and the like. The auditor, with his inevitable tendency to "strain at a gnat and "swallow a camel," will spend, perhaps, hours in the pursuit of sixpence in the Cash Book, while the expenditure of thousands of pounds in respect of stores is allowed to pass unchallenged.

Yet, in regard to stores, the auditor is bound to see—

(1) That only stores consumed are charged to Store Account.

(2) That as rigid a discrimination between revenue and capital stores is exercised as between revenue and capital cash.

(3) That reasonable care is taken to prevent theft of stores.

(4) That, when a detailed audit of Stores Accounts is impossible, he should call for the Stores Sheets and agree them with the Stores Account in total.

A kindred subject to stores is stock. When it is remembered that a direct increase of stock is a direct increase of profit it will be seen how important the subject is. It is an axiom of accountancy that the stock should be taken at cost price, or, if at the time the market price be lower than the cost price, at market price. Otherwise, stock taken at selling price is an anticipation of profit. This it is obviously necessary for the auditor to see done, as also to make sure that the stock at the beginning of the period is dealt with on the same basis as the stock at the end. It is important also to check the value of the stock as well. I mean, for example, that it would not be correct to take a linen-draper's stock, which included many items of obsolete, and therefore unsaleable, pattern, at cost price. A percentage would have to be deducted for the change in fashion. Or again, on the other hand, a wine merchant laying down wine would be entitled to appreciate his stock by a percentage of its cost for the enhanced value of the wine.

But the chief difficulty of stock for the auditor is not in regard to its price but to its value. We are often enough glibly told that extensions should be checked, say four a page, as I read in a recent lecture. I should like to see the gentleman who proposed this performing it in the case of stock of any magnitude, or of one which consists of many small quantities of differently-priced articles. I am very much afraid that the next stocktaking would appear before he had emerged from checking the extensions of the last one.

Of course, Stock Sheets should be cast. Articled clerks and others know that to their cost. Equally of course, we should not place much value upon that as a check. But the best check will be an examination and comparison of the amount of stock with that of former years. Given that so much stock, plus so much purchases, less so much sales and stock at the end, produce so much profit in one year, a proportionate profit should be produced in any other year. True, so long as the buying and selling prices remain constant; but what if they vary from day to day, as I understand is the case in some businesses? I must leave the answer to those who are so much better enabled to answer it than I am. If they received the decision of Mr. Justice Vaughan Williams in the case of the *Kingston Cotton Mills* with delight, they will doubtless have an answer.

The managers' signed certificates of stock will be taken by the auditor for the amount in each of their departments, failing the possibility of his personally inspecting it, which is next to impossible, or to his having presented to him a valuer's certificate of the amount, which is highly improbable.

As regards capital and revenue it is the duty of the auditor to discriminate between them. The natural tendency of companies will be to overcharge capital and reduce the charge of revenue; and, equally, the duties of the auditor will lie the other way, since a charge on revenue will mean a decrease of the profit available for dividend. Here, as everywhere, the auditor will derive a great advantage from the comparison of revenue charges of one year from those of another, and from the specific enquiry as to the cause of any variation. On the other hand, the auditor will not allow capital work to be paid for out of revenue, except, indeed, as a temporary expedient, pending the calling up of fresh capital.

In the case of the certificate of profits given to a firm which is being converted into a company, the auditor is bound especially to see that he only certifies actual facts, and that the profit shown has actually been earned. He should also be careful, if possible, to give the separate actual figures of profit from year to year, and not an average of any number of years, so that a bad year may be made up for by a good. He must examine the last Balance Sheet very carefully, and thoroughly satisfy himself that every asset is correctly valued, and that adequate depreciation has been made in every case.

The auditor will do well to create, as far as possible, a system of internal checks by which his work may be materially assisted, or even lessened. By allowing one department to have the checking of the accounts of another, a sufficiently reliable safeguard of accuracy is produced; and often a slight alteration of the system in vogue will be sufficient to ensure this, without upsetting the general routine of work.

A comparison of the figures in one set of accounts with those in the preceding, affords the auditor one of the best and simplest methods of checking any abnormal differences. This may often be made easier by a system of percentages whereby, in the accounts of a large business, the results from year to year are rendered more easy of comparison. The importance of a series of percentages cannot be too much insisted upon.

Having now briefly touched upon one or two points of importance to the auditor, I will proceed to say a few words on the general aspect of his duties and responsibilities. The public, as a rule, are far too apt to regard him as an ultimate and perfect check upon the accounts of a company; they expect from him a degree of perfection and an absence from error that would, were they a fact, make him almost a deity; and if their belief in him is shattered, as it sometimes is, by a false certificate or an undetected fraud, they are liable to go as far the other way and proclaim him altogether useless. "The falsehood of extremes" is here evident. It is a mistake to imagine that a system of audit ensures absolutely the non-occurrence of a fraud, and the sooner the profession allow the public to understand this, the better will it be for them; but, unfortunately, the tendency of auditors is to give countenance to, rather than deny, their infallibility, and they rest in ease because they know that the accounts of the majority of companies and firms are *bonâ fide*, and such belief is not likely, therefore, to be disturbed.

In theory no doubt every fraud is possible to be found out, in theory every crime is possible to be detected. But we ought no more to expect infallibility from the auditor than we do from a detective. Both are liable to be hoodwinked, yet both are invaluable in their special positions. Lord Justice Lopes, in the case of the *Kingston Cotton Mills*, said that the auditor was not bound to be a detective or approach his work with suspicion. He said that their duties must not be made too onerous, and they must not be made liable for tracking out ingeniously laid schemes of fraud when there is nothing to arouse their suspicion, and when those frauds, too, had been perpetrated by tried servants, and had been undetected for years by the directors.

I should be much misunderstood if it were imagined that I thought that auditors should accept this definition of the Court. It is quoted here merely as an instance from the Judges themselves as against the popular idea. There will be few auditors who will not take a most serious and responsible view of their duties, and the above might fairly represent the irreducible minimum of their duties and responsibilities.

What, then, in my humble opinion, an auditor provides is another addition to the series of checks upon the accuracy and freedom from fraud of accounts. If it is said that this is too low a level on which to place him, we should remember that instances of failure are not so few or far between that auditors can afford to boast of their immunity from error. The law of auditing is small, and the literature of auditing is small, and even now auditors may be likened to some African explorer who is pushing his way into a hitherto unexplored country, on the whole with great success, but at times with failure. Such a one will not boast of his achievements till his end is attained.

The case of the *Kingston Cotton Mills* clearly shows that there is nothing definite to be obtained of the law at present. The too severe judgment of the Court of first instance becomes the too lenient judgment of the Court of Appeal, and as regards one of the most unfortunate points in auditing—stock—the legal responsibility of the auditor is much where it was. How far such responsibility may be altered or modified it is for the future alone to decide.

If I may be allowed to recapitulate, then the general result seems to me to be that the limits of an auditor's responsibilities and duties are indefinite, and different in different cases. He has certain limits to which he is bound to attend, namely:—

(1) The articles of association;

(2) Any special Acts governing the class of audit on which he is engaged;

(3) The certificate;

but beyond these he has the limit of his own discretion. It is to this limit and to this limit alone that in the bulk of cases the auditor has to refer, and in closing may I be allowed to say that only by making his duties as great and his responsibilities as onerous as is possible for him, by regarding not so much the legal as the wider horizon of his moral responsibility, will the auditor add to or even preserve the growing trust that from day to day is evidently being placed in the last, but not the least, of the professions throughout the length and breadth of the country.

THE LIABILITIES OF AUDITORS UNDER THE COMPANIES ACTS (1898)

Lawrence R. Dicksee

Dicksee argues that the Institute of Chartered Accountants, not the courts, should judge allegations of negligence brought against accountants. So severe were the legal penalties that "A doctor who by his lack of skill killed a whole hospital full of patients would get off more lightly" than a negligent auditor.

Chartered Accountants Students' Society of London.

The Liabilities of Auditors under the Companies Acts.

By Mr. LAWRENCE R. DICKSEE, F.C.A.

THE following paper was read at a meeting held on Tuesday, 3rd May 1898, by Mr. LAWRENCE R. DICKSEE, F.C.A., Mr. ERNEST COOPER, F.C.A., in the chair:—

IN view of the grave and increasing responsibilities which are being cast upon auditors, I feel that no apology is due from me for my selection of the above subject upon which to address you this evening; but, while striving to make the most of the time which I have before me to do justice to this important subject, I feel that it is one upon which so much might advantageously be said, that it is practically impossible for me now to do more than deal with the single question of the liabilities to which the auditors of joint stock companies may find themselves subjected.

When I first undertook to deliver this paper, I had intended to include also the questions of the rights and duties of auditors, together with some remarks as to the nature and manner of their appointment, but I found, upon further going into the question, that it was practically impossible to embrace these points, and at the same time do anything like justice to the question of the auditor's liabilities. I have, therefore, abandoned the attempt altogether, and shall confine myself to the question of an auditor's liabilities, in the event of its being subsequently ascertained or even alleged that the accounts which he has certified are in point of fact inaccurate.

At the outset, however, I should like it to be very clearly understood that I am not for one moment advocating auditorial irresponsibility. I see no reason why auditors, like other persons, should not be held responsible for their own wilful acts and defaults, and nothing which I am about to say must be taken as contradicting that statement of principle; but what I wish to particularly draw your attention to is that the responsibilities which, as I believe, were intended to be placed upon auditors by the Legislature, have been very much enlarged by the Courts, while in the first instance they were in many cases unreasonable, as I shall show hereafter.

In dealing with the question of the liability of auditors, it is necessary, in the first instance, to consider the precise relationship between the auditor of a company and that company. This relationship is in the nature of a contract, the basis of which is the articles of association of that particular company, or (in the absence of special articles of association) by Table "A" of the Companies Act 1862.

This statement, however, requires some modification in the case of the auditors of banking companies incorporated under the Companies Act 1879, as there are certain statutory provisions in these cases, as follows:—

7.—(1) Once at least in every year the accounts of every banking company registered after the passing of this Act as a limited company shall be examined by an auditor or auditors, who shall be elected annually by the company in general meeting.

(2) A director or officer of the company shall not be capable of being elected auditor of such company.

(3) An auditor on quitting office shall be re-eligible.

(4) If any casual vacancy occurs in the office of any auditor, the surviving auditor or auditors (if any) may act, but if there is no surviving auditor, the directors shall forthwith call an extraordinary general meeting for the purpose of supplying the vacancy or vacancies in the auditorship.

(5) Every auditor shall have a list delivered to him of all books kept by the company, and shall at all reasonable times have access to the books and accounts of the company; and any auditor may, in relation to such books and accounts, examine the directors or any other officer of the company: provided that if a banking company has branch banks beyond the limits of Europe, it shall be sufficient if the auditor is allowed access to such copies of, and extracts from, the books and accounts of any such branch as may have been transmitted to the head office of the banking company in the United Kingdom.

(6) The auditor or auditors shall make a report to the members on the accounts examined by him or them, and on every Balance Sheet laid before the company in general meeting during his or their tenure of office; and in every such report shall state whether, in his or their opinion, the Balance Sheet referred to in the report is a full and fair Balance Sheet properly drawn up, so as to exhibit a true and correct view of the state of the company's affairs, as shown by the books of the company, and such report shall be read before the company in general meeting.

(7) The remuneration of the auditor or auditors shall be fixed by the general meeting appointing such auditor or auditors, and shall be paid by the company.

8.—Every Balance Sheet submitted to the annual or other meeting of the members of every banking company registered after the passing of this Act as a limited company shall be signed by the auditor or auditors, and by the secretary or manager (if any), and by the directors of the company, or three of such directors at the least.

It will be seen that these regulations do not in any material way differ from those which usually obtain, except that section 7 (5) distinctly limits the liability of auditors in the case of undertakings having branches beyond the limits of Europe. I may point out in passing that while this provision is no doubt very necessary for the protection of auditors resident in this country, it has the practical effect of reducing the audit of the accounts of a non-European banking company almost to a matter of form.

There is another distinction which has been drawn by the Court of Appeal between auditors under the 1879 Act and the auditors of other companies, viz., that the former are in all cases officers of the company, whereas it is a question for consideration under each separate case whether the latter are officers of the company or not. This is a point which I shall have to revert to again, but at the moment it is perhaps convenient that I should draw your attention to the practical effect of this very material distinction.

Now, the position of an auditor with regard to the company being on the basis of a contract, it is obvious that from the first the company always had a remedy against any auditor who by failing in his duty could be shown to have committed a breach of contract. That remedy would be by way of action, and might be taken either by the company itself, or, if the company were being wound up, by the liquidator in its name, and would be by way of damages which could be shown to be the result of such negligence or breach of contract. Now, so far as I am aware, there is no recorded case which appears to suggest that this remedy, which a company undoubtedly had in the case of an auditor failing in his duty, was so difficult to enforce as to render the assistance of the Legislature necessary in the public interest. It is true that there are very few cases on record in which such actions have been brought against auditors, but the reasonable inference here is that (in at all events the vast majority of cases) there has been no considerable negligence upon their part, and as the few actions which have been brought against auditors have been almost invariably successful it certainly cannot be suggested that, as a matter of experience, it was found extremely difficult to obtain judgment, when, as a matter of equity, it ought to have been given against the auditor.

Yet—notwithstanding the fact that there was always a means of bringing negligent auditors to book, and further that but few cases had arisen in which this was necessary, and those which had been brought were almost uniformly successful—it is noteworthy that, under the Companies (Winding-up) Act 1890, a new procedure was inaugurated, affording greater facilities for bringing legal proceedings against auditors who were thought to have been negligent; and as at the time there certainly seems to have been no necessity for this change of procedure, and as, moreover, the question as to precisely how it came to find the place in the Statute Book seems to have been forgotten, it will perhaps not be amiss if, before considering the effect of section 10 of the Companies Act 1890, we pause for a moment to inquire how this section ever came to be incorporated in the Bill.

Probably you are all of you well familiar with the wording of section 10—the "misfeasance section" as it is generally called - but it is, perhaps, desirable that I should refresh your memory as to its precise terms, which are as follows :—

> 10.—(1) Where, in the course of the winding-up of a company under the Companies Act, it appears that any person who has taken part in the formation or promotion of the company, or any past or present director, manager, liquidator, or other officer of the company, has misapplied or retained or become liable or accountable for any moneys or property of the company, or been guilty of any misfeasance or breach of trust in relation to the company, the Court may, on the application of the Official Receiver, or the liquidator of the company, or of any creditor or contributory of the company, examine into the conduct of such promoter, director, manager, liquidator, or other officer of the company, and compel him to repay any moneys or restore any property so misapplied or retained, or for which he has become liable or accountable, together with interest after such rate as the Court thinks just, or to contribute such sums of money to the assets of the company by way of compensation in respect of such misapplication, retainer, misfeasance, or breach of trust, as the Court thinks just.
>
> (2) The provisions of this section shall apply in the winding-up of any company under the Companies Act, whether the same is being wound up by, or subject to the supervision of, the Court, or is being wound up voluntarily, and whether the winding-up commenced before or after the passing of this Act, and notwithstanding that the offence is one for which the offender may be criminally responsible.

When the Companies (Winding-up) Bill was first printed, in February 1890, it contained no such clause as the misfeasance section, which I have just read; but in its place we find the following, which was clause 9 of the original Bill :—

> 9.—(1) If it appears from any report of examination under this Act that any person has :—
>
> (*a*) Signed or made himself responsible for any false or misleading prospectus, notice, statement, report, or Balance Sheet ; or
>
> (*b*) Misapplied or retained in his own hands, or become liable or accountable for, any money of the company ; or
>
> (*c*) Been guilty of any fraud, misfeasance, or breach of trust in relation to the company or the promotion or formation thereof ; or

(*d*) Been party or privy to carrying on the business of the company after having reason to believe that it was insolvent; or

(*e*) Been party or privy to any rash or hazardous speculations by which the insolvency of the company has been brought about in whole or in part; or

(*f*) When the company was unable to pay its debts as they became due, given an undue preference to any of its creditors, and that loss or damage has been thereby caused to the company, or to the creditors of the company:

The Court may order him to contribute over and above any sums for which he may be otherwise liable, such sum as it may think just towards the assets of the company.

(2) For the purpose of any proceedings under this section, the report shall be *prima facie* evidence of the statements therein contained.

Now, this clause met with a considerable amount of opposition, both in Committee and also in commercial circles outside Parliament; and among the representations which were made upon the subject I may quote the following from a memorandum prepared by the Council of the Institute of Chartered Accountants:—

"Clause 9 covers much the same ground as section 165 of "the Companies Act 1862 and section 38 of the Act of 1867, "which have frequently been put in force against delinquent "directors and others; but it so far differs as to make the "construction of the three enactments together extremely "difficult, and to tend to unsettle the law as established by "the decisions on these sections. The liability attached to "directors and others by subsections (*a*), (*d*) and (*e*) is so "serious, that it would certainly deter men who have any-"thing to lose from accepting such positions. Directors and "others might apparently be rendered responsible under it "even for mistakes made by employees which it might be "next to impossible to discover. Subsection (2) would "make the statements contained in the report of 'the pre-"'scribed officer' *prima facie* evidence against any person "named therein, though he might never have been heard or "have had an opportunity of being heard. It is suggested "that the clause requires to be modified and entirely recast, "so as to show distinctly how far it proposes to amend and "extend the law contained in the above-mentioned sections "of the Acts of 1862 and 1867, and the decisions thereon. "Provision will also be requisite, if any part of the clause is "retained, for initiating proceedings under it, and for the "costs of proceedings."

As a result of the numerous objections that were raised to it, the Attorney-General withdrew the clause altogether, and in the following May submitted a new clause, to the effect that where, in the course of winding-up of a company under the Companies Act,

(1) It shall appear that any person who has taken part in the formation or promotion of the company, or any past or present director, manager, official or other liquidator, or any officer of the company has misapplied or retained or become liable or accountable for any moneys of the company, or been guilty of any misfeasance or breach of trust in relation to the company, the Court may compel him to repay any moneys so misapplied or retained, or for which he has become liable or accountable, together with interest, or to contribute such sums of money to the assets of the company by way of compensation as the Court thinks just.

(2) Where, in any such winding-up as aforesaid, it shall appear

(*a*) That any person who has taken part in the formation or promotion of the company, or is or has been a director, manager, clerk, or other officer of the company, has knowingly or negligently signed, issued, or caused to be published any false or misleading prospectus, notice, report, Balance Sheet, or other statement relating to the company or its affairs, and that any contributory or creditor of the company at the commencement of the winding-up who was deceived by such false or misleading statement has, in consequence thereof, sustained loss or damage; or

(*b*) That any such promoter, director, manager, clerk or other officer of the company as aforesaid has been party to the carrying on of the business of the company after (after reason to believe that) it was insolvent, or been guilty of any fraud, misfeasance, or breach of trust in relation to the formation or promotion of the company, or the carrying on of the business thereof, whereby loss or damage has been occasioned to the company, the Court may compel him to contribute to the assets of the company, and to pay to the injured creditor or contributory such sums of money by way of compensation for the loss sustained as the Court may think just.

(*c*) The provisions of this section shall apply in the winding-up of any company under the Companies Acts, whether the same is being wound-up by or subject to the supervision of the Court or is being wound-up voluntarily, and whether such winding-up commenced before or after the passing of this Act, and notwithstanding that the offence is one for which the offender may be criminally responsible.

The following is an extract from the reported discussion of this clause in Committee:—

"The Attorney-General explained that the first part of the clause incorporated the 165th section of the Act of 1862, while the second part of it provided for those new matters which were not contained in that section.

"Sir John Lubbock said he had not a word to say against the incorporation of clause 165 of the Act of 1862 in this Bill.

He quite admitted that the Court ought to have the power, under certain circumstances, of compelling directors to pay damages to shareholders whom they had misled; but it occurred to him that a director might have to pay twice over for the same fault, the Court ordering him to pay something to the shareholders generally, and the shareholders then bringing separate actions against him. It ought to be made clear that if a director was made to pay something by order of the Court, that absolved him against individual actions. It would be an injustice for a director to have to pay twice over for the same mistake.

"The clause was read a second time, and on the question that it be added to the Bill,

"Mr. Warmington pointed out that this proposal to make directors compensate shareholders applied only in cases under this Bill where there was a winding-up order. It would not apply at all to cases where there was no winding-up order, and he maintained that directors ought to be subject to liability for the issue of an untruthful Balance Sheet, whether there was a winding-up order or not. He thought the matter would be better dealt with by separate legislation.

"Sir Julian Goldsmid said the facility with which directors lent themselves on many occasions to very extraordinary proceedings was remarkable, and ought to be checked by a new provision of the law. At the same time he was inclined to agree with Mr. Warmington, as this Bill only applied to the cases where companies were wound up, that it would be better to deal with the question of directors' liability in a separate measure, which would be applicable to all companies alike.

"With reference to the proposal in the clause,

> "That any person who has taken part in the formation or promotion of the company, or is or has been a director, manager, clerk, or other officer of the company, has knowingly or negligently, alone, or in conjunction with any other person, signed, issued, or caused to be published any false or misleading prospectus, notice, report, Balance Sheet, or other statement relating to the company or its affairs, shall be liable to pay compensation to any contributory or creditor of the company who has sustained loss,

"Mr. Dixon Hartland proposed to omit the words 'or other officer,' as he did not quite know who this would include.

"Mr. Quilter agreed that the leaving in of these words might be a very serious matter to auditors, who might have placed upon them a responsibility which they ought not to be called upon to sustain.

"Sir Julian Goldsmid said it was impossible to specify every officer who was meant, and he thought it might safely be left to the discretion of the Court to determine who was liable.

"The amendment was negatived.

"Mr. Dixon Hartland next proposed to leave out the words 'or negligently.'

"The Attorney-General said it was for the Committee to determine whether or not there ought to be this liability on the part of directors for negligence.

"Sir Julian Goldsmid was of opinion that the word 'negligently' ought to remain, and he thought auditors, for example, who were appointed for the protection of the shareholders ought to be made liable for negligence in the performance of their duties. He was quite sure auditors would take care they received remuneration commensurate with the liability they incurred. Again, he should say, with regard to officers generally, that the secretary of a company might be very negligent in the discharge of his duties; and if there was on his part what, in the opinion of the Court, amounted to criminal negligence, he ought to be punished for it.

"Sir M. Hicks-Beach said it was very desirable that the Committee should be able to come to some agreement on this matter, and he would suggest that after the word 'affairs' they should insert these words: 'In matters with which, in 'the opinion of the Court, it was the duty of such person to 'be acquainted.' His idea was that the liability should be confined to those matters which the Court would hold it to be the duty of a director or other officer to have known about if he had properly carried out the duties of his office.

"Mr. Dixon Hartland said those words would be satisfactory to him, and he asked leave to withdraw his amendment.

"With regard to subsection (2):—

"The Attorney-General said he was informed that there had been several serious cases lately in which directors had carried on a very large business and obtained very large quantities of goods when their company was insolvent. They had no means to pay with, and when the companies came to be wound up there were found to be no assets at all. There was a similar section to this in the Bankruptcy Act, and it seemed to the Government that this provision of the Bankruptcy Act might very usefully be applied to the company law.

"Mr. S. Smith thought it would be necessary to have a proper definition of the word 'insolvent' before the Committee agreed to the clause as it stood.

"Mr. Kimber thought that to prevent all insolvent companies from trading would be a great hindrance to business. It would absolutely prevent any mine in the future from being carried on by any respectable man, because, in the experience of every mining company, there was no point of time at which it was not possible for a mine to give out. It would also strike at a number of insurance and other companies.

"After some discussion the words contained in the clause were struck out, and the following words, suggested by Mr.

Warmington, inserted: 'Any such director, manager, secretary, or other officer of the company who has wilfully incurred on behalf of the company any liability which there was no reasonable prospect that the company would be able to satisfy' shall be liable, etc.

"The following portion of the clause was then considered:—

> "The Court may, upon the application of the said officer of the Court, or of the liquidator of the company, or of the creditor or contributory injured as aforesaid, examine into the conduct of such promoter, director, manager, clerk, or other officer of the company, and compel him to contribute to the assets of the company, or to pay to the injured creditor or contributory, as the case may be, such sums of money by way of compensation for loss or damage sustained as the Court may think just.

"Sir Julian Goldsmid moved to omit the words 'or to pay to the injured creditor or contributory, as the case may be,' on the ground that the delinquent directors and officials ought not to be called upon to pay money over to individuals, but should be ordered to pay it to the assets of the company.

"The Attorney-General and Mr. Warmington opposed the amendment on the ground that the Court ought to have the discretion of ordering payments to individuals who had been misled or defrauded by directors.

"The Committee divided, when there voted:—

For the amendment	17
Against	15
Majority	2

"Sir Julian Goldsmid's amendment was accordingly carried, and the words were then struck out of the clause."

Now, it will be seen that this "misfeasance section" took the form in which it at length became law after a most full discussion in Committee, and that such modifications as were made in the original wording of the clause were made with the object of relieving some of the liabilities imposed on persons who might act as directors of companies, and that from first to last the liability of auditors, all important as it is, seems to have been almost entirely lost sight of. You will also notice that, while relieving the position of directors somewhat, the final wording is very much stronger against auditors than the original draft—assuming, of course, that the interpretation of the Court of Appeal is correct, and that auditors were intended by the Legislature to be included under the term "officers of the company." But—in view of the fact that auditors were only once mentioned during the course of the whole debate, and then as *possibly* coming under the operations of the section—it seems to me that there is room for serious doubt as to whether it was ever really the intention of the Legislature to include auditors under this section, which obviously is primarily directed against persons having more or less directly the actual handling of the properties and moneys of the company. For my own part I am inclined to think that it was never intended by the Legislature to include auditors under this section; for it is, to my mind, inconceivable that, had they been intended to be included, so important a class of persons would not have been specifically mentioned; both in the text of the section itself and also, and more particularly, in the course of the debate as to the wording of that section.

It has, however, been decided by the Court of Appeal that not only are auditors of banking companies registered under the Act of 1879 officers of the company, but further that under some (and, probably, under most) articles of association the auditor of an ordinary joint stock company is an "officer." As I have already pointed out, however, the point is by no means free from doubt, because no decision has yet been come to on the matter by the House of Lords; while [illegible] is an open secret that at all events one of the leading Law Lords is very strongly of opinion that auditors are not included under its provisions. As a further proof of the legitimate doubt as to the precise application of this section I may mention that in the Companies Bill to which I have already referred, an attempt is specifically made to clear up this point in clause 34, which reads as follows:—

> 34.—If any director, manager or auditor of a company knowingly violates any of the provisions of this Act with respect to accounts and audit, he shall, without prejudice to any other liability, be guilty of a misfeasance within the meaning of section 10 of the Companies (Winding up) Act 1890.

Now, this clause would be wholly unnecessary if the question were to be regarded as finally settled, and I take it that it can be considered as conclusive evidence that the framers of the Companies Bill share the doubts which I have already expressed as to the soundness of the decision of the Court of Appeal on this subject. I am glad to notice that Mr. Frederick Whinney, F.C.A., has drawn the attention of the Select Committee to the point, and that there appears to be some prospect of the clause being omitted or amended. It is because of the great importance of the matter in the interests of all accountants that I have selected this subject for my lecture to you to-night.

Now, before pointing out to you in detail the disadvantages under which we—as accountants—labour by reason of the present legal interpretation of the misfeasance section, I should like to again repeat that I object to this interpretation, not because I am desirous that auditors should be exempt from all responsibilities for misconduct or negligence, but simply because the procedure under this section is most vexatious and expensive, while placing the respondent to a misfeasance summons under most serious disadvantages which would not obtain were he proceeded against by way of action. More over, as I have already pointed out, this change of procedure is altogether uncalled for, inasmuch as there was never any difficulty experienced in enforcing the liability of auditors by way of action.

Having now explained at some length my motives for dealing with the matter, let me draw your attention to the precise difference between the two classes of procedure.

Now, in procedure by way of action the first step is for the party aggrieved to issue a writ, stating in general terms his ground of action. The counter step to this is for the defendant to enter an appearance (which is a small expense), and then the next step that must be taken by the plaintiff is to deliver his statement of claim, in which he virtually has to state in detail the particular points which he proposes to prove, and upon which he seeks to base his claim for compensation. At a later stage the usual affidavits of discovery of documents are made, and the result of this procedure (which, I may remind you, is the usual procedure in all civil cases, and practically in all criminal cases, and which it has never ever been suggested is insufficient for this purpose) is that at the earliest possible moment the defendant knows the exact nature of the case that will be made against him, and has an opportunity of preparing his defence, without at the same time showing his hand to the other side. The procedure thus gives a slight advantage to the defendant so far as the moves of the game are concerned; but, in view of the fact that the English law invariably assumes a man to be innocent until he has been proved to be guilty, it must be conceded that, in so far as there is to be an advantage upon either side, it is only equitable that it should be with the defendant, and not with the plaintiff. In the great majority of actions, moreover, if the plaintiff can be shown to be impecunious, the Court will, upon application, order him to find security for costs, so as to prevent defendants from being wantonly put to expense by plaintiffs who cannot pay even if they lose.

Now, as I have before pointed out, this was the procedure which could be taken against auditors previous to the Act of 1890 coming into operation, and (as you will readily understand) in those few cases where it appeared that auditors had been lacking in care or skill, there was nothing whatever in the form of procedure which made it difficult for the liquidator to formulate his case. Since the 1890 Act came into operation, however, no proceedings have been taken against auditors by way of action, which, in itself, is sufficient to show that the misfeasance procedure is more favourable to the liquidator and less favourable to the auditor. But when we go into the matter a little further, you will see that this considerably understates the actual position of affairs.

Even before the 1890 Act came into operation, there was no difficulty whatever in a liquidator examining on oath any person whom he might think could give him information upon the company's affairs, and the result of such examinations would not infrequently be to put the liquidator on a scent which subsequently enabled him to bring an action against the directors, auditors, or officers of the company. But it was not open to him to use the shorthand notes of such examinations as evidence in the action, although, of course, it was open to him to call anyone who had been examined as a witness, and in the event of their evidence differing materially from that which they had previously given at their examination, they would have been liable to a prosecution for perjury.

Under the 1890 Act, however, it was deemed desirable to assimilate liquidation procedure with bankruptcy procedure; and, among other changes, that of the public examination of directors, auditors, and others was instituted, the avowed purpose of such public examination being to make the persons examined as uncomfortable as possible. Matters did not stop here, however. The public examination is a proceeding in the liquidation, and a misfeasance summons is another proceeding in the liquidation; consequently the shorthand notes of any person's examination became legal evidence against him at the hearing of a misfeasance summons. Now, I need only mention that these examinations very frequently date back to matters which occurred as much as six years previously, and that they deal not only with figures, but also with actual conversations which transpired at the time, and ideas which were passing through the minds of the parties concerned, to show you that—with any ordinary luck and a cross-examining counsel of anything like ordinary ability—it is a comparatively simple matter to trick a witness into one or two statements or explanations which could be twisted to the greatest advantage at a later stage of the proceedings. No one can reasonably object to the actual facts drawn out at these examinations being utilised at the hearing of a misfeasance summons with a view to saving the expense of a double examination, but it may reasonably be objected that nothing but the actual facts should be reproduced.

Moreover, if the evidence is to be used before a Judge it should be taken before a Judge, or at least before someone presiding in a judicial capacity. As matters stand at present, questions which are clearly inadmissible as evidence are frequently asked, and when objected to by the legal advisers of the parties to be examined, the Registrar usually says that he will admit the question and the answer, and that it is a point for the Judge to consider later on whether they are admissible as evidence. This, of course, means, in point of fact, that all sorts of improper suggestions come before the Judge in the form of evidence, which he may (or may not) eliminate from his mind when dealing with the matter.

Now, with regard to another point. No doubt with the praiseworthy view of checking wholesale and unfounded accusations, the Legislature has provided that no misfeasance summons shall be issued without the leave of the Court; but for the purpose of obtaining such leave an *ex parte* statement of the liquidator—which is not a statement of facts verified by affidavit, but an advocate's indictment, containing all sorts of false conclusions, conjectures, and suggestions of bad faith—is regarded as *primâ facie* evidence, and this, although no opportunity for cross-examination is afforded to the respondent. The result is, of course, that the liquidator gets the ear of the Judge at a time when the respondent is not before the Court. In other words the respondent is, in the first instance, tried in his absence. Moreover, when mere suggestions are allowed to take the place of evidence, it is important to remember that it is often easier to suggest the false than to show the truth. Again, the mere fact that the Court has given its sanction to the initiation of these proceedings necessarily commits the Court to the view that there is at least some ground for their being instituted, and thus the Judge who ultimately hears the summons (who will usually be the Judge who allows the summons to be issued) is necessarily prejudiced against the respondent from the outset.

I do not use this term "prejudiced" in any offensive sense, nor with a view to suggest that the Judge will not honestly try to weigh the case on its merits when it comes before him; but I do wish to very strongly point out that the procedure is open to justifiable attack where a Judge who has eventually to try a case should in the first place be asked to give an opinion upon its merits on *ex parte* evidence. Moreover, it must be borne in mind that when the liquidator is the Official Receiver he has, as an officer of the Court, personal access to the Judge in his private room, not only before the proceedings have been commenced, but even while they are pending or actually in course of hearing.

We have now got to the point of the issue of a summons, which is equivalent to the issue of a writ under a procedure by action. The next step is on the part of the respondent, to enter an appearance in the same way as he would in an action. Then, instead of a formal statement of claim, the liquidator is required to file particulars.

Now, this term "particulars" is very vague. In the early days of the working of the 1890 Act the particulars were so scanty that the respondent had practically to come into Court without knowing what charges would be levelled against him, and it may even be added that the applicant not infrequently went into Court not quite knowing what charges he proposed to make. The actual hearing of the summons was thus not an inquiry into the foundation existing for specific charges, but rather in the nature of a second edition of the fishing expedition which had been previously undertaken at the public examination. Matters have been somewhat improved in this respect of late, but the particulars furnished by the liquidator need not even now be so definite as to bind him to specific issues. Consequently the respondent still has to be at the expense of getting up a defence which will be a complete answer to *any* charge that may be raised, instead of being allowed (as every other defendant would be) to confine his energies—and limit his expenses—to defending himself against specific issues.

I may here break off for a moment to remind you that, as the applicant would invariably base some of his case upon admissions made by the respondent at his examination, it necessarily follows that, to defend his case the latter is obliged to obtain a copy of the notes of the examination. This copy will be supplied by the other side, but only upon payment; and as the examinations are frequently long, and the price of copies most expensive, this means that before the respondent can instruct his solicitor for the defence it is necessary for him to incur heavy initial expenditure—a state of affairs which finds no parallel in a procedure by action. Another difference is that under no circumstances can the respondent obtain security for costs, even although it may be beyond dispute that the liquidator has little or no funds in hand.

While still on this question of costs, I may point out that they are very seriously increased by the auditor being tried "in a batch" together with, perhaps, half-a-dozen or more directors and other officers. Not only has he to pay counsel to be in Court during a hearing which may take ten times as long as the hearing of his own case would, but he has virtually to get up a defence against the evidence brought forward against all his co-defendants as well as himself. Moreover, if it should happen that there really is a good case against the directors, it is almost inevitable that the auditor's case will suffer most seriously from being tried at the same time, as it is extremely unlikely that the auditor's case will be altogether dissociated from circumstances which are not strictly evidence against him, but which are evidence against the directors.

There is yet another important point, which considerations of time alone prevent my discussing fully. I allude to the utter disproportion between the offence of even a grossly negligent auditor and the punishment meted out to him under the present procedure. No other offence known to our judicial system meets with so severe a punishment. A doctor who by his lack of skill killed a whole hospital full of patients would get off more lightly. Moreover, the money recovered from an auditor might under this rule even be distributable among the shareholders themselves, who, having already had their capital back in the form of dividends improperly paid out of capital, could not by any stretch of imagination be said to have suffered pecuniary loss by the auditor's neglect. Since the draft of this lecture was written, two of the Law Lords have expressed a doubt as to whether the present law really does make an auditor responsible for dividends improperly paid out of capital; but whether this may be taken as a hint of what the House of Lords would decide in such a case, or whether it is merely a refreshing example of "judicial innocence," it is impossible to say.

Now let us recapitulate these points, as contrasted with the procedure by action. We find in the misfeasance procedure a harassing, lengthy, and expensive examination at the outset; a Judge, who has heard the other side *ex parte* and has committed himself to an expression of opinion that there is a *primâ facie* case against the respondent; expense in procuring particulars of the precise charges raised against the respondent; the absence of detailed pleadings; the disadvantage of being tried with others who perhaps are not above reproach; and the great damage to the respondent's reputation which even a successful issue to the hearing must necessarily entail: and I ask you, is it wonderful under these circumstances that the vast majority of cases which are commenced by liquidators are settled out of Court? The number of such cases does not to my mind suggest that there are any material number of instances of auditors who have really rendered themselves liable. It merely suggests that any wise business man, knowing as he must know that even to successfully rebut such charges would damage his reputation, and in the end cost him far more than to effect an early settlement with the other side, will naturally of the two evils choose the lesser. In this connection I may draw your attention to the last two reports of the Inspector-General in Company Liquidation, which each showed that proceedings against auditors were pending in three cases, of which two were afterwards settled out of Court, and the remaining one was decided in the Court of Appeal in the respondent's favour.

Now, I should like to ask you again—even in the event of its being considered that there are reasons sufficiently urgent to justify a method of procedure with regard to these alleged offences which is adopted for no other purpose in this country, and is considerably more disadvantageous to the defendant than even the criminal procedure of France—even in this event, is it expedient, is it desirable, that such procedure should be initiated by the liquidator of the company? That liquidator will under all normal circumstances be either an Official Receiver or a professional accountant. Now, with regard to the Official Receivers, without wishing to make the least suggestion against any one of their number personally, or even against the staff as a whole, I should like to point out that, by virtue of their office, Official Receivers are the professional opponents of accountants; and, particularly in view of the fact that the vast majority of proceedings which they institute never come on for hearing (and therefore the Court never has an opportunity of really inquiring into their merits), I would like to suggest whether it is not too much of a temptation to place in the hands of any Government employee (who is expected to make his department pay, but fails to do so because he cannot oust professional accountants, whom it was virtually formed to extinguish) to be in a position to increase the assets of the various estates which may come into his hands, by threatening or instituting proceedings of this character, which, as we have already seen, are generally settled without coming to trial, and which in only one case during the past seven years have ever proved to be successful? In the case of professional liquidators, there is not, of course, the same competition between officialism and non-officialism; but against that, there is the far worse evil of the competition of professional rivals. It is not every professional accountant—and not even every Chartered Accountant—who is above all feelings of professional jealousy, and I should like to ask you whether it is not a serious danger, which each one of us may have one day to meet, when the liquidation of a company of which we have once been the auditor falls into the hands of an unscrupulous man. This latter danger is infinitely greater than that of unfair treatment from Official Receivers, for at least the latter will act in what they conceive to be the interests of their department, and the estate will always get the benefit of any moneys paid to settle such proceedings. But it by no means follows that an unscrupulous private liquidator will act in the interests of the estate he is winding up, nor does it follow that all moneys paid in settlement would invariably go to the benefit of the estate.

Now, I have taken you to the point of showing that, notwithstanding the fact that auditors were always liable to be proceeded against by way of action, they are now (so long as the present decisions are upheld) liable to be subjected to misfeasance proceedings, which are so very much more disadvantageous, and so very unfair in working, that in the majority of cases auditors with reputations and money to lose prefer to settle these claims rather than face the inevitable worry, damage, and expense. I have also shown you that, in spite of the enormous facilities which this procedure affords to liquidators, the actual results clearly show that there is not the slightest occasion for any special legislation upon the subject. They also show—and I would direct your special attention to this point—that in no single case has the initiation of these proceedings ever proved to be to the advantage of those who are entitled to dividends in the company liquidation. The Inspector-General's reports show that only nine cases have been concluded, and none were still pending at the date of the last return. Of these, six were compromised upon terms which could in no case have exceeded the costs of the liquidator, two were eventually decided (on appeal) against the liquidator with costs, and in the sole instance in which the liquidator was successful, the amount which he was actually able to recover on his judgment must have been far below his out-of-pocket expenses. It will thus be seen that not only is the misfeasance procedure an unfair tribunal to auditors, but it is not even successful financially from the point of view of creditors.

There is another aspect to the matter which claims attention here. It is that there seems to be a growing appreciation upon the part of Her Majesty's Judges of the iniquity of these proceedings, and (if I may say so without being taken to imply any comment upon the merits of any particular case) a growing disinclination upon their part to give judgment against respondents. A particularly noteworthy instance of this occurred in connection with the last misfeasance summons which came on for hearing—in which, however, the auditors were not concerned. In this case, Lord (then Mr.) Justice Vaughan Williams adopted the most unusual course of endeavouring to induce all the parties to consent to the case being tried by a jury; you will remember that, as this was not assented to, his Lordship subsequently tried the case alone, and afterwards dismissed the summons with costs.

It is, of course, very difficult to generalise upon so very limited a number of instances, but it would certainly appear that, from every point of view, the misfeasance procedure has totally failed as a means of increasing the dividends distributable among creditors in company liquidations.

Now, up to the present I have been comparing misfeasance procedure with procedure by action, and have shown that from every point of view the latter is by far the most suitable; but I do not for one moment wish it to be thought that because procedure by action is preferable to misfeasance procedure it is at all a proper tribunal to try questions of professional negligence. I submit to you that it is absolutely impossible for any single Judge (or, for that matter, for any number of Judges) to form an opinion which is entitled to the respect of the community upon so highly technical a question as that which is involved in the consideration of whether or not an auditor has, under the circumstances of any particular case, honestly discharged his duties with reasonable care, diligence and skill. It is notorious that all lawyers are poor accountants, and, probably, of all lawyers Judges are the poorest accountants. It is also noteworthy that although Judges are lawyers they never in point of fact venture to try a question as to whether or not a solicitor has so neglected his professional duties as to render himself liable to a client. All such claims against solicitors are by law referred in the first instance to the Disciplinary Committee of the Incorporated Law Society, which Committee, as a body of experts, goes into the case on its merits and reports its conclusions to the Court, while the Court takes such report as a final settlement of the facts of the case and then gives judgment accordingly. Now, if such a procedure is necessary or desirable in the case of solicitors, how much more necessary and desirable is it in the case of accountants, whose profession is one with the ramifications of which Judges—and, indeed, all lawyers—must necessarily be quite unfamiliar?

It is greatly to the advantage of the accountancy profession that the public should know that the liability of accountants (whether as auditors or otherwise) is neither unduly harsh nor, on the other hand, a dead letter, and I would suggest to you that the proper method for the Legislature to adopt in dealing with this important subject would be that any person claiming redress from an accountant should apply to the Court, which should accordingly refer the facts of the case to a committee of experts, the ultimate judgment of the Court being based upon the contents of the committee's report. This course would have the merit of greatly reducing the expense of such inquiries, so that in the event of the accountant being held liable there would at least be a reasonable chance of the parties aggrieved actually benefiting pecuniarily, while, *per contra*, in the event of the accountant vindicating his position, the costs which would necessarily fall upon him would be far more moderate than at present. Moreover, the question of accountants being liable for neglect would then become a real thing, instead of being—as it is now—the arbitrary decision upon a technical matter of one who has little knowledge of the subject.

With regard to the composition of the committee of experts, we have such a committee ready made, in the shape of the Investigation Committee of our Institute. But, should it be thought that this recognition of our Institute would constitute an unfairness to other accountants, then it would be the simplest matter possible for the Legislature to constitute a Standing Committee, upon the same lines as the Inspection Committee of Trustee Savings Banks, or to leave it to the Judge making the reference to nominate his own committee, consisting of, say, five or six accountants who have been upwards of ten years in practice.

Now, the great point which I wish to finally impress upon you is that no single one of us can, by the exercise of even the greatest care and circumspection, place himself beyond the risks of these iniquitous misfeasance proceedings, instituted, perhaps, altogether unwarrantably by an unsuccessful and unscrupulous rival. It is, therefore, of the utmost importance to us all that the legislation upon the subject should be promptly amended. Hitherto—for what reasons I do not care to discuss—the subject has been most unaccountably neglected; but seeing that, as I have now been able to show, reform is as necessary in the interests of the public as in our own, there is now no longer excuse for lethargy upon our part, and it will be to our disgrace as well as to the detriment of our own interests if we neglect the opportunity offered by the Companies Bill now before Parliament to press upon the Legislature the necessity for equitably and adequately dealing with this all-important question.

APPENDIX.

Statement Supplied by Messrs. Vaughan & Hornby.

ℓe Western Counties Steam Bakeries Company and Parsons & Robjent.

The company was incorporated on the 13th January 1888.

Messrs. Parsons & Robjent, by their accountant clerk McDonald, prepared a Balance Sheet for the year ending 31st ecember 1888, and audited the accounts of the company for the ear ending 31st December 1889.

A prospectus inviting subscriptions for further shares was issued y the company in February 1890.

On the 25th April 1891 the company was ordered to be wound p by the Court, and E. G. Clarke was appointed liquidator.

On the 20th October 1892 the liquidator issued his preliminary nd further reports.

Following these reports certain of the directors and officials of he company were publicly examined at Bath.

These examinations were held on the 29th and 30th November 892, and 13th and 23rd January and 10th March 1893.

Notice of these appointments were given to Parsons & Robjent, nd they were present with their solicitor on each occasion.

On the 24th May 1893 an order was obtained by the liquidator nder section 115 of the Companies Act 1862 directing Parsons & objent and McDonald to attend and be examined at Bath, and hey accordingly attended with their solicitor on three occasions, iz., the 3rd and 10th June and the 10th July 1893.

Nothing was paid to Parsons & Robjent for their expenses on hese occasions.

In November 1893 the solicitors to Parsons & Robjent were in-ormed that the liquidator was about to commence proceedings gainst them (Parsons & Robjent) and the directors to recover 1,200 paid in dividends in 1890, and other sums.

On the 16th February 1894 three actions were commenced gainst Parsons & Robjent and the directors by three share-olders.

In May 1894 criminal proceedings were commenced against two f the directors, and in June 1894 these directors were tried at the Vells assizes and acquitted.

McDonald was a witness on subpœna for the prosecution.

On the 29th April 1895 the liquidator took out his misfeasance mmons against Parsons & Robjent and the directors.

A summons was at once taken out by Parsons & Robjent that e liquidator should find security for costs.

On this summons no order was made as to costs, but the liqui-ator's summons was ordered to stand over until after the hearing the shareholders' actions.

The shareholders compromised with the defendant directors, d the actions as against Parsons & Robjent came on in arch 1896, when judgment was given for the defendants.

The summons for security for costs was then restored and no der was made, the liquidator admitting that he was personally ble.

On the 5th June 1896 a summons was taken out by Parsons & Robjent to stay all proceedings under the liquidator's summons, on the ground that Parsons & Robjent were not officers of the company within section 10 of the Companies (Winding-up) Act 1890.

Evidence in connection with this summons was taken on affidavit, and on the 2nd July 1896 the summons came before the chief clerk, and he adjourned same to the Judge for directions.

On the 13th July 1896 the summons came before the Judge in chambers, and was adjourned by him into Court.

On the 12th January 1897 the adjourned summons was heard before Mr. Justice Stirling, and judgment reserved.

On the 27th January 1897 judgment was given against the summons to stay, with costs to the liquidator.

On the 2nd February 1897 application was made to Mr. Justice Stirling for leave to appeal, and leave given.

On the 5th February 1897 notice of appeal was given, and the appeal set down.

On the 24th February 1897 the appeal was heard, and judgment reserved.

On the 11th March 1897 judgment was delivered and the appeal allowed, with costs against the liquidator, and all further proceedings ordered to be stayed against Parsons & Robjent on the ground that they were not officers of the company within the meaning of section 10 of the Companies (Winding-up) Act 1890.

Subsequently the costs were taxed and paid by the liquidator.

The Chairman: I am sure you will all agree in one thing, namely, that we are very much indebted to Mr. Dicksee for the great labour he has given to this valuable and interesting paper. You will also, I am sure, agree with him that no apology is needed for the choice of subject, for this subject of our position in regard to the Companies Acts, as auditors, is probably the question of questions for us — the most important question, I think, that we can consider. At present there is no doubt that we can none of us feel perfectly safe. In conducting our duties as auditors we never know whether we may not make some mistake or be guilty of some weakness which may get us into trouble. The paper has taken so long to read that we shall not have much time for discussion, but I hope some questions will be put to Mr. Dicksee and that some discussion will take place, and with that view I should like to make a few observations. First, with regard to the Companies Act of 1879, I cannot quite follow Mr. Dicksee's reading of the words which deal with the limiting of the right of an auditor to the returns from branches. Mr. Dicksee takes the view that that limits the responsibility of the auditor. This, however, is a view I have never taken. It simply limits our right to ask for fuller information; I think, too, it is going a little far to say that when our audit is based upon returns it is a mere matter of form, or almost that. I think that is rather further than we can go, because a large part of our work must be and is based upon returns. Mr. Dicksee says that owing to the extent of the subject he has had to confine himself to the auditor's liabilities. There we must agree with him. This whole question could not be dealt with in one lecture. Now, what are our liabilities? As Mr. Dicksee points out, we enter into a contract when we accept the audit of a company. We take the liability, in the first place, to fulfil that contract. We take the liability for any breach or negligence in carrying out that contract, and, I am afraid, for all consequences of that. Then, of course, we also take the liability for wrongdoing, for misfeasance, the remedy for which is enforced under section 10. Then there are two other points as to which there is some doubt, I think, as to our liability. One is as to the misfeasance of our clerks, and the other is as to whether we are liable to refund for the benefit of shareholders the amount of dividends which have been paid to them. So far as I know, there is no decision on either of those questions yet. Mr. Dicksee alludes to the second question casually and says that we might be liable. It seems to me that there is an answer to that. The claim could only be for damages, and as the company, if it received that money, would have to pay it to the shareholders and would have a right of set-off—a right of credit in account with the shareholder for the dividend he has received—the damage must be *nil*. Still, that question will come up some day, no doubt, Then, as to clause 10, I cannot quite agree with Mr. Dicksee in the importance he attaches to the alterations in, and the long and interesting account he has given us of the passing of, the section. Section 10 is simply a re-enactment of section 165 of the 1862 Act, exactly the same as regards auditors, unless it be that power is given to the Official Receiver to apply for a summons. The only other alterations of any account in that re-enacted clause are that promoters are brought in, very properly, and that property is added to money as something for which we or anyone brought under the section would be accountable. Clause 165 has been held, as Mr. Dicksee will know, by the Court of Appeal to confer no rights, and therefore it can impose no liabilities, but it simply deals with the manner of enforcing, by summary proceeding, rights which already exist. Therefore, I do not think section 10 can be said to introduce any new procedure, and it certainly introduces no new rights that were not in the Act of 1862, none, at all events, that are material to us. He says the Act of 1890 inaugurated new procedure. Well, that, as I have said already, I cannot quite see. Perhaps he will have time before we go to give us a little more light on that, but I cannot see that anything in that 1890 Act inaugurated any new procedure at all in regard to auditors. Then Mr. Dicksee compares the procedure for misfeasance under section 10 and the procedure by action. It seems to me that the objects aimed at are very often different. For negligence, simply, so far as I know, there is no right to proceed under section 10 at all. You proceed now, just as you did before, by action. Perhaps Mr. Dicksee can enlighten us a little on that. Then he tells us that before 1890 the examination notes could not be used in an action. Well, they cannot be used now in an action. Before the Act of 1890 they could be used, of course, in a misfeasance summons, and they can be used in precisely the same way now, I think. I do not think the Act of 1890 has made any change at all in that respect. He tells us that before 1890 there were actions, and he suggests there were a great many. Well, I only know of one in the whole of 28 years and that is the *Leeds* case, which was decided 25 years after the Act of 1862 and only three years before the Act of 1890; that is, in 1887. That, I think, is very extraordinary, but I believe it is the only case, and certainly in the *Leeds* case it is mentioned in argument that an auditor had never been joined in an action of that kind before and had never even, I believe, been joined in a misfeasance summons, at all events publicly. So that I think we have not many cases before, and as Mr. Dicksee says, there have been none since. But there have been, oddly enough, two actions against auditors within the last few weeks, but these have not been company cases and unfortunately, or perhaps fortunately—I do not know which to say—they have been settled and not tried out. Mr. Dicksee calls our attention to what we consider the injustice under which we lie of having *ex parte* evidence used against us, and having our rivals, the Official Receivers, to attack us, and having the Judge who has directed proceedings and whose mind may perhaps unintentionally be possibly prejudiced—not, I think, very seriously—against us on trial. He also calls attention to the disproportion of the penalty. There is another point to which he draws attention, and that is that we are put up for trial along with the directors who had control of the funds, and we all go in together, which seems unfair. Another very important matter is that we are deprived of the right to trial by jury We may have a decision given against us by a Judge which may sweep away all our life's earnings, and we have no right to a jury, which surely we ought to have, if we choose. I do not say that in all cases we should care to. There is only one other point. Mr. Dicksee suggests that lawyers are dealt with in a different way, namely, by the Law Society. That, I think, must be a complete mistake. I think a lawyer is dealt with in regard to negligence exactly as an accountant or anybody else is. An action is brought against him and it is tried in Court. The Law Society, so far as I know, has nothing whatever to do with the question, and certainly I hope the Investigation Committee of our Institute has nothing to do with the trying of cases of negligence by us; at all events, it would be interfering with things that we can very much better leave to the Courts. We must not all of us be taken to agree with everything that Mr. Dicksee says as to professional rivalry. I cannot imagine that we need fear professional rivals deliberately bringing proceedings of this kind against us; at all events, I have never heard of such a thing since the Act of 1862 and I hope there is no such Chartered or any kind of accountant to be found. With these few remarks I have much pleasure in moving that a vote of thanks be given to Mr. Dicksee for his able and very interesting paper. (Applause.)

Mr. R. F. W. Fincham seconded the motion, which was carried unanimously.

Mr. Dicksee: In thanking you very much for your kind vote of thanks to me for my paper this evening I do not propose at this late hour to detain you much longer, but there are just one or two points which the Chairman was kind enough to refer to which I should like to clear up a little more. One was with regard to whether section 10 was to be taken as being primarily responsible for the difference in the form of procedure which now appears to be customary as contrasted with what was in force before 1890. I think that perhaps the real cause of the difference does not lie in section 10, but there is another section—of which I cannot tell you the number at the moment but which I think you will all remember—which says that for the purpose of these proceedings the notes taken at the public examination shall be evidence. It is expressly enacted in the 1890 Act, and, so far as I remember, and so far as the legal gentlemen who were kind enough to help me with this paper were aware, it was freshly enacted at that time. With regard to actions before 1890, I believe with Mr. Cooper that the *Leeds* case is the only reported case, but I have been given to understand that there were one or two unimportant cases which were not reported, somewhat similar to the few which have occurred, curiously enough, during the last few weeks, and which are not really company cases at all. Then, with regard to the question as to whether an auditor is liable for mere negligence, none of the decisions which have been given really settle that point, but I think it has been frequently said in the course of judgments that an auditor is expected to bring to bear a reasonable amount of care and skill in the discharge of his duties. Well, I take it that the absence of reasonable care would be negligence, and it would never do as a defence to that to plead that there was no absence of skill. Then, with regard to the question of the liability of lawyers, the Chairman thinks that that must be somewhat of a misapprehension. I do not, of course, pretend to give that on my own authority, but it was certainly stated to me by a very good solicitor, so that it is well worth inquiring, I think, as to what the precise position is. This gentleman was good enough to look through the proof of this lecture before I came here, and is so responsible for it, and beyond that I cannot explain how the matter could have passed him if, in point of fact, it is inaccurate. With these few words I beg to thank you very much for your kind vote.

The Chairman: Of course, the lawyers have their own discipline—a committee of discipline, which deals with any improper conduct of a solicitor and reports to the Court. That, of course, we are acquainted with from seeing occasionally a solicitor struck off the rolls on the report of the Law Society. That, I think, must be the proceeding to which Mr. Dicksee's remarks should refer, if I am right.

On the motion of Mr. Langham, a vote of thanks was passed to Mr. Cooper for presiding, and the Chairman having briefly acknowledged the compliment, the proceedings terminated.

THE LIABILITIES OF AUDITORS
(1898)

Editorial from The Accountant

A generally favorable comment on Dicksee's paper.

Leading Articles.

The Liabilities of Auditors.

IT would be difficult to over-estimate the importance and interest of the subject on which Mr. DICKSEE read a paper before the London Students' Society—a paper which we published at length in our last issue. The exact position of an auditor who fails completely to do his duty is not as clear as it might be, and as even the best are likely to make occasional slips—though the lack of reported cases shows how seldom this happens—all want to know how they will stand on such inauspicious occasions. Unfortunately, the time at Mr. DICKSEE'S disposal did not allow him to go into this part of the question. Those suffering under a wrong want to know two things—what are their legal rights, and how they can be enforced. Mr. DICKSEE dealt mainly with the latter point. His paper is really an attack upon the procedure of the misfeasance summons.

The substantive liability of an auditor is, to a certain extent, clear. Those who employ him are entitled to expect that he will do his work with reasonable care and with such skill as men of the class to which he professes to belong habitually hold themselves out as possessing. No Chartered Accountant can, or will, object to this general proposition. But there are two difficulties, the one in applying it, the other in determining the amount of damages payable for breach of the duty stated in this proposition. No general rule can be laid down as to the application; the facts of each case differ so much one from the other that the Court—whatever its constitution—must decide on the evidence brought before it. We wish Mr. DICKSEE had given the students the benefit of his knowledge in a discussion of these points; but he was anxious to pass on to the question he had set himself to consider.

We find the historical account of the passing of the 10th section of the 1890 Act interesting, and, notwithstanding Mr. COOPER's criticisms, think a very useful purpose has been served by its inclusion in the lecture. Whatever be the cause, the misfeasance section is very obnoxious to accountants, and it is well to learn how it found its way in to the statute book. It may be, as Mr. COOPER says, that the law was but little changed by the section under discussion. But if we grasp Mr. DICKSEE's view aright, his point is that, had the matter been understood at the time, Parliament would either have altered the law or made it clear and beyond a doubt that auditors were to be included within the purview of the new section, and in the latter case would have had clearly brought before it the question of the amount of damages payable by a delinquent.

We are in agreement with Mr. DICKSEE's main proposition, that auditors have a real grievance if they can be included within a misfeasance summons, but we do not quite go with him in all his arguments. For instance, he says that the misfeasance summons as a procedure is more expensive than procedure by way of action. We do not care to dogmatise, but we should have thought the very reverse to be the case. It may be—indeed, it is—hard that an Official Receiver's report should be evidence; but surely this rule tends towards cheapening the whole process. Mr. DICKSEE has forgotten some of the steps in an action, *e.g.*, the pleadings beyond the statement of claim; he refers very casually to the "usual" affidavits of discovery, affidavits which lawyers and Judges alike look upon as a cause of endless expense and trouble, but which—recent reforms notwithstanding—cannot altogether be got rid of in an action. When he talks about an action he is thinking of some practice altogether different to what prevails, for he says that he is speaking of the procedure usual "in all civil cases, and practically in all "criminal cases": but the procedure in each differs one from the other in nearly every particular. Mr. DICKSEE, in making the remark that it has never even been suggested that this procedure is insufficient for the purpose, has evidently overlooked the celebrated report of the Judges made in 1892, the sharp criticisms at every meeting of the Law Society, the complaints in Parliament, and the indignant articles in the daily newspapers. The Commercial Court has been formed to avoid some of the very difficulties which arise in actions, and not under the procedure of the misfeasance summons.

Mr. DICKSEE says in the majority of actions, if the plaintiff be impecunious, the Court will order him to find security for costs. Would it were so! Pauperism is no bar to an action—the proprietors of newspapers could tell a tale about this. But in this respect those attacked under the procedure we are discussing are better off than the usual run of defendants. Security for costs can be obtained against a litigating insolvent company, and this rule extends so far that a liquidator issuing a misfeasance summons can be ordered to give security for costs; as to this see PALMER'S *Precedents*, Part II., pp. 549-560. In the well-known *Western Counties Steam Bakeries* case, STIRLING, J., refused an order for security, but only on an admission by the liquidator that, if unsuccessful, he *personally* was liable to pay the costs, a liability which the Court subsequently enforced.

In connection with Mr. DICKSEE'S remark that the shorthand writer's notes of a public examination are available as evidence against the person examined, it should be added that no public examination can take place unless there is *prima facie* evidence that the person to be examined is guilty of a fraud. We believe we are right in saying that since this was declared to be the law, no professional auditor has been publicly examined.

The phrase in which it was suggested that the procedure of the misfeasance summons may possibly prejudice the Judge against the defendants doubtless does not mean what at first sight appears, especially coupled as the statement is with another to the effect that the Official Receiver has personal access to the Judge in his private room, and that the leave of the Judge to bring the summons, obtained *ex parte*, commits the Court to a one-sided view. The practice of applying *ex parte* for leave to commence proceedings is by no means confined to misfeasance matters nor to company cases; not only are applications often made *ex parte*, but injunctions and similar orders are daily granted *ex parte* where the whole effect would be spoilt if notice were given; yet when the trial comes on the Court by no means is hampered by its former decision—it hears the case on the merits, and nobody complains. Even in an action the Judge hears one side fully before the other side addresses the Court. But the best answer to Mr. DICKSEE'S argument on this head is his statement—true enough—that the procedure has proved inefficient, and that auditors are, in fact, not hit by it. If the procedure is so harsh, and the Judge so placed that it is difficult for him to escape prejudice, how is it that success is so seldom attained by the Official Receiver?

Mr. DICKSEE prefers an action to a misfeasance summons, but he suggests a tribunal of another sort. He says let the Council of the Institute deal with allegations of negligence against auditors. There is probably one all-sufficient reason why this suggestion will not be considered: the public would, we think, not allow it. In one part of his paper, and referring to another matter, Mr. DICKSEE says that private liquidators may attack rivals under cover of the misfeasance summons—the public would fear just the reverse; it would say that a body of professional men would never condemn one of themselves. Such being the case—and it is no use arguing to the contrary with the average man—it is useless to discuss this matter. The analogy to the Law Society's Committee of Discipline does not hold; Mr. COOPER disposed of this question. If an accountant and a solicitor are guilty of a misfeasance, they are both equally liable to be proceeded against by action or summons—as the case may be—and in addition the solicitor may be brought before the Law Society and eventually be reported to the Court; he may, also, be proceeded against for any criminal offence arising in course of the transaction. But the Law Society's report and the criminal liability are additional to, not in substitution for, his liability to the company. Indeed, he may—illogical though it be—be condemned to pay the damages to the company, and be acquitted by the other tribunal, or *vice versa*.

But though we are at issue with Mr. DICKSEE on these few points, we are with him in the result. It is a hardship that an Official Receiver's report should be evidence against the auditor, not on account of the expense or prejudice, but on account of the difficulty in meeting charges when the witnesses are not produced in Court, and because it is so easy for the Official Receiver—with perfect *bona fides*—to report what he could not actually prove. It is a hardship to be tried *en bloc* with the directors and others, the length of time during which the auditor and his advisers must attend being thereby prolonged, and the opportunities of getting in evidence "sideways" being so much increased. This hardship would, we should think, be got over by a rule authorising the Court—if it has at present no authority—to order separate hearings. But the chief objection, it seems to us, is moral rather than material. An auditor may have been negligent—the directors may have taken advantage of this to defraud; this is not a normal case, but it is one which readily strikes the general public. Hence, whenever auditors and directors are lumped together and attacked by a misfeasance summons, there is danger that an impression will go abroad that the auditor is dishonest. The proverb "Birds "of a feather," etc., has much to answer for. The remedy, we think, is to permit an auditor to apply for separate trial, and—if he wishes it—to apply that the case be tried with the formalities of an action.

We have considered it our duty to differ from Mr. DICKSEE's statements in these few particulars, but in so doing we must not be taken to have overlooked the excellencies of his paper; indeed, it is his very ability which has caused us to refer to his views. A similar paper read by one less known and less able would not need to be criticised at this length.

LETTER TO THE EDITOR ON "THE LIABILITIES OF AUDITORS" (1898)

Lawrence R. Dicksee

Dicksee's reply to the preceding editorial, clarifying his position taken in the original article.

The Liabilities of Auditors.

(To the Editor of The Accountant.)

SIR,—The great interest manifested in this subject, and which is admitted in your able article which appeared in your issue of the 21st inst., is my apology for occupying your space further with the matter.

I notice that, in general terms, you agree with the conclusions which I have arrived at in my recent lecture to the Chartered Accountants Students' Society of London, although you see fit to take exception to some of my arguments; but I would like to point out to you that the main object of the attitude which I have adopted seems to have been somewhat missed in your article upon the subject. This may, however, be my fault rather than yours. The original draft of my lecture when completed was considerably more than twice the volume of the lecture as actually delivered and it became absolutely necessary for me to ruthlessly curtail the original draft to meet the requirements of time and space. That being so, it may well be that I have not really sufficiently clearly expressed myself upon all the various points to which I desired to direct attention, and consequently it is not altogether surprising if you should have failed to appreciate the particular point to which I have in the main addressed myself in this paper.

In general terms you are quite right in assuming that my paper is really intended to be an attack upon the procedure of the misfeasance summons, but you do not altogether gauge my motives when you suppose that my attack upon this procedure is based upon any hardship which may in consequence result from an auditor having failed to do his duty, whether from lack of skill or attention, or from what you aptly describe as an "occasional slip." I yield to no one in my conception of what the duties of an auditor should be, and probably if I were to detail these exhaustively, it would be generally thought that my standard upon the subject was unduly high. My motive for attacking the misfeasance procedure was not because inconvenience might thereby be caused to auditors who had—from whatever cause—failed in the complete discharge of their duties, but because after a careful examination of various reported cases and consultation with the victims of these and also of unreported cases, I have deliberately come to the opinion that the misfeasance procedure may be made a cloak for blackmailing pure and simple. There is, of course, much to be said in favour of offenders being given a fair trial according to the ordinary laws obtaining in this country; but, if that be granted, there is far more to be said in favour of protecting persons who have done nothing wrong from being harassed and put to wanton expense—and, indeed, being blackmailed—simply because the procedure which at present obtains offers facilities for this purpose.

Having thus quite clearly put before you the motives which led me to deal with this important subject, I may, perhaps, be permitted to express myself a little more clearly upon the various points which you raise in criticising my paper.

With regard to the actual proceedings, I am, of course, prepared to defer to you upon points in which an accountant must necessarily speak from hearsay, but by way of showing that I have not been speaking absolutely widely and without due inquiry, I may mention that the original draft of my lecture was submitted to a solicitor who is certainly not without mature experience upon this particular branch of jurisprudence, and met with his unqualified approval.

Passing on to take some of your various criticisms in the order in which they appear in your article, while quite agreeing with you that the admission of the Official Receiver's report as evidence may tend towards cheapening the process as a whole, I would point out that this is a very different thing from cheapening the process of the auditor compiling his defence. As I have already said, in the event of its being clearly shown that an auditor has failed in his duty, I do not consider myself interested in facilitating any legal procedure by which he may be enabled to wriggle out of his just responsibilities. But the point to which I have mainly addressed myself is the one towards simplifying the process by which an auditor who has done his duty may clear himself from an unjust accusation; and I think that, upon mature reflection, not only accountants, but also all impartial persons, will agree with me that this is the line upon which all our laws should be laid down.

With regard to the procedure under actions, which I very shortly dealt with in my paper, I was not attempting to state in detail the whole process, but was drawing attention to the manner in which this procedure differed from that obtaining under a misfeasance summons. What you style as the "usual affidavits of "discovery" obtains, I have every reason to believe, in both procedures in precisely the same degree, and therefore it did not appear to me to call for any detailed comment. Unfortunately, it is a most vexatious and a most costly process, but, inasmuch as neither the vexatiousness nor the costliness had been increased by the introduction of the misfeasance summons, I do not feel called upon to deal with it at further length. As to the question of the efficacy of actions, I was confining myself strictly to the point at issue, viz., the liabilities of auditors; and, in spite of "the celebrated report of the "Judges made in 1892, the sharp criticisms at every "meeting of the Law Society, the complaints in Par-"liament, and the indignant articles in the daily news-"papers," I maintain that there is no case upon record in which an action against an auditor has failed to produce a judgment against him, when the facts showed that a judgment ought to have been so given. That being so, I think I am entitled to say that the procedure by way of action had not proved to be an ineffective way of enforcing the liabilities of auditors.

Then as to the question of the shorthand writer's notes at the public examination being available as evidence against the person examined, I may point out that perhaps the most serious grievance that may be raised against this is that in practice these notes will not merely be held as evidence against the person examined, but they are also treated as evidence at the hearing of a case in which perhaps half-a-dozen persons are being tried *en bloc*. One has only to read the verbatim reports of judgments that have hitherto been delivered to see that the actual practice of at least some Judges is to regard all the evidence given at such examinations as evidence against all persons who afterwards come before them to respond to a misfeasance summons. Of course, this is directly contrary to the law, but in practice it is what actually seems to obtain. The evil does not stop here, however. It is, as you point out, the fact that, since it was laid down that a public examination could not take place unless there was *prima facie* evidence that the person to be examined was guilty of fraud, no auditors have been publicly examined; but there is nothing whatever to prevent a private examination being held under the Act of 1862, and there is nothing whatever to prevent the shorthand writer's notes of such examination being produced as evidence. This was a point which, in the condensation of my paper, appears to have been cut out, but it is a very important one notwithstanding, and, indeed, constitutes a greater grievance than the fact that the notes taken at a public examination can be used in evidence, if only for the simple reason that the persons examined at a private examination may perhaps not have the remotest idea of any proceedings being contemplated, and may not be even represented by solicitors or counsel at the time of their examination.

With regard to the next paragraph in your article, without wishing to particularise unduly, I may perhaps be allowed to say that I do not in the least wish to take advantage of the kind opportunity you give me for minimising the importance of the point to which I drew attention. I am satisfied that there is a great deal in my contentions, as originally put forward, and (to quote one concrete instance) I may mention that of Lord (then Mr.) Justice Vaughan Williams, who, without the consent of the auditors, actually interviewed in private some of the witnesses called upon either side, so that they might explain to him the various entries in the books. This, as you will remember, the Court of Appeal held was absolutely contrary to law, and although no doubt it was to be attributed mainly to an excess of zeal, it shows, I think, as conclusively as anything could possibly do, that there is ample opportunity for an official charged with an advocate's enthusiasm for his case to very unduly influence even a Judge of the High Court in the discharge of his duties, who after all is but a human being like the rest of us.

Respecting the suggested alternative tribunal at which allegations of professional misconduct might be heard, I would like to point out that my suggestion was not, in essence, that the Council of the Institute should deal with these matters, but that the questions should be heard before an impartial body of experts, and I suggested various methods by which this body might be constituted. I notice that you think the public would not have confidence in the impartiality of a tribunal consisting of the Council of the Institute, and—however regrettable this might be—I am inclined to agree with you that probably such a tribunal might be thought open to objection. There is, however, so far as I am aware, not the least reason why my alternative suggestion should not be adopted, that a permanent body of assessors should be constituted, formulated in some such manner as the Inspection Committee appointed to supervise Savings Banks. The precise method of appointment is a matter of detail, and not a matter of principle; but it is a matter of principle that the tribunal having jurisdiction should be one competent to form a judgment entitled to every respect of persons having technical knowledge of the particular matters at issue, and it is a fundamental part of the proposition which I put forward in my paper that such a tribunal does not at present exist to deal with these matters. It is, of course, true that this is a disability under which lawyers and others suffer as well; but, however unfortunate this may be to them pecuniarily, lawyers have at least the satisfaction of being simultaneously tried by a body which not only has jurisdiction to deal with their offence, but is also competent to express an opinion thereon, and in the event of the finding of that body differing from that of the Courts, the accused will (so far as intelligent persons are concerned, at all events) be absolved from blame, if not entirely free from expense in the matter. In practice, however, actions and misfeasance summonses are never commenced against lawyers except in cases of absolute misconduct. The Disciplinary Committee (a real jury of their "peers") is in reality the only tribunal before which they are tried.

As to the question whether either Official Receivers or professional liquidators should be competent to initiate proceedings, there is, of course, room for a considerable diversity of opinion. It is satisfactory to learn, through the medium of your columns, that the public would probably think that "no professional man would ever "condemn another"; but, however much this might apply (and does no doubt apply) to the medical and legal professions, I personally am very much inclined to doubt whether the accountancy profession as yet possesses sufficient solidarity to admit of the point being seriously discussed. I am afraid that we have still very much to learn in this direction, and it is no use blinking at facts.

The present unfortunate position of the law with regard to the liabilities of auditors—upon which in general you clearly agree with me, although you differ upon a few points of detail—is, I believe, entirely due to the Legislature not having been made sufficiently well acquainted with the various technical ramifications of the position. It is, perhaps, invidious—and also hardly profitable at the present time—to say whose fault it is that this unfortunate position of affairs exists; but I trust that you, and the majority of your readers, will agree with me that it is a position of affairs which should no longer be allowed to continue, if by any means it can be prevented; and I hope that I am able to carry you with me when I suggest that the present time—when company law amendment is being so fully discussed—is an appropriate one for the matter to be brought more fully home to the attention of the Government, and also of independent Members of Parliament.

Hitherto few accountants appear to have had the courage to grapple with the situation, apparently feeling that they might be thought to be advocating and encouraging professional irresponsibility. It seems to me that this is a weakness which is hardly worthy of us as a professional body, and I sincerely trust that some of your readers will in future issues agree with me, that the whole matter is one which should be boldly taken in hand, and fully placed before the Legislature, so that at least it may be cognisant of the actual facts when called upon to give its ultimate decision as to what the law shall be in the future.

At the present time the legislation existing upon the subject, as interpreted by the Judges, is such that the utmost facilities are afforded for harassing and causing expense to auditors, not by any means necessarily because they have failed in their duties as such, but simply because they happen to have been connected with concerns which have ultimately proved to be unprofitable. That might, perhaps, be a *prima facie* reason for causing annoyance and expense to directors, who are responsible, more or less, for the financial success of an undertaking; but it is, in itself, no ground whatever for putting an auditor (who has nothing whatever to do with the carrying on of the business of a company) to either trouble or expense; and although, of course, it is impossible to altogether prevent proceedings being wantonly brought against any person, I think that this is peculiarly a matter in which the Legislature should, if anything, go out of its way to protect auditors, rather than leave them at the mercy of every company wrecker or blackmailer. It is important that the public should be able to secure the services, as auditors, of men of substance, good repute, and skill; but, unless some relief is soon afforded to auditors, I am convinced that such men will be found increasingly difficult to secure in proportion as they begin to realise more fully the enormous risks that they at present incur in return for fees that are altogether inadequate.

I am, Sir,

Yours faithfully,

LAWRENCE R. DICKSEE.

THE LIABILITY OF AUDITORS
(1898)

Editorial from The Accountant

Dealing with two questions raised by Ernest Cooper at the Dicksee lecture, the editor asks: what liability has an auditor for misfeasance by his subordinates? and what liability has an auditing firm when dividends are improperly paid?

Leading Articles.

The Liability of Auditors.

IN dealing with the lecture recently delivered on the above subject, by Mr. LAWRENCE R. DICKSEE, F.C.A., we omitted notice of two questions of some little interest, which were raised by Mr. ERNEST COOPER, F.C.A., in his vote of thanks to the lecturer.

Mr. COOPER'S words, as reported in our issue of the 14th ult., are as follows, viz.: "There are two other points as to which there "is some doubt, I think, as to our liability. "One is as to the misfeasance of our clerks, "and the other is as to whether we are liable "to refund for the benefit of shareholders the "amount of dividends which have been paid to "them. So far as I know, there is no decision "on either of these questions as yet. Mr. "DICKSEE alludes to the second question "casually, and says that we might be liable. "It seems to me that there is an answer to "that."

Taking first of all the question as to the liability of an auditor for the misfeasance of his clerks, it is true that, in the Companies Act 1890, and also in the Act of 1862, there is no mention whatever of the question of clerks; but there is, as in all other matters, the general rule of law that a principal is answerable for the acts of his agents, and more particularly that an employer is answerable for the acts of his employees. Cases are by no means infrequent in which the secretaries of companies have been liable for the dishonesty of their clerks when their own actions in regard to those companies have been absolutely above suspicion, and although, of course, their liability in such cases is limited to a civil liability to make good the damage done by their employees, the point is, it seems to us, useful as affording an analogy in this case. An accountant would most likely be liable for any loss occasioned to his clients by the dishonesty of his clerks, and that being so, we think that the same liability would exist with regard to any damage whatever sustained by reason of the acts or omissions of the accountant's clerks. Such a liability would certainly be enforceable by way of action, and (although, as Mr. COOPER says, the point has not yet been raised) we do not think it likely that the mere question that the acts or omissions were the work of a clerk and not of the principal would be regarded as a good defence against a misfeasance summons. Although there is no actual decision upon the point, it is worth while to remember in this connection that in the case of the *Western Counties Steam Bakeries Company, Lim.*, it was in evidence that the actual work that was complained of had been performed not by the respondents to the misfeasance summons but by a clerk of theirs. Their preliminary defence, it will be remembered, was that, not having been regularly appointed auditors to the company, they were not officers of the company within the meaning of section 10 of the 1890 Act; and, as they succeeded in this contention on appeal, it may, of course, be said that the real question of their responsibility was not argued upon its merits. But, at the same time, if we are to assume (and perhaps it is, in the absence of any express decision upon the point, only reasonable to assume) that they were well advised as to the nature of their defence, we may take it for granted that it was deemed inadvisable to add, as a counter-defence of a preliminary nature, the fact that the work which was complained of had not been performed by the respondents themselves, but by their clerks. If we are right upon this point, it would seem to show that the respondents in this particular case were advised that they had not a very strong defence in the nature of that suggested by Mr. COOPER upon the question of an auditor's liability for the misfeasance of his clerks. But, as the point is of considerable interest, and of not a little importance, to accountants, it would no doubt be very advantageous to the profession generally, if the respondents in this case would kindly place at our disposal some further information as to how they were advised upon this particular point.

The second question raised by Mr. COOPER is one which is entitled to a more detailed consideration. Where it is proved to the satisfaction of the Court that there has been misfeasance, and where, in consequence, dividends have been paid to shareholders which ought not to have been paid, thereby reducing the assets of an insolvent company which are available for the distribution among the creditors, one can understand that, from one point of view at least, the measure of damages should be the amount of such dividend, however inequitable this may be in other respects from the auditor's point of view. But Mr. COOPER suggests a doubt—and the doubt is one which we have already expressed in these columns in times past—as to whether the Courts could reasonably hold that a similar measure of damages existed in cases where the company was not insolvent, and where in the subsequent liquidation there existed sufficient assets to repay the creditors the amount of their claims in full. Such a condition of affairs would, it is true, not usually arise in practice; but it is none the less well worth discussing in the abstract, the more so, inasmuch as Mr. COOPER points out, there are no actual decisions directly bearing upon the point.

It must be borne in mind, however, that, in point of fact, there is really only one decision in respect of the liability of an auditor for misfeasance which has been upheld against the auditor on appeal, viz., the case of the *London and General Bank*, in which case the auditor (jointly and severally with the other respondents of the misfeasance summons, who had not previously compromised the Official Receiver's claim) was held liable in respect of certain dividends that had actually been paid out of the assets of the company. Now this was the case of a company in compulsory liquidation, and insolvent; but the position of affairs up to the present date is such that already dividends amounting to 17s. 6d. in the £ have been paid to the creditors in the liquidation, and further unrealised assets remain in hand which, in course of time, should be sufficient to pay to the creditors, if not 20s. in the £, at least something very nearly approximating thereto. It is further to be remembered that the judgment given against the respondents to this summons was not for the amount of dividends improperly paid out of capital, or such proportion thereof as might represent the ultimate loss to creditors in the liquidation, but for the dividends paid out of capital, pure and simple; while in this particular case (the only reported case on record) there seems to be a considerable likelihood that, had the whole amount in respect of this judgment been recovered, there would have been a very handsome surplus after payment of creditors in full, with interest. And this, it must be remembered, is a result which was not brought about by the misfeasance proceedings themselves—for these certainly resulted in actual diminution of the assets available for the general body of creditors, by reason of the costs of the proceedings far exceeding the amount that was actually recovered from the respondents.

It will therefore, we think, be seen that, although the point was not expressly raised in the *London and General Bank* case, yet this was a case in which judgment was given against the respondents for the amount of dividends improperly paid out of capital, wholly regardless of the question as to whether it was necessary that such monies should be contributed to the estate for the purpose of increasing the assets available to a sufficient sum to make a return in full to creditors.

It seems therefore that, so far as the existing decisions go, they incline to the view of the lecturer. But, however that may be, it will, we think, be generally conceded that such a position of affairs is so wholly unsatisfactory that, in the interests of the profession, the matter should not be allowed to stay here; and we hope that, should a case arise upon which the point may be fought, the decision of the highest tribunal will be obtained upon the question.

In this connection the highly suggestive remarks made by the Lord Chancellor and Lord DAVEY upon the occasion of the examination of Mr. FREDERICK WHINNEY, F.C.A., before the Select Committee of the House of Lords on Company Law Amendment, must not be lost sight of. It will be remembered that their Lordships expressed their surprise at Mr. WHINNEY'S *resumé* of the existing state of the law, and distinctly suggested that such decisions could not be regarded as being altogether authoritative. There is, we think, every reason to believe that, were the House of Lords called upon to express an opinion upon a misfeasance case, they might take quite a different view from that as yet held upon the subject by the Courts below; and from this point of view there is, no doubt, much to be said in favour of the doubt expressed by Mr. COOPER upon the question of the measure of damages which actually obtains when misfeasance has been proved to have been committed.

It is, however, of all things desirable to be practical in these matters, and therefore, pending a revision of the existing interpretation of the law, it may, we think, be reasonably asserted that the measure of damages in the case of proved misfeasance is the amount of dividends which have been improperly paid out of capital, wholly irrespective of the question as to whether or not it is necessary that such sum should be contributed to the assets of the company in order to secure a payment in full to the creditors thereof. That such a decision is absolutely in contradiction to all laws of equity in regard to the matter is a point which has already been sufficiently dealt with in these columns; but it is, after all, only one of the many inequitable phases of the subject which arise in connection with misfeasance procedure as a whole. It seems to us that the practical view for accountants to take of the situation is to do their best by all constitutional means to secure a revision of a position of affairs which is so clearly inimical, not merely to the interests of the accountancy profession, but also to those of the general public by reason of the fact that the present decisions press so hardly upon auditors as to afford a direct discouragement to men of ability, substance, and repute to undertake the onerous duties which an auditor is called upon to perform.

We are somewhat surprised to find that this subject has hitherto attracted so little attention in these columns. Probably the majority of the members of the profession are (or think themselves) too busy to engage upon a point which in all probability will never touch them personally, but it is impossible for *any* accountant to so arrange matters that he can say for certain he will never be called upon to respond to a misfeasance summons; and, that being so, although the number of cases up to the present may have been comparatively few, the fact remains that every professional accountant must live perpetually under the risks of this procedure until it is modified or altogether abandoned. The whole question is therefore not only a most interesting one, but also one of paramount importance, and we trust that it is one which will appeal to accountants generally as being worthy of their most careful and immediate attention.

THE LIABILITIES OF AUDITORS OF COMPANIES, WITH ESPECIAL REFERENCE TO THE COMPANIES ACT, 1900 (1901)

J.M. Easton

The provisions and statutory liability implications of the first Companies Act to require annual corporate audits.

The Liverpool Chartered Accountants Students' Association.

The Liabilities of Auditors of Companies, with especial reference to the Companies Act, 1900.

By Mr. J. M. EASTON, Barrister-at-Law.

A paper read before the Liverpool Chartered Accountants Students' Association, 28th March 1901.

THE auditor is no longer a luxury which a company may, or may not, according to its pleasure, possess. By virtue of the Companies Act, 1900, he is a compulsory institution, and acquires increased importance from the provision which compels a new company to insert his name in its prospectus.

The compulsory auditor is not an entire innovation. We have been accustomed to him in the case of what we may call "heavy" companies, such as railway companies and other companies incorporated by special Act of Parliament, and also, more recently, in the case of banking companies. But in the case of the ordinary commercial company registered under the Companies Act, 1862, it has, hitherto, been left to its discretion to insert such audit clauses as it pleased in its articles of association, or, if it preferred, to do entirely without auditors. The importance of auditors upon fraudulent or reckless companies is now fully recognised by the provisions of the Companies Act, 1900, which render it necessary for every company registered under the Companies Act, 1862, and the amending Acts—whether it be a limited or unlimited company and, if limited, whether limited by shares or by guarantee—to have at least one auditor.

There are three sections of the Act—the 21st, 22nd, and 23rd—relating to auditors: the first two dealing with their appointment and remuneration; the last, with their rights and duties. Let us deal with these matters in their logical order, and first see who may be appointed and the manner of their appointment.

The Act requires no qualifications for an auditor. He need not be a Chartered Accountant: he need not even be able to add up figures. Of course, the articles of association may provide some qualification; but so far as the Companies Act, 1900, is concerned, it has been thought better to leave it to the common sense of the shareholders to see that no incompetent person is appointed, only providing that the prospectus shall give notice to intending shareholders who the auditors are at the date of its issue. But while there is no qualification necessary, there is a disqualification. The Act says "a director or officer of "the company shall not be capable of being appointed "auditor of the company." As to a director, I think there is little difficulty; but who is an "officer" of a company? A similar provision has generally been inserted in the articles of association of commercial companies, but so far as I know the Courts have never been called upon to adjudicate upon such a clause. There is, however, a section of the Companies Act, 1900, popularly called the "misfeasance section," which provides a summary remedy against "the director, manager, liquidator, or other "*officer*" of a company who has been guilty of misfeasance or misappropriation of the funds of the company. There have been decisions upon the word "officer" in that section. It has been decided on the one hand that neither a banker nor a solicitor, except under very special circumstances, is an officer within the meaning of that section. But it has been held that an auditor is; and I think that another clear example of an officer is the secretary. With regard to the decisions as to auditors being officers, that, I believe, is a point upon which accountants generally have felt a little sore. It is an honour they do not desire. There are, however, two decisions of the Court of Appeal where auditors have been held to be officers. The first was the well-known one of the *London and General Bank* (1895, 2 Ch. 166), where the auditors were subject to the provisions of the Companies Act, 1879, which contains provisions as to the auditors of banks; in the second case, that of the *Kingston Cotton Mills* (1896, 1 Ch. 6), the auditors were subject to articles of association containing similar provisions as to audit to those in the Act of 1879. In this latter case the Court of Appeal held themselves bound by their previous decision, though there were expressions used in the judgments indicating a doubt whether that decision was right. In the *Kingston Cotton Mills* case an appeal to the House of Lords was lodged, but before that appeal came on the auditors—fortunately for themselves, unfortunately, as regards this point, for their profession—obtained a decision in their favour upon the merits. They consequently abandoned the appeal on the technical point.

With the two cases of the *London and General Bank* and the *Kingston Cotton Mills* must be compared that of the *Western Counties Bakeries Company* (1897, 1 Ch. 617), where an auditor, appointed only to make a special audit, and appointed by the directors and not by the shareholders, was not an "officer" of the company. I have, however, little hesitation in saying that auditors appointed under these sections of the Companies Act, 1900, with which we are now dealing, are more like the auditors of the first-named companies than the last, and that such auditors must submit to the indignity of being labelled officers of the company, at any rate until someone is found with a long enough purse to take the question up to the House of Lords. I may add that I believe in the recent *Dumbell's Bank* case, the learned gentleman who occupied the temporary position of Deemster ruled that the auditors of that bank were "officers" of the company within the meaning of the Falsification of Accounts Act, 1875.

It may be said that all this is irrelevant to the point in hand—viz., the question of the disqualification of persons to be auditors of a company, because such a provision as that "an officer of the company shall not be capable of "being appointed auditor" would be absurd. I must confess, gentlemen, that such a criticism has my sympathy; but it was necessary for me to deal with the point because of two contentions that I have heard, based on the ground that auditors of a company are officers. The first contention is that an auditor, being an officer, cannot be elected two years in succession. Perhaps no one really seriously holds this opinion, but the second one has more weight behind it. The second contention is that the Act will put a stop to a practice which has grown up in certain small companies, where the secretarial duties are light. The practice alluded to is where, say, A. and B. are in partnership, and A. is personally appointed auditor and B. is appointed secretary. This, it is said, the Act prohibits, because, apparently, B. being an officer, his partner is tainted with his incapacity. I have a little difficulty in dealing with these two highly ingenious contentions; but it seems to me that the whole burden of proof lies on those who set them up, and I have heard no argument convincing me that either of them is based upon a true construction of the Act. The arguments are, perhaps, such as can only be appreciated by lawyers, and I do not intend to burden you with them. All I can say is that my own opinion, whatever it may be worth, is, that auditors are eligible for re-election, and that there is nothing in the Act or the general law to prohibit the practice—whether it be a good one or a bad one—followed in some companies of making one member of a firm of accountants the auditor and his partner, or a clerk in the office, the secretary.

Turning now to the method of appointing auditors we find that the Act provides that this is to be done at each annual meeting, for the office of auditor is an annual one only. If there is any failure to appoint at the annual general meeting, then the Board of Trade has power to appoint on the application of any member of the company. The remuneration of auditors is likewise to be fixed by the company, or by the Board of Trade, where that body appoints. There is a principle underlying these provisions which all auditors of companies will do well to bear in mind: as it is the company which appoints and fixes their remuneration, the duty of auditors lies towards the shareholders and not the directors. There are, however, two cases in which the directors have power to appoint—viz., (1) in the case of any casual vacancy arising, and (2) in the case of first auditors, before the statutory meeting has been held. Remember, after the statutory meeting this power of the directors lapses. The first of these two cases calls for no comment, but the second raises a difficulty. The directors may appoint auditors before the "statutory meeting" of the company. The statutory meeting seems to be that which Section 12 provides shall be held within three months from the date when a company is entitled to commence business. Section 12, however, applies only to the case of a company registered after the 1st January 1901, and limited by shares. There is now no statutory meeting for an unlimited company or a company limited by guarantee. What, then, is the meaning of empowering the directors of such a company to appoint auditors before the statutory meeting? It is not easy to say how this difficulty is to be got over. It may be that it is a matter which can be dealt with by articles of association, or it may be that such companies will have to do without auditors until the first annual general meeting. It may be noted that auditors appointed by the directors before the statutory meeting are to hold office until the first annual general meeting "unless previously removed by a reso-"lution of the shareholders in general meeting." This power to dismiss preserves the principle that even such auditors are responsible to the company and not to the directors.

Let us now suppose that our auditors have got their appointment secured and turn to see what are their rights and duties. First, it is their duty to at once study the articles of association of the company unless they have previously done so. It was really the neglect of this precaution that got the auditors into trouble in the case of the *Leeds Estate Company v. Shepherd* (36 Ch.D. 187). They did all they honestly thought to be their duty, but they did not do all that they were required by the articles to do, and their plea that they had never read the articles did not help them. There is no reason why the articles of association of a particular company should not supplement the provisions of the Companies Act, 1900, as to audit. Of course, if the provisions of the articles are inconsistent with those of the Act, the Act must prevail, but an auditor may be rendered liable for neglect of merely supplementary provisions (see *per* Lindley, L.J., *London and General Bank*, 1895, 2 Ch. 673). Questions may, perhaps, hereafter arise as to whether the provisions of articles of association are or are not inconsistent with those of the Act in the case of old companies, but I anticipate that in the case of companies registered after 1st January 1901 the practice will grow up of inserting in articles of association provisions as to auditors similar to those in the Act. Such a practice will certainly be a convenient one.

There is one duty that the Act requires of the auditors of a new company which it may be convenient to refer to here. Previous to the statutory meeting, to which I have already alluded, of a new company a report has to be sent by the directors to every shareholder giving them certain information. Amongst other things this report must state the total number of shares allotted, the total amount of cash received by the company in respect of such shares, and an abstract of the receipts and payments of the company on Capital Account to the date of the report. In respect of these matters the report of the directors must be certified as correct by the auditors (if any) of the company.

We are now, I think, in a position to consider the very important Section 23, relating to the general rights and duties of auditors. The section is as follows:—

> Every auditor of a company shall have a right of access at all times to the books, and accounts, and vouchers of the company, and shall be entitled to require from the directors and officers of the company such information and explanation as may be necessary for the performance of the duties of the auditors; and the auditors shall sign a certificate at the foot of the Balance Sheet, stating whether or not all their requirements as auditors have been complied with; and shall make a report to the shareholders on the accounts examined by them, and on every Balance Sheet laid before the company in general meeting, during their tenure of office; and in every such report shall state whether, in their opinion, the Balance Sheet referred to in the report is properly drawn up so as to exhibit a true and correct view of the state of the company's affairs, as shown by the books of the company; and such report shall be read before the company in general meeting.

The first part of the section deals with the auditor's rights, the last part with his duties. Observe, first of all, that the auditors are to have a right of access to the books of the company "at all times." This provision seems to me to make the auditors regular officers of the company and not merely strangers called in once a year at the time of the annual balance. The books to which the auditors are to have access are, in my opinion, all the books of the company and not merely the account books. The right to examine the directors and officers of the company seems to require no comment except to say that if the directors or officers refuse the required information the auditor's only remedy would appear to be to report the matter to the shareholders.

The duties of the auditors required by the Act are (1) that they certify at the foot of the Balance Sheet whether or not their requirements have been complied with; and (2) that they make a report to the shareholders upon the accounts. There has been some discussion as to this certificate and report—whether the certificate should contain this and the report that, or *vice versa;* whether there must be two separate documents, or whether the report and the certificate may be embodied in one, and, if so, whether the auditors must sign their names once or twice. My own opinion is that these matters are mere technicalities, and the last thing this section was intended to be was technical. The auditors must carry out the spirit of the section, and, if they do so, I do not believe they will be held liable for some slight departure from the words. Take an instance. The auditor has to certify at the foot of the Balance Sheet whether his requirements have been complied with. But suppose there is no Balance Sheet? There is nothing in this Act of Parliament or any other Act of Parliament to compel the ordinary commercial company to have a Balance Sheet. Can, then, an auditor avoid certifying whether his requirements have been complied with, on the technical ground that there is no Balance Sheet to which he can affix his certificate? Well, all I can say is that I should be very surprised if any Court of law would listen to such a plea. So I think there is no objection to making certificate and report one document, so long as the report reaches the shareholders. I think, again, that if the auditors' requirements have not been complied with, they ought to inform the shareholders in what particulars they have not been complied with; but whether these particulars be given in the certificate or report is, in my opinion, immaterial. As to the contention that if the certificate and report form one document the auditors must still sign their names twice over, I can find absolutely nothing in the Act to warrant any such view. In fact, the section does not seem to require that the report should be signed at all, though, of course, as a matter of convenience, for purposes of identification, it always will be signed.

The report is, perhaps, the most important thing required of auditors. It must be read before the company in general meeting—a most important protection both for the auditors and the shareholders. It is to be made to the shareholders and not to the directors. The auditor's liability will depend, I expect, almost entirely upon whether or not he has reported to the shareholders what he ought to have reported. The Act itself describes in merely general terms what is to be inserted in the report. The auditors are to "report on the accounts examined by "them and on every Balance Sheet laid before the com- "pany in general meeting; and in every such report shall "state whether in their opinion the Balance Sheet referred "to in the report is properly drawn up so as to exhibit "a true and correct view of the state of the company's "affairs as shown by the books of the company." That is fairly vague language; and we must consider what an auditor must do before he will be justified in giving such a certificate. The auditors will not have fulfilled their duty to the shareholders by merely verifying the Balance Sheet by the entries in the company's books. Such a contention may seem to receive some support from the fact that this Section 23 only requires a certificate that the Balance Sheet exhibits a true view of the state of the company's affairs "as shown by the books of the company." The object of this expression, however, is merely to relieve the auditor from any responsibility as to affairs of the company kept out of the books and concealed from them (*per* Rigby, L.J., *In re London and General Bank* (No. 2), 1895 2 Ch. 692).

We are practically dependent for our law on the subject of auditors' liabilities on two cases decided in the Court of Appeal—viz., *In re London and General Bank* (No. 2) (1895, 2 Ch. 673), and *Re Kingston Cotton Mills Company* (No. 2) (1896, 2 Ch. 279). Let us look at the facts of these two cases. That seems the best way to appreciate the decisions. I have always thought that the importance of the actual decision in *Re London and General Bank* has been greatly exaggerated by accountants and others. The London and General Bank was one of what were known as the "Balfour group" of companies, in which the notorious Jabez Balfour was the moving spirit. The chief business of the bank appears to have been to finance the other companies of the group. In the year 1891 the chief asset in the Balance Sheet of the bank was a sum of £346,975 put down as "Loans to customers and other "securities" which was treated as a good asset to its full nominal value; and, by doing this, the company was enabled to appear in flourishing circumstances and to declare large dividends. As a matter of fact, nearly the whole of this large sum had been advanced to the allied companies and a few special customers, and, of course, when the smash came, the asset did not realise anything like its face value. Now the point to be noted, which, I think, has been often overlooked, is that the liquidator sought to make Mr. Theobald, the auditor, liable for the dividends that had been paid from the year 1886 (I believe I am correct) onwards, but that he only succeeded in making him liable for that paid in the one year 1891. Yet the auditor seems to have done his work in exactly the same manner in each year. The difference was that his suspicions with regard to this asset increased from year to year as its amount grew, so that in the year 1891 he felt it to be his duty to report to the directors that he considered that the asset ought not to be treated as of the value inserted in the Balance Sheet and that no dividend ought to be declared. That report, however, never reached the shareholders; and he was held liable for that year because, according to his own admission, he thought the Balance Sheet did not show the true condition of the company, yet he neglected to inform the shareholders. If it had not been that the suspicions of the auditors were proved to have been aroused, I think he would have escaped liability altogether.

Therefore, to my mind, the later decision in *Re Kingston Cotton Mills Company* is of more importance. There the company was made to appear prosperous by a gross over-valuation of a mill and of the raw cotton in stock. The auditors relied on the certificates of the manager, who was a man of great business ability and high repute, as to these values and made no further inquiry. Their suspicions were not, in fact, aroused, but it was said that if they had done a simple arithmetic sum they would have discovered that something was wrong. If they had taken the value of the cotton at the beginning of any year, had added the amount spent during the year in purchasing cotton and deducted the amount of the year's sales, they would have seen that the statement of the value of the stock-in-trade at the end of the year required explanation. The Court held that there was no duty upon the auditors to make that calculation and that they were not liable. I may, perhaps, give here a few extracts from the judgments delivered in these two cases, giving, as they do, some opinions of the Judges as to the duties of auditors:—

London and General Bank.—"It is the auditor's business "to ascertain and state the true financial position of the "company at the time of the audit, and his duty is confined to that. But then comes the question. How is he "to ascertain that position? The answer is, by examining "the books of the company. But he does not discharge "his duty by doing this without inquiry and without taking any trouble to see that the books themselves show "the company's true position. He must take reasonable "care to ascertain that they do so. . . . His first duty "is to examine the books, not merely for the purpose of "ascertaining what they do show, but also for the purpose "of satisfying himself that they show the true financial "position of the company. . . . An auditor, however, "is not bound to do more than exercise reasonable care "and skill in making inquiries and investigations. He is "not an insurer."

Kingston Cotton Mills.—"An auditor is not bound to be "a detective or to approach his work with suspicion or "with a foregone conclusion that there is something "wrong. He is a watch-dog, and not a bloodhound. He "is justified in believing tried servants of the company in "whom confidence is placed by the company. He is "entitled to assume that they are honest and to rely upon "their representations, provided he takes reasonable care. "If there is anything calculated to excite suspicion he "should probe it to the bottom; but in the absence of anything of that kind he is only bound to be reasonably "cautious and careful."

You may say that all this is very vague, and it is true that it is vague; but I do not think, gentlemen, that you would desire much greater exactness. You are a skilled profession, and I am sure you would feel sore if the Judges of the land or the Legislature were to start to teach you your business. The whole advantage of employing a respectable firm of Chartered Accountants, rather than an amateur, is that the former will bring to bear upon the accounts they audit the experience that they have gained in auditing other accounts of a similar character; whereas the latter will probably be a mere checker of figures. Take, for instance, the question of valuation of assets. An auditor clearly is not a valuer, but, obviously, a report on the financial condition of a company will be of comparatively little value if it ignores entirely the question of the value of assets. And so a skilled accountant is generally able to detect, by means of the experience gained from auditing the accounts of other companies carrying on a similar business whether stock has been grossly overvalued. If an auditor were to allow accounts to pass in which stock was valued at a figure which his experience told him was utterly unwarranted, I cannot see that that auditor ought to be allowed to escape civil liability when he had neglected to mention the matter to the shareholders.

Of course, in the case of the vast majority of companies everything is regular, but, unfortunately, there are some exceptions. Once your suspicions are aroused, then probe the matter to the bottom. Make use of your right to question directors and other officials, and if you discover that your suspicions are well founded, you must make up your minds to speak out. I do not mean to say that you will be justified in immediately rushing to report to the shareholders; you may, and generally ought to, begin with the directors, and, if they rectify what you consider wrong, then nothing more need be said. But if the directors refuse your advice, then you must report to the shareholders and in no veiled terms. The auditor in the case of the London and General Bank pleaded that he had *hinted* to the shareholders that something was wrong by giving his certificate in a somewhat unusual form. But you have to report to shareholders who may be totally ignorant of what the usual form of certificate may be, and the plea did not avail the auditor of the London and General Bank.

Before concluding this paper, I think I ought to say a word or two on the subject of dividends. There is only one point of view from which this matter concerns the auditors. Provided there is a profit, it is no concern of theirs whether the profit is divided up to the hilt or whether a part of it is carried to reserve. That is a matter for the directors and shareholders. But the auditors are concerned, to some extent, at any rate, to see that, if a dividend is paid, there are profits out of which it may properly be paid. It is illegal for a limited company to pay a dividend out of capital—that is a well established rule of law. Of course, if the directors and shareholders were to deliberately declare a dividend out of capital, the auditors would not be responsible; but if the accounts were so presented to the shareholders as to show a profit, when no such profit had in fact been earned, and it was the auditors' fault that they were so presented, and acting on the faith of those accounts the shareholders were to declare a dividend, then the auditors might be held liable. It is, of course, not an easy matter to determine what is the exact profit on a year's working, as you know better than I do. But there is an important question which has come before the Courts for decision which I ought to allude to, and that is, supposing your Revenue Account shows a profit, but your Capital Account shows a loss, must you make good the loss upon Capital Account before you distribute a dividend, or may you divide the whole of the profit appearing on the Revenue Account? It has been held in certain cases that you may divide the profits without making good loss or depreciation on capital. These are the well-known cases of *Lee v. Neuchatel Asphalte Company* (41 Ch.D. 1) and *Verner v. General Trust* (1894, 2 Ch. 266, 1895, 2 Ch. 254). In the latter case much stress was laid upon the difference between "fixed" and "circulating" capital, and it was said that loss or depreciation of fixed capital need not be made up out of profits, but that loss or depreciation of circulating capital must be. However, it seems to me that the value of such a distinction has been greatly reduced by the recent case of *Re National Bank of Wales* (1899, 2 Ch. 629). In that case funds of the bank were advanced on loan to customers and lost. It was held that this was a capital loss and that the bank was entitled to distribute profits without making it good, though as I understand the meaning of "circulating capital," there could hardly be a clearer instance of it than money advanced by a bank by way of loan to its customers.

These decisions have met with plenty of criticism, both from accountants and lawyers. Accountants say that they encourage unsound finance. It has, however, never been the province of Judges and lawyers to teach commercial men what is sound finance, all they have to decide is, what is legal finance? But the cases have not been received as good law by many lawyers. Perhaps the two greatest living authorities in company law are at hopeless disagreement on the point. However, the case of *Re National Bank of Wales* has been appealed from and argued in the House of Lords, though judgment has not yet been delivered. When it has, perhaps we shall get an authoritative exposition of the law relating to this difficult question. But even if the case be affirmed, accountants must not jump to the conclusion that in no case need capital loss be made good. There are many matters to be considered before that conclusion can be arrived at in any particular case, and I should always advise accountants, when they find a company about to distribute dividends on the footing of the profit shown in the Revenue Account without making good loss on Capital Account, to urge the company to take the opinion of counsel whether it is entitled to do so.

I have purposely refrained in this paper from dealing

with the criminal liability of auditors. This remains the same as it was before the passing of the Companies Act, 1900, except that Section 28 provides penalties for wilfully false statements in the auditor's certificate and report.

CODIFICATION OF AN AUDIT
(1902)

Ernest Crewdson

The author argues that it is possible and desirable to make a standarized list of procedures which every auditor must perform before he can write his opinion and collect his fee, and that it is also possible to frame a standard scale of auditor's charges.

Manchester Chartered Accountants Students' Society.

President's Address.

Codification of an Audit.

By Mr. ERNEST CREWDSON, F.C.A. (President).

AT a meeting of this Society, held on the 3rd inst., Mr. CREWDSON read the following paper:—

There were present upwards of 70 members, including Mr. W. Moss, Vice-President; Messrs. Fred Scott, W. H. Nairne, A. S. Brewis, R. N. Carter, John Hamer, A. Charlesworth, and others.

When some months ago I intimated to your able and energetic Honorary Secretary at a meeting here the intended subject of my Presidential Address, I did not contemplate travelling beyond the strict limits of the title; but when I came to try and crystallise my rambling thoughts into the form of an address I found that the subject led me much further than I had expected.

I found, for example, that as soon as you begin to try and codify an audit you have to strike off a number of departments of the work which though not technically forming part of the auditor's duties have, either through his complaisance or his desire to do all possible in the interests of his client, come to be accepted as part of his duties.

I was thus brought to see that there is a great distinction between the *duties* of an auditor *quâ* auditor and the extent of the work habitually done under that name, that much of the work, if done at all, should be done in another capacity—*i.e.*, as accountant specially retained and paid for the special services so rendered.

The importance of this was not so apparent until comparatively recently, but since the legislation of the past few years and the decisions of the Courts have added, or rather created, responsibility which did not previously attach to the office of auditor, it is essential in our own interests and for our own security that an attempt be made to define and codify the principles and practice of the auditor.

Hitherto the efforts of the writers of text-books, recognising with perfect truth that the importance and value of our work receives scant recognition from the public, have been directed to show rather how *much* an efficient auditor might and should do, and how far-reaching and deep were his researches into the accounts of the company for whose shareholders he was acting.

Now, however, that auditors are recognised as important factors in every company, and have to bear a weight of responsibility often quite out of keeping with the fee which is usually voted for the work, I think it is time someone raised his voice on the other side, and, without encouraging in the least any neglect of the duties, boldly claim a definition of the duties to which attach this grave responsibility, and claim, further, that all and sundry the many departments of investigation and research which are now deemed part of the audit shall, if done by him at all, be done not as auditor, but as accountant, investigator, or what not, and paid for as such.

It does not come within the scope of my address to attempt to define the various tasks which fall within and without the function of the auditor. This would be impossible, for lack of time, if for no other reason; but, indeed, it would in any case be presumption on my part to attempt to do that which, in my judgment, can only be adequately done by a number of the leading members of the profession in conference.

My efforts to-night are confined to an endeavour to show that such a definition and separation is possible and desirable, that it is even urgently called for as a protection to us, and incidentally as a means of bringing our work more into harmony with the relatively small remuneration it procures for us.

As soon as I touched the question of remuneration it became apparent to me that there, not less than in the matter of the work itself, was the principle of codification to be desired. I have, therefore, ventured to put forward under this head some suggestions which have long occupied my mind, and which are, I hope, deserving of your consideration.

Lastly, there comes the question of the means by which such changes can be introduced and made effective, and here, too, I have endeavoured to indicate very briefly what I think is required.

To what purpose would such a code be applicable, and what is the real object of framing it?

The purpose is, as already stated, at once to limit and define the region of our duties, so that, firstly, these may be publicly recognised, and the efficiency and utility of the audit more generally acknowledged than at present; secondly, that remuneration may be made more adequate than in many cases it is for the responsibilities undertaken and the work which has to be done; and, thirdly, that a proper criterion may be established which can be followed in the event of disputes, legal or otherwise, arising out of differences between auditors and the companies who employ them as to whether their work has been properly done or not.

The profession of an accountant in his capacity as auditor, like all other professions, comprises two sets of duties—

(1) The rendering of efficient service;

(2) Obtaining adequate payment for services rendered.

I naturally do not refer to the thousand and one calls upon his skill and time which come to him in the practice of his profession as a consulting accountant, but solely with regard to his duties as auditor, and in particular as auditor to public companies.

In his private practice an accountant must be guided by his own judgment, and the measure of his skill and opportunity is largely the measure of his success: but it is in public practice—*i.e.*, where he appears before the public as the auditor of a public company—that there is, in my judgment, urgent need for the establishment of some recognised code to define the limits of his duties.

At present the reply to the question, "What is an Audit?" is that an audit is whatever a man considers to be an audit when he signs the accounts, and the shareholders accept the signature as sufficient evidence that all that is necessary has been done, even though the auditor may have done no more than add up the Balance Sheet and ascertain its correctness *per se*.

Out of any hundred shareholders at the ordinary meeting of any company to-day, I doubt not there are those who in their hearts believe that this *is* the limit of the auditor's duties, or, at all events, that it is the limit of his performance.

If, on the other hand, we turn to the text-books, we find that the desire on the part of the writers has generally been to range as far as possible, and make the term "audit" include the examination of every possible department and all possible books.

To make matters worse, while many a shareholder believes the audit to be more or less of a farce, and that the auditor does the least possible amount of his work for the money, and while the text-book provides that he shall do the greatest possible amount of work, should loss unfortunately arise to the shareholders, whether through mismanagement, fraud, or defalcation, at once it is assumed that the auditor has neglected his duty, and directors and shareholders alike search keenly amongst the various text-books for some justification for an accusation, while the hapless auditor will be fortunate indeed if he has not done or omitted something which brings him into conflict with one or other of those writers who pose as authorities on the subject.

In plain English, while I believe there is to-day no profession the members of which believe more thoroughly in themselves and in the importance of their duties, or who as a whole do their work with a more elaborate conscientiousness, those who have the best opportunities of judging will admit that the public do not as yet greatly believe in us; and, on the other hand, in the effort to prove that our services are valuable, writers have sought to extend as far as possible the field of our operations, without regard to the liabilities which were thereby imposed upon us.

It will not, I hope, be imagined that in what I have just said I desire in any way to reflect upon the text-books or the writers.

On the contrary, I have the highest respect for them and for their work, which has been of inestimable value to the profession; but their own words are themselves the very best proof of the lack of that for which I plead—viz., Codification in regard to the work of the auditor *quâ* auditor to public companies.

It is precisely for lack of this that the various writers, seeing that certain things were required to be done by someone if the shareholders were to be properly protected, and finding that the directors of companies as a whole declined to recognise any personal responsibility, have assumed that responsibility on behalf of the auditor, constituting him, in fact, a sort of counting-house scavenger, whose duty it is to clear out holes and corners and to clean up every mess which had been left neglected by others.

Now, in this matter dates are of some importance, and it is worth while to point out that most of the writings on this subject of an auditor's duties—of those writings, at least, which are accepted as authorities—appeared prior to the recent decisions and legal enactments which have added so largely to our personal liability and responsibility.

On the other hand, the Act of 1900 by no means imposes upon auditors the sort of roving commission which I have described, and I think that, as we are bound to accept the responsibility imposed upon us by law and Parliament, it is our right, and even our duty, to decline to extend the scope of those responsibilities.

The extreme divergence of view will be made at once apparent by comparison of the Act with the text-books.

What we know as the audit clauses of the Act of 1900 are well known, and run as follows:—

> "23.—Every auditor of a company shall have a right of access at all times to the books and accounts and vouchers of the company, and shall be entitled to require from the directors and officers of the company such information and explanation as may be necessary for the performance of the duties of the auditors, and the auditors shall sign a certificate at the foot of the Balance Sheet stating whether or not all their requirements as auditors have been complied with, and shall make a report to the shareholders on the accounts examined by them, and on every Balance Sheet laid before the company in general meeting during their tenure of office; and in every such report shall state whether, in their opinion, the Balance Sheet referred to in the report is properly drawn up so as to exhibit a true and correct view of the state of the company's affairs as shown by the books of the company; and such report shall be read before the company in general meeting."

That is the Act. Now, what do the text-books say?—

> "The duty of the auditors is to investigate the affairs of the company. . . ." (Gore-Browne, p. 248.)

If that is so, why does not the Act prescribe it? and, if not, why put the burden upon us? An investigation of the affairs of a company is a proceeding which always presupposes a suspicion of something wrong.

On the other hand, what do the Judges say?—

> L.J. Lopes:—". . . . An auditor is not bound to be a detective, or . . . . to approach his work with suspicion, or with a foregone conclusion that something is wrong. He is a watch-dog, not a bloodhound. He is justified in believing tried servants of the company in whom confidence is placed by the company. He is entitled to assume that they are honest, and to rely upon their representations, provided he takes reasonable care. If there is anything calculated to excite suspicion he should probe it to the bottom; but in the absence of anything of that kind he is only bound to be reasonably cautious and careful. . . . He does not guarantee the discovery of all fraud."

A still greater divergence from the wording of the Act is to be found in the writings of a writer of authority, with whose work you will all be familiar.

> "The object and scope of an audit.—The next point to be considered is the object and extent of an audit. The object of an audit may be said to be threefold:—
>
> "(1) The detection of fraud.
>
> "(2) The detection of technical errors.
>
> "(3) The detection of errors of principle." (Dicksee, "Auditing," p. 7.)
>
> "The detection of fraud is a most important portion of the auditor's duties. Auditors, therefore, should assiduously cultivate this branch of their functions." (Dicksee, p. 8.)
>
> "Advantages of an audit.—It may be pointed out that in the event of an auditor through his negligence failing to discover fraud or embezzlement on the part of the employees of the client, he may be held liable in damages for the amount lost as a result of his negligence. A complete audit conducted by a responsible firm of accountants thus virtually becomes almost as good as a guarantee policy of the honesty of all employers, and that at probably but little greater expense than such a policy would cost." (Dicksee, p. 11.)

Comparing these extracts, where would it be possible to find more wide discrepancy or better evidence of the need for a system or code which shall define our duties as auditors of public companies?

To the author I have last quoted there is clearly no difference between the legal position of the auditor of a public company's accounts on behalf of 1,000 shareholders, and whose duties are supposed to be prescribed by law, and his duties as accountant and auditor of a private firm, where the appointment is almost always in the nature of a personal engagement.

Again, the author proceeds:—

> "It is well to remember that, however desirable it may be to know exactly the bare extent of the legal responsibility, the real professional responsibility to c... r, an a ... ssion i... onsi- b... f his p...

In ... riend to ou... nfine withi... ing to a pos... .

Th... or is emin... s *quâ* audit... d, be separ...

We actually arrive at this point, that while the Court of Appeal says of an auditor (Gore-Browne, p. 245), "He is not an insurer," our text-book says "A complete audit ". . . virtually becomes almost as good as a guarantee "policy of the honesty of all employees." Truly a gratifying statement for us as accountants, but a dangerous one in the hands of a client who has lost money by defalcation.

There is a valuable note by Mr. F. W. Pixley (Worthington-Evans, p. 79) which seems to come very near to laying down a well-defined general principle, but it does not adequately cover the ground of my subject:—

> "In addition to seeing that the Balance Sheet agrees with the Ledger balances, it is considered the duty of auditors to examine securities representing the investments which appear on the credit side, and satisfy themselves of the correctness of the bank balances.
>
> "Although, possibly, no part of their legal duty, professional auditors should, in practice, endeavour to ascertain if all the liabilities have been brought into the Balance Sheet, whether they appear in the books or not, and endeavour to guard against errors of omission as well as of commission. It is really in this respect that the superiority of the professional over the amateur auditor is most apparent; the amateur merely contents himself with bare checking, while the professional auditor of experience brings to bear that experience on the Balance Sheet of every company he audits, and by comparing it with the Balance Sheets of companies doing similar business he is able to institute enquiries which lead to a very different Balance Sheet being ultimately placed before the shareholders to the one originally placed before him for signature."

It is a good many years since the celebrated *Kingston Mills* case was decided and afterwards reversed, but I may be pardoned for alluding to it for a moment. You will say, perhaps, "Oh! but this was a too preposterous decision, and, moreover, it was reversed on appeal."

Quite true, but that did not undo the cruel suffering to the auditors, nor the damage to their name and position; and as to the judgment itself, I have always felt that its preposterousness was its gravest feature, for it shows the defencelessness of our position when every Judge feels free to construct his own theory of the duties of an auditor.

I must admit that I think we are ourselves partly to blame for the want of due appreciation by the public, because each of us has his pet ideas on the subject of our work, and there has been a tendency to make rather a mystery of it, so as to encourage the idea that it was not merely better done than that of our rivals, but that it has special characteristics of method or system to which *special* merit attached.

I do not say that these special characteristics do not exist; far from it. I claim that they do, and in particular I claim a special merit for what is known as "Jones's system," which my firm have used for many years to a greater or less extent; but I hold it a mistake, from the point of view of our position with the public, to introduce the element of mystery into the matter in any way.

In discussing the question before us, however, that of the possibility of codification, we are not concerned with the question of how to do the work, but rather of what the work consists. For instance, within what lines are the duties of the auditor of a bank comprehended, or the auditor of a manufacturing concern, or of a merchant's business; and it is in defining these that I think something in the nature of codification is very greatly needed.

I have to confess at this point that the question of how to enforce anything of the kind presses upon me; but that brings me to a third branch of this subject, on which I hope to say a few words before the close of this address.

But passing that by, and assuming that a code once established could be enforced so as to be recognised by authorities and in Courts of law, I proceed to give a few illustrations of the points at which it would apply:—

In the case of the audit of a bank's accounts, for instance, leaving on one side all the recognised duties which are easily defined and generally recognised, there is the great question of how to deal with the Branch accounts.

Some auditors visit the Branches and examine the accounts of each exactly as they examine them at the Head Office. Others accept the certified returns from the Branches. Both alike claim to have audited the accounts, but it is obvious that the amount of work entailed and the staff required for the work is wholly different in the two cases.

You will, perhaps, say, "Each states in his certificate what he has done," but that does not, in my judgment, deal with the question in a satisfactory way. Possibly—probably, perhaps—it gives us legal protection, but I must frankly say I do not think it is quite fair to the public. The certificate is the work of an expert, and I fear it often requires the knowledge of an expert to interpret it.

Now, the public are not experts, and our certificates should aim to be written down to the level of the average man's understanding rather than up to the highest reach of our own. For example, how often, or how seldom rather, do you find in a certificate or report any statement of anything the auditor has *not* done—*e.g.*, "We "have not visited any of the Branches, but we have "accepted their certified returns of the Branches sent to "the Head Office."

The question is, What ought to be done before the auditor has earned his fee, and before he can conscientiously sign the Balance Sheet as correct?

Such a code as I have in my mind would define this question.

Probably the class of business which presents the fewest difficulties is that of the ordinary manufacturing concern. But here, again, there are certain points at which the practice varies largely, and where a code would be of inestimable value, alike to young accountants who wish to know what their duties comprise, and to those who—as will happen to the best of us from time to time—find themselves face to face with differences between themselves and their clients.

The subject would be a much less difficult one were it not obscured by the fact already referred to—that the duties of an auditor and the duties of an accountant are not necessarily the same. The duty of an auditor, as I have shown, not being *primarily* to discover fraud and defalcation, but to ascertain the correctness of the accounts as they stand; in fact, to certify that they present a proper picture of the business in its then present condition.

If defalcations have occurred, and have been hidden in such a way that an audit of this kind discloses them, well and good; but if the defalcations have been so covered up that the audit does not disclose them, the auditor, as such, has still discharged his duty although they may be undiscovered.

Such is the fact, and such also is the law, but it is quite contrary to the popular supposition, and woe betide the auditor who tried to defend such a case in Court. If, however, a distinct code existed, and this had been fully complied with, the case would then be comparatively clear.

It is a fact of some significance that there have been very few decisions of actions against accountants arising out of defalcations or misappropriations. This does not mean, I need hardly say, that there are no cases in which accountants are made to suffer for the wrongdoings of others, but rather, as I am assured by a leading London solicitor, that the accountant does not think it worth while to carry the case into Court, well knowing that he would start so handicapped by the weight of presumption against him that rather than face the troublesome and annoying publicity, with small chance of success, he makes the best terms he can and pays what he must.

At present I do not suppose that any two firms in Manchester would audit any given set of books in exactly the same way, or would carry the work exactly to the same extent. Some believe in calling-over everything; others call-over at haphazard and in parts only; some believe that the books required to be audited do not extend behind the official Cash Book, Day Book, Invoice Book, &c.; others will pursue their investigations into every available book, primary and waste.

Which is right? And, if opinions differ, where is the authority to settle the question?

Suppose a code existed which stated that for the purpose of an audit the primary and waste books were to be ignored, and that any investigation of these was outside the limit of the auditor's duties proper, and should be undertaken by request as an investigation *quâ* accountant and paid for separately, an intelligible basis of audit would thus be provided for everyone.

I think this matter is important, not only in the interests of the auditor, who often finds it impossible to obtain adequate remuneration for the elaborate research which is sometimes suggested as necessary, but in the interests also of the efficiency of the audit, for much of the detail which is now imposed upon the auditor as part of his audit must be rushed through under great pressure, and would be done better and more effectively at other times of the year if it were part of his duties as accountant.

I am aware of the strong feeling which exists in some minds against an auditor doing what is called accountant's work at the books of which he is also auditor. If this objection be urged, then I say let some other accountant do that work. We should not suffer, for each of us would do what I term the investigation work of accounts other than those we audit; and in this way I hold that we should not lose but rather gain, for we should learn to work together and in harmony, to the great advantage of all, each being responsible for his own department.

It is always dangerous to attempt broad definitions dealing with complex subjects, and, as I have already said, the codification of an audit is too large and complex a subject to be undertaken by one man, or adequately dealt with in an address of this kind. I venture, however, to suggest that the ruling idea should be that the auditor stands between the shareholders and the board, while the investigating accountant, in my view, stands between the directors and the staff.

An accountant has been described by one of Her late Majesty's Judges (in a quotation already given) as a kind of watch-dog. Well, I submit that the auditor is the watch-dog of the shareholders, and the investigating accountant is the watch-dog of the directors.

Turning to the second department, the question of Charges for work done.

If the state of the accountant's profession as regards the definition of his duties as auditor is confused, the state of its condition with regard to charges is certainly no better.

There is no criterion; there is no standard; there is no basis.

By far the larger number of audit fees paid to-day to accountants have been fixed at haphazard; and while many of them are inadequate, they are retained from fear that in disturbing them the otherwise pleasant relations between the auditors and the shareholders should also be disturbed.

In dealing with this part of the question, just as in the previous part, I exclude all question of the accountant's charges in matters connected with his private practice, or, as above explained, as investigating accountant. These are necessarily a matter of arrangement, and it is his own fault if he cannot make a satisfactory one. But in the case of public companies, the audit is often inadequately remunerated because there is no basis existing for comparison, and the shareholders, while wishing to do justice, are afraid of being foolishly generous.

How, then, would it be possible to frame a code of auditors' charges?

I maintain, gentlemen, this is a much simpler matter than framing a code of auditors' duties. Of course, in framing a code of charges we should have to take the rough with the smooth, and sometimes the result would be against us; but, on the whole, I believe it would be favourable.

What basis, then, do I suggest?

There are two in my mind, both of which have been tried, and one of which has, to my knowledge, worked well:—

(*a*) A percentage on the assets comprised in the Balance Sheet.

(*b*) A percentage on the turnover.

There is a third basis, but this hardly applies to public companies, and that is a percentage upon the income. This last is already generally recognised in estate work.

With regard to the other two, although at first sight they may seem visionary, I do not think they would prove so. In point of fact, my firm is at present paid by one company a minimum fee of 50 guineas merging in a fee of ¼ per cent. upon the turnover, and the result has been eminently satisfactory to both of us.

In other instances it has been possible to arrange a percentage upon the capital sum comprised in the Balance Sheet.

For this purpose, I need hardly say, you take the whole right-hand side of the Balance Sheet, not merely the capital of the company, and such a basis as the following might apply:—

Up to £100,000, £1 per mille, with a minimum fee of 10 guineas.

Above £100,000 up to £1,000,000, 5s. per mille.

On all above £1,000,000, 2s. 6d. per mille.

I merely put forward these rates as illustrations, without reference to their relation to the ordinary rates of remuneration; but I deem it would be part of the object in framing a code to obtain an increase in the rate of payment which, in view of the responsibilities which now attach to the auditor's position, is in my judgment quite inadequate in a large proportion of cases.

Assuming for the moment that the principle of codification, some idea of which I have endeavoured to lay before you, is admitted to be desirable, the question which arises is, How is it to be attained, and if codes be prepared and approved how are they to be enforced?

This is the third and last portion of my subject, and here, alas! we are to-day in a position of great weakness. Our authorities have no mandatory power, and our resolutions and opinions carry no weight in Courts of law.

There was a time, some years ago, when endeavours were made to bring about a fusion of all accountants, and a Bill was prepared which would have had the effect of giving a legal status to the profession.

I am far from desiring to enter upon any controversial matter to-night, but I believe that the older members of the profession (who, like myself, though disliking much about the measure, deemed it the only way out of the difficulty) were somewhat remiss in that we did not use much pressure upon the younger members, who not unnaturally protested against the apparent throwing away of the advantages which they had gained so recently, at so much trouble and cost, to enable them to become members of the Accountants' Institute.

Had that Bill become law, the temporary disadvantages it brought with it to the younger members of the Institute would long since have disappeared, and they themselves would have been verging on seniority, and we should have had to-day a legal status and the power to enforce arrangements, such as I am suggesting, made for the common good.

Is it too much to hope that if the question is brought forward again at some not distant date, those who are then our juniors will eschew the counsel of Rehoboam, and be guided by the counsel of the old men.

Without some such enactment as that Bill, schemes of codification seem little better than visions, but I give them to you in the hope that they may direct your minds to the importance of this part of the subject, and one day help to bear fruit in the extended power and usefulness of our profession, which, in my opinion, can only be attained when we have common practice and a common basis of charges.

LETTER TO THE EDITOR ON "CODIFICATION OF AN AUDIT" (1902)

Lawrence R. Dicksee

Rebutting Mr. Crewdson's proposal: "We do not find medical men discussing in detail the amount of care and attention which they must give to their patients, if they wish to avoid a conviction for manslaughter in the event of their dying...."

Codification of an Audit.

(To the Editor of The Accountant.)

SIR,—I was much interested in the able address of Mr. Ernest Crewdson, F.C.A., on the above subject, which appeared in your last issue. The question is one upon which the fullest possible discussion is, I think, desirable; but I may perhaps be allowed to express the view that such discussions are frequently apt to be unprofitable if new and special meanings are to be arbitrarily attached to words that already have other well-known significations. Mr. Crewdson, in his desire to limit the legal responsibilities of auditors, suggests that the auditor stands between the shareholders and the board of a company, while the investigating accountant stands between the directors and the staff. That such a distinction is not justified by the existing facts must be clear to anyone who reflects that, assuming the correctness of the distinction, auditors could not exist apart from directors and shareholders, whereas, of course, the term has for years been employed in connection with those who audit the accounts of private traders and of public institutions other than companies.

The suggestion that there should be an auditor appointed by the shareholders, and an investigating accountant appointed by the directors, has already been anticipated. It is mentioned on page 13 of my book as the "ideal" audit, and has to my knowledge been employed to the greatest advantage to all concerned in several cases. It is, however, open to question whether this would have the effect anticipated by Mr. Crewdson of diminishing the responsibilities of the shareholders' auditor. If it had that effect, it would presumably equally limit the responsibilities of the directors' auditor, but, so far as I remember, no such division of responsibility was recognised in connection with the *Liberator* failure. The statement that, in my view, there is "clearly no difference between the legal position of "the auditor of a public company's accounts on behalf "of 1,000 shareholders, whose duties are supposed to be "prescribed by law, and his duties as accountant and "auditor of a private firm, where the appointment is "almost always in the nature of a personal engage-"ment," is, I think I may fairly say, not borne out by any but the most hasty perusal of Chapter I. of my work. Chapter IX. is devoted to the consideration of the different positions occupied by the auditor under several conditions, while the auditor's liability under different circumstances is dealt with in Chapter X. It is true that the fresh light thrown upon the subject by the Companies Act, 1900, is not considered, for the reason that the current edition was completed and printed before that Act was finally settled, and it was therefore only possible to reproduce those sections affecting auditors in the form of an additional Appendix. This deficiency will, of course, be remedied in the next edition, which I am now preparing, and which will, I hope, be ready in about six months.

At the same time it is, I think, very possible to exaggerate the importance of the recent legislation, and I must beg to entirely differ from Mr. Crewdson's statement that "recent decisions and legal enactments have "added largely to our personal liability and responsi-"bility." As I understand the Act of 1900, it limits rather than increases our liabilities, while the Act of 1890 merely provided a novel (and in my opinion somewhat objectionable) means of enforcing a liability that already existed. I am entirely in agreement with Mr. Crewdson as to the desirability of an auditor's liabilities being kept within reasonable compass, but I cannot agree with him that the bare legal limit of liability should be regarded as the standard of professional conduct, or the standard which it is desirable that writers of text books should inculcate in the minds of students and young practitioners. Personally, I cannot help thinking that continual discussions, having for their object the whittling down of the duties which an auditor can reasonably be expected to perform, are to be deprecated. We do not find medical men discussing in detail the amount of care and attention which they must give to their patients, if they wish to avoid a conviction for manslaughter in the event of their dying; and I cannot help thinking that, if we found the members of Students' Societies giving up their time to debates upon the number and nature of mistakes which they ought to be permitted to make without being called to account by their principals, we should think twice before offering an appointment to those who took a prominent part in such advocacy of irresponsible inaccuracy. I am not prepared to accept Mr. Crewdson's statement that "the public do not as yet greatly believe in us" as a profession; but if any such view is at all prevalent, it is more likely to be encouraged than refuted by a suggestion that "he is the best friend of "our profession who helps to confine within the "narrowest possible limits the duties attaching to the "position of auditor."

Apart, however, from the expediency of the discussion, it may be pointed out that an attempt has already been made by the heads of the Institute to endeavour to agree upon a codification of the auditor's duties, which proved entirely unproductive. Moreover, such a code, even if agreed upon, would in no way limit the responsibilities of auditors, nor is it likely that any legislation will ever be enacted that will enable the profession to limit its own responsibilities.

In conclusion, perhaps you will allow me to add to this already lengthy letter the following extract from my book, which appears to have escaped Mr. Crewdson's attention, and upon which I should be glad to hear his views :—

> "In this connection it may be pointed out in passing that, even with regard to such important questions as the value of assets, provision for depreciation, the assessment of profits earned, and the distribution of unrealised profits, the Courts have shown a marvellous disinclination to lay down any general rules which could be regarded as principles for the safe guidance of auditors in the future. In carefully and laboriously shirking their duties in this respect, however, the Courts have been most ably seconded by the Legislature, which has been particularly cautious in abstaining from laying down any exact rules as to what the duties of an auditor may be. No doubt it has acted wisely in adopting this course, however, because any attempt to state explicitly what the duties of auditors are in all cases would inevitably fail in not a few, and would afford the best possible excuse in such cases for the insufficiency of the audit that had been performed. Any Act of Parliament which attempts to classify the duties of an auditor under stereotyped headings must at least profess to be at the same time exhaustive, and as the latter is impossible, it seems to follow that the former is very inexpedient."

Yours, &c.,

LAWRENCE R. DICKSEE.

February 24th 1902.

CODIFICATION OF AN AUDIT
(1902)

Editorial from The Accountant

Codified auditing duties would be hard to specify, and requiring an accountant to follow standardized procedures could decrease his sense of personal responsibility for the work he has done.

Leading Articles.

Codification of an Audit.

MR. ERNEST CREWDSON, F.C.A., in his able Presidential address to the Manchester Chartered Accountants Students' Society, deals with a difficult subject, of great interest to the profession, which has in the past been before the Institute with entirely abortive results. Indeed, we think it would be almost impossible to frame a "code" capable of governing every case. Assuming, however, that such a "code" was arranged, we do not think it would exalt the profession if it was formed on the basis of restricting the liability of the auditor as far as possible. We cannot, therefore, agree with Mr. CREWDSON when he says that "he is the best friend of our profession who helps to confine within the narrowest "possible limits the duties attaching to a "position (*i.e.*, auditorship) which carries such "grave responsibilities."

In our opinion, the auditor should not consider his responsibilities adequately dealt with until he has seen that his clients' interests in the particular matter—so far as such interests come within his (the auditor's) sphere—are properly safeguarded. Again, looking at the matter from the selfish standpoint of the auditor's own protection, how much greater is the danger of the auditor who sails along on the very edge of his legal responsibilities, doing no more than he is legally compelled to do, compared with the auditor who goes further away from the line—who discharges his moral, as well as his legal, responsibilities? The danger of sailing so close to the wind is evident. By all means let the auditor keep well before him the extent of his legal responsibilities, but on no account should he confine himself to them.

The difficulties of "codification" exist, not only in the large variety of the concerns to be audited, but also in the different conditions which may govern companies engaged in similar trades, &c. Auditing, like many other things, to be conducted successfully, requires a large amount of common sense. Codes, rules, and regulations are all very well up to a certain point, but if that point is passed there is a danger of the auditor becoming a mere machine. The "epitome" found in many accountants' offices for different audits is a mild form of "the code," yet the epitome, though useful to a certain extent, is liable to encourage the auditor to become a piece of mechanism. The sense of relying upon oneself is in danger of being undermined.

The lecturer is to be commended for his remarks discouraging the tendency (most prevalent among the younger members of the profession) to create the impression in the mind of the layman that there is a mystery attached to auditing which can only be divulged to members of the mysterious circle.

The latter portion of Mr. CREWDSON's paper hardly comes under the title selected by him for his address; in fact, he admits that "Codification of an Audit" does not furnish a proper diagnosis of the ground he covers. Legislation for the profession would, however, be necessary, as the lecturer says, before any code could be enforced. Legislation will probably come; but if it does not come from within, so much the worse for the profession.

THE DUTIES AND RESPONSIBILITIES OF THE PUBLIC ACCOUNTANT (1902)

Arthur Lowes Dickinson

The training and duties of public accountants, as interpreted for an American audience by a leading English Chartered Accountant, and including suggestions for adapting English accounting methods to American practice.

The Duties and Responsibilities of the Public Accountant.

A PAPER read before the Illinois Association of Public Accountants on February 25 1902, by ARTHUR LOWES DICKINSON, M.A., of the firms of Jones, Cæsar & Company and Price, Waterhouse & Company, Chartered Accountant and Fellow of the Illinois Association of Public Accountants.

The profession of public accountant, in the modern sense of the term, is a product of the Nineteenth Century, and owes its existence and progress to the great expansion of industry and commerce for which that period is remarkable, and in particular to the rapid growth of that form of partnership represented by the joint-stock company or industrial corporation.

The first public recognition of the importance of the profession dates from the Royal Charter granted in Scotland to the Scottish Institute of Accountants in 1856. Twenty-four years later a similar Charter was given to the Institute of Chartered Accountants in England and Wales, a body formed by the consolidation of various pre-existing Societies. Both the English and Scottish Charters provided for a compulsory course of training prior to admission to either Institute, comprising five years' continuous service in the office of a practising Chartered Accountant, coupled with examinations in accounts, in certain branches of law and (in Scotland) in the elements of actuarial science. The growth of the profession in Great Britain since the date of these Charters has been very great, and Associates and Fellows of the two Societies are now to be found in every English-speaking community.

In tne United States the development, while equally rapid, has proceeded on somewhat different lines. In place of granting special privileges to certain leading Societies the Legislatures of the States of New York, Pennsylvania, California, and Maryland have passed Acts providing examinations for the degree of "Certified Public Accountant," commonly known as "C.P.A." The examinations comprise practically the same subjects as those in England and Scotland, but no period of service under a practising accountant is required. In connection with the examination in the State of New York, a School of Commerce and Accounts has been organised in the University of New York, and is developing a very complete system of preliminary training, including bookkeeping and accounts, law, and the principles of economics. The importance to the profession generally of such an organised scheme for preliminary education cannot be overrated, and it is desirable that the educational authorities in other States should follow this example. There are also many local Societies whose members are as a rule public accountants in practice; but no special qualifications attach to membership, and they have not adopted or required any special form of training. The principal of these Societies are the following:—Illinois Association of Public Accountants, New York Society of Certified Public Accountants, American Association of Public Accountants, and the Incorporated Accountants of Massachusetts.

While at the present time there is here no obligation to serve an apprenticeship in the office of a public accountant, the great importance of this part of the education is generally recognised, and it may safely be stated that, with few exceptions, the members of the profession are all qualified both by the degree of "Certified Public Accountant" or "Chartered Accountant," and, further, by a continuous practical experience extending over many years.

The experience gained in the period of training comprises not only all the branches of auditing and accounting, but also a general knowledge of the principles of commercial law, including the law of corporations and the law of bankruptcy, especially in so far as these laws have relation to accounts, the desire being that the accountant should have a sufficient legal knowledge to make him an intelligent client to his lawyer without in any way usurping the functions of the latter.

It is necessary to emphasise the fact that, while the bookkeeper or accountant or comptroller of a large corporation may have and should have a thorough knowledge of accounts, yet, from lack of the special training which can only be acquired by several years' practical experience in the office of a public accountant, he cannot be considered a member of the latter profession in the modern sense of the term. A public accountant is not merely a bookkeeper, a statistician, or a man of figures, nor only a good man of business, but if he be successful in his profession he must combine all these qualifications, and in addition have a general knowledge of all industrial undertakings, of the forms of accounting most suitable to each, and of the general principles, both legal and economical, which govern them. The training referred to above is only the first step to the attainment of such a position, and must be supplemented by many years of practical experience as assistant or manager in the office of a public accountant, where, in the midst of innumerable problems in accounts calling for the exercise of skill and judgment, opportunities for acquiring efficiency in accounting in its highest sense can alone be found.

In addition to training and experience, there are two most important principles upon which the position and reputation of the public accountant rest. The first is what may be called "the doctrine of personal responsibility." He alone is responsible to his clients for the results of his work; he cannot excuse himself by attaching blame to his subordinates, who are selected and trained by himself and imbued with his personality, and are thus qualified to act as his deputies in obtaining the information and statistics he requires. Being himself the absolute head, holding in his grasp all the threads of his business, subject to no control by directors, and free from all influence which might bias his judgment, he is in a position to accept, and does accept, the whole responsibility. His reputation and his success in his profession, and his personal fortune, are all dependent on his appreciation of the responsibility of his position and upon his continued endeavours to attain the high ideal at which he aims.

The second principle is that of absolute secrecy regarding all matters which may come before him in the course of his business. This rule is impressed upon his assistants from the earliest stages, and is recognised as so essential that breaches thereof are practically unknown; and the business community may feel thoroughly assured on this point when they avail themselves of the services of a member of one of the recognised bodies of public accountants.

Duties.

Having passed through his period of training and subsequently gained as an assistant or manager in the office of some senior member of the profession several years of general experience, the young accountant is qualified to practise on his own account, and his work may be classified under the following heads:—

First.—The audit of accounts, entailing such examination as will satisfy him that the accounts laid before him are substantially correct and enable him to certify to this effect.

Second.—The establishment of systems of bookkeeping and Cost Accounts, including such a system of internal checks between departments as will minimise, if not entirely prevent, the possibility of frauds.

Third.—The investigation of frauds.

Fourth.—The supplying of trained assistants to help his clients in times of emergency in the keeping of their books and accounts.

Fifth.—The investigation of the accounts of firms and companies with a view to certifying the profits or verifying the assets and liabilities on conversion of the same into public or private corporations, either by sale or by the consolidation of several concerns into one large corporation.

Sixth.—The preparation of the accounts of assignees in bankruptcy, with special reference to the form in which the accounts have to be submitted to the Court.

Seventh.—Devising, opening, and keeping books for Executors' Accounts, Estate Accounts, and Trust Accounts.

Eighth.—The investigation of claims for compensation.

Ninth.—The calculation of sinking funds for repayment of loans or redemption of bonds, interest calculations, and general problems in connection therewith.

A more detailed examination of the nature of the work of the public accountant and the responsibility which he is prepared to undertake is the object of the remarks which follow.

I.—The Audit of Accounts.

This may be divided into:—

(*a*) The continuous daily or weekly or monthly audit, in which all the details of the business will be examined and verified.

(*b*) The half-yearly or yearly preparation and audit of the Balance Sheet and Profit and Loss Account, also involving a full, detailed examination of all the accounts.

(*c*) A financial audit of the accounts as prepared by the officials of the firm or company, not necessarily involving a detailed examination of all the transactions.

In small concerns, where there is no special system of internal check, a detailed audit would seem to be almost a necessity. The head of the firm, or the president and board of directors of the company, while naturally having a full knowledge of the methods of conducting the business, have neither the time, nor in most cases the requisite technical knowledge, to supervise the accounting department. This must necessarily be left to an official, whose work is often to a great extent unchecked, or only checked by his subordinates, who, in all questions involving the exercise of judgment, would hesitate to express an opinion at variance with that of their superior. Experience shows that where frauds occur they are in the majority of cases committed by men in a confidential position who have been implicitly trusted, but have abused the confidence placed in them. The head of a business owes a duty to his employees, as well as to himself, to see that there is such a check upon all the transactions of his staff as will obviate opportunities for wrongdoing; and no better means of exercising this check exists than a continuous verification of the accounts by an independent auditor. A public accountant filling such a position is an assistance to the heads of the business by ensuring accuracy, both in principle and detail, and a correct statement of profits earned; and by giving the benefit of his advice and experience on any difficult points that may arise. He is further of assistance to the head of the accounting department by means of his general supervision of the work of the subordinate officials, and because from his wider experience he can point out any weak points in the system, and the remedies therefor, and can frequently make suggestions for saving labour.

Some large employers have so recognised the advantage to themselves of an independent audit that they make arrangements for the daily attendance of one of the auditor's assistants to check up the cash transactions and to certify to the correctness thereof; but in the majority of cases a monthly or quarterly examination is considered sufficient. It may be noted here that the cost of such an audit is less than the salary of a permanent auditor as a member of the staff, at any rate, in all corporations of moderate size, and, in view of the comparative qualifications of the independent and salaried auditor, the advantages to the employer must be largely on the side of the former.

In questions of foreign exchange, depreciation, valuation of inventories, reserves for bad and doubtful debts, the treatment of wasting assets, and other problems of a like nature, the experience of the public accountant, gathered as it is from years of close contact with all kinds of business, should be invaluable, and the employer who has availed himself of these services continuously can feel that he has done everything possible to insure himself, not only against fraud, but also against errors of calculation and errors of principle in the accounting department of his business—errors which frequently result in serious overstatement of profits.

In certain concerns, when the principals do not consider the expense of a more frequent audit desirable, it is the practice to employ a public accountant only at the half-yearly or yearly balancing periods to conduct a complete audit of the transactions of the period and prepare the Profit and Loss Account and Balance Sheet. While such an examination is not so effective a check as a more frequent one would be, especially in connection with possible frauds or errors in accounting resulting in loss to the employer, the same advantages would accrue in other respects and the report or certificate of the independent auditor attached to the accounts is a guarantee of their substantial accuracy.

In the case of large corporations such a detailed audit as that outlined above is as a rule unnecessary, even when the expense involved does not render it impracticable. The corporations referred to may be defined as those whose transactions are so numerous that they can employ their own staff to carry out the continuous audit described above; and, provided that a sound system is designed and (what is of equal importance) properly carried out, this is quite sufficient. It will, however, nearly always be found that the final preparation of semi-annual or annual accounts is left entirely to one official, who is checked only by his subordinates, and, like all other human beings, is liable to errors of principle upon points on which his subordinates' opinion would not be available. Here, too, therefore, appears the necessity for the independent auditor; firstly, to satisfy the general manager of the business that the system is as good as it can be; secondly, to test the system in varying ways, and to see that it is properly carried out; and, thirdly, to supervise the work of the corporation's auditor or comptroller by a verification of the final accounts, and, incidentally, to discuss and settle with him doubtful points, such as frequently arise, which can be settled better by two heads than one.

One incidental advantage of such an audit by a public accountant is that he has before him, by means of his trained staff, a complete view of the company's affairs in a condensed form, and can oversee the transactions as a whole more effectively than the corporation's officials, who deal with each point as it arises, and are necessarily involved more or less in a mass of details.

Perhaps, however, the most important feature of the independent audit of the accounts of a corporation, large or small, is the verification of the assets and liabilities in the Balance Sheet, the determination of proper and adequate rates of depreciation, and of proper reserves for bad and doubtful debts. The experience of most public accountants goes to show that the estimates of managers are often too sanguine, and the auditor is able by inquiries into the status of the various book accounts, by a comparison of prices in the inventory with current market quotations, by a close examination of Cost Accounts, and in many cases by an actual test of quantities remaining on hand as compared with quantities purchased and sold, to satisfy himself whether the valuations both of book debts and of inventories are fair and reasonable, and frequently to suggest increased reserves which are generally justified by subsequent experience.

The modern practice of publishing monthly statements of net earnings which are necessarily based on approximate inventories renders the employment of an expert accountant even more desirable. The wisdom of the frequent publication of such statements, which are necessarily only approximate, inasmuch as they are published before there has been time to ascertain the absolute correctness thereof, may be open to question, but so long as such statements are required, whether for publication or for the board of directors of the corporation, it is of the utmost importance that the basis upon which they are prepared should be accurate. Cases have occurred where from some mistake of principle in the calculation of an approximate book inventory, the statements so prepared have been utterly wrong, and the true facts subsequently ascertained by the investigation of an expert accountant have caused not only disappointment but loss to all concerned.

Accountants are often asked whether their periodical examination of the books of a concern will be an absolute safeguard against fraud. It is as well to make clear at once that it will not. If there is a bad system, frauds are comparatively easy, and, even with a good system, the collusion of two or more people may render it possible; but it may safely be said that the periodical examination of books and accounts by an independent auditor puts very much greater difficulties in the way of such frauds and renders their detection within a reasonable time of their commission almost a matter of certainty.

Reports are frequent of frauds which have remained undetected for long periods, and have been discovered only on the temporary absence of the confidential clerk, trusted implicitly by his employers, and apparently wholly devoted to their interests, who has made himself invaluable by his constant attention to business, uninterrupted by any annual vacation. The large defalcations thus accidentally brought to light would be rendered almost impossible if the accounts were inspected in detail at regular or irregular intervals by a responsible public accountant. And it may be safely said that, if the large body of trusted officials of firms and companies, among whose ranks these comparatively few black sheep are found, would recognise the benefit to themselves of such a periodical detailed audit and urge it upon their principals as an additional safeguard, the number of these unfortunate incidents would be materially diminished.

II.—The Establishment of Systems of Bookkeeping and Cost Accounts.

The importance of employing the best possible systems of accounting must be admitted as an axiom. Without a good cost system, no manufacturing concern can expect to show the best results, and, although at first sight such a system may appear to some in the light of an expensive luxury, there can be no doubt that practical experience shows that the expense is amply compensated by savings in cost of manufacture. But while this is generally admitted by the leading manufacturers, there are many who either have no such system or such an incomplete one that it is of little, if any, use. One of the most important services which the public accountant can render to the business of the country is by urging upon his clients the importance of a proper cost system and employing his wide experience to establish it. The objects to be arrived at are, firstly, to ascertain not only the actual cost of any piece of work when completed, but also the cost of the different stages of manufacture. Secondly, to enable an approximate inventory to be taken at any time from the books without any physical valuation, thus enabling periodical statements of profits to be prepared; and, thirdly, to ascertain readily from the books the quantities of any class of stores or materials on hand, and to effect economies by taking advantage of the markets for replenishing supplies. It is claimed, and will, as a rule, be readily admitted, that the experience in all forms of Cost Accounts, suitable to all kinds of businesses, which the public accountant should have, renders his advice and assistance in these matters of the greatest value to his clients.

A good system of bookkeeping is of equal importance with a good system of Cost Accounts, and much unnecessary labour can be saved by adapting the books and accounts to the nature of the business and by suitable sub-divisions thereof, so that work which, under one system, could hardly be done in the ordinary hours of business, is, under another and better one, easily accomplished. One essential of any system is that it should provide safeguards against fraud, and, as the records of such frauds show, even the largest institutions occasionally leave loopholes which the training and experience of the public accountant would, in all probability, have enabled him to detect and fill up. The practice of relying upon the honesty of individuals instead of a good system of bookkeeping is not to be commended.

The preparation of suitable forms of daily, weekly, or monthly returns to show as concisely as possible the results of the trading with a summary of the most interesting detail contained therein is another branch of this important work. The information conveyed to directors by such statements is entirely dependent upon the shape in which they are presented, and it requires some skill to make it concise and yet at the same time complete in all important details. For such work the public accountant is eminently qualified.

III.—The Investigation of Frauds.

The unravelling of fraud is a complicated piece of work, which can more satisfactorily be carried out by a public accountant whose business it is to know exactly where to put his finger on the weak spots than by the ordinary staff of the concern defrauded, who are, as a rule, wholly inexperienced in such investigations. If the defrauding official has to be prosecuted the evidence of the expert accountant will be required; his independent report will carry greater weight, as a rule, with a surety company than the report of the officials of the concern who are claiming against it; and there is the further advantage that such a report could be made by a public accountant without such interruption to the ordinary business routine of the office as would be involved if a greater part of the staff were engaged thereon.

IV.—The Supply of Trained Assistants.

In an emergency, whether due to the illness or absence of a trusted accountant or bookkeeper, to the pressure of work or to other causes, the advantage to clients of availing themselves temporarily of the services of a confidential and skilled man will be appreciated by all who know what it means in such a case to have to depend upon the services of a more or less incompetent substitute. The public accountant always has in his employ trained assistants, competent to undertake any work of this class.

V.—The Investigation of the Accounts of a Business for Purposes of Sale, &c.

This branch of the profession of accountancy is, perhaps, that which, up to the present, has been most in evidence in this country, and its importance can hardly be overrated. In every case of purchase and sale it is the desire of the seller, without necessarily any intent to defraud, to put the best complexion possible upon that which he has to sell. It is clearly to the interest of the buyer to know the exact facts about the business which he is buying, stripped of the gloss thrown over it by the views of the seller. An overstatement of profits or assets by the vendor may be deliberate or it may be due to ignorance or to mistakes of principle resulting in an honest belief on his part that his figures are correct; or the purchaser may only have to combat the sanguine views which a vendor is naturally inclined to take of the value of his own business. The position of the business, the nature of the assets and liabilities, the profits it has earned, and the distribution thereof (that is, whether they showed a rising or falling tendency), the existence of important future contracts not disclosed by the vendor, the omission of large liabilities under existing contracts which would materially affect the profits, the adequacy of the provision made for depreciation and bad debts; charges to Construction Account of expenditures on renewals and maintenance of plant, machinery, and other fixed assets, which should properly have been charged against profits; all these, as affecting not only the profits, but the values of the assets, are matters of the greatest moment to the purchaser, who has probably neither the time nor the technical knowledge necessary to investigate the accounts for himself; and, unless he deliberately chooses to rely upon the vendor's statements, they can only be ascertained by an exhaustive examination of the books and accounts by a public accountant. As a new corporation, taking over either by purchase or consolidation one or more concerns, is frequently capitalised on a basis which will yield 10 or 12 per cent. on the capital stock of the new company, any error in the past profits forming the basis of the contract is multiplied in the same proportion in the capitalisation of the new corporation.

VI.—The Accounts of Assignees in Bankruptcy.

Much trouble and expense might be saved in all bankruptcy cases if a public accountant were instructed in the first instance to prepare the inventory of the firm in the form required by the Courts, and to decide the manner in which the accounts of the estate should be kept. While the employees of the bankrupt firm may have a complete knowledge of its transactions, and be competent to keep its books, it should be remembered that the accounts which the assignee has to render are not such as would be required for a continuing business; and, if they are not kept in proper form in the first instance, they may have to be rewritten at a later date when the materials and information required are not readily available. A proper system started at the date of the assignment and written up concurrently with the books of the old firm and under the supervision of a public accountant will ensure the complete record of each transaction as it occurs in the form in which it is eventually required; and the final statements required by the Courts are then readily compiled.

VII.—Executorship Accounts.

This is a branch of accounting of which it may be said that there is only one really correct and clear way of keeping the accounts, while there are many ways which are neither clear nor correct, and yet are very generally adopted. The record of the transactions of a trust estate in a simple and complete form requires much skill and experience, as well as a knowledge of the principles of law involved, and executors would be well advised if they relied upon the services of a public accountant to open the books of the estate and to audit them periodically. In fact, in many cases it would be found the most satisfactory course to leave the entire bookkeeping in the hands of the accountant, who would then be responsible for its accuracy.

VIII.—Compensation Cases.

The amount of compensation awarded in cases of personal injury generally depends to a large extent on the loss of income arising therefrom. For an accurate determination of the amount of such loss an examination of the accounts of the business or profession of the claimant is essential. His own statement of a decrease in profits or earnings subsequent to the injury should not be relied upon, partly because it is his interest to make it as large as possible, and partly because the decrease may be due to quite other causes than the injury. An investigation of the accounts by a public accountant for a period, both before and after the injury, will bring together all the facts necessary to form a correct estimate of the loss sustained and the amount of compensation that should be awarded. Similar cases often arise of compensation for loss of trade or business resulting from other causes, and an investigation by a public accountant is equally necessary.

IX.—Interest Calculations.

Many public accountants have, and all should have, a thorough knowledge of this subject. Such calculations as sinking funds for redemption of leases, the instalments payable on car-trust obligations, amounts required to redeem bond issues or repay loans over a series of years, and other kindred points, are only a few of those matters of everyday occurrence in ordinary business affairs upon which a public accountant is generally qualified to advise his clients.

Responsibility.

So far the subject of the utility of the public accountant has been considered from the point of view of assistance to principals who are responsible for or interested in the accounts, either as partners in a private firm or as directors or managers of a commercial corporation. But there is a much wider responsibility which the public accountant is qualified and willing to undertake, and which it is becoming increasingly the custom to throw upon him—viz., responsibility to the general public, who, either as sleeping partners or as stockholders, or as creditors, are interested in various undertakings as to the details of which they can necessarily have no knowledge.

The prospectus or invitation to the public to subscribe for stock in a corporation should always contain a certificate by public accountants as to the profits earned and the value of the current assets to be acquired. For their own purposes the promoters would obtain such a certificate, and in order to enable the public to judge for themselves of the value of the undertaking, and the fairness of the purchase price, it is only reasonable that they should be furnished with a certificate of past results. If the large body of influential promoters of the undertakings which are offered for public subscription would adopt this practice they would materially aid in preventing the flotation of rotten concerns by unscrupulous speculators; for the absence of any certificate of profits would carry with it a warning to the public to be on their guard. The promoters would at the same time strengthen their own position by throwing a share of the responsibility for the statements contained in the prospectus upon those experts who alone can properly certify to their correctness.

It would seem to be a self-evident proposition that stockholders in a corporation are entitled to all the information in connection with its operations which can safely be made public without damage to its interests; and the most important part of this information is a full statement at regular intervals of the profits of the company and of its true financial position. As stockholders are for various reasons unable to verify such statements for themselves, it is natural that they should depute a representative to examine the books on their behalf, and satisfy them by a comprehensive certificate that the accounts as stated to them present a true and correct view of the condition of the corporation's affairs. The only qualified body whose members are fitted to undertake this duty is that of public accountants, and there can be no doubt that, if such an examination were made compulsory by law or preferably adopted as a universal custom, stockholders would be more effectually protected against losses arising either from deliberate or accidental misstatements of fact. There can be little doubt that to all properly-managed corporations a certificate to the annual Balance Sheet by an independent auditor would be of great value, and, if public opinion insisted upon such certificates, the losses arising from fraudulent, dishonest, or badly-managed corporations would be minimised.

It may be useful to state the position which public accountants claim to take up in giving their certificates. Accounts should show the actual facts—that is to say, the profits stated should be as far as possible the actual profits earned by the undertaking, and the wording adopted therein should be such as to truly and correctly describe the nature of the various items; the Balance Sheet should show the true value of the assets, or, where that is not possible or expedient in the interests of the stockholders, should state the basis on which the valuation thereof is taken, and the excess, if any, over actual value; and the wording adopted should be such as would explain to any reasonable business man the nature of the items included in each group of figures. The accounts are those of the directors, and they are necessarily the final arbiters of the form which they should take. But, if the independent auditor objects to any of the items as not being properly described, or to the statement as a whole as not showing the true profits or the true values of any of the assets or liabilities, it will be his duty to qualify his certificate by embodying his objection therein. If, on the other hand, the auditor is appointed by the directors to assist them, his responsibility is to them alone; he can only advise and report to them and has no discretionary power beyond the right to prevent the directors publishing his signature to any report or statement of accounts without his consent. If he were appointed by the stockholders, it would be his further duty, in the event of the directors declining to affix his certificate to the accounts, to take the earliest opportunity of communicating his views directly to the stockholders. The reason of this attitude is that the corporation is the property of the stockholders and not of the directors as such, the independent auditor being, in this case, the representative of the stockholders to carry out fully that inspection of the accounts which, in a private partnership, each partner would undertake for himself. The directors, being appointed by the stockholders to manage the undertaking, are entitled to state the accounts in any manner they think fit before presenting them to the auditor. It is then the duty of the latter either to certify that the statement is correct and shows the true financial position of the corporation or to specify in what particulars it fails to do so; the stockholders having appointed the auditor are entitled to know his opinion as the result of his investigation, and he is therefore bound to report to them direct if the directors refuse to transmit his report.

Publicity.

The subject of the regulation of trusts is now before the public, and the President's message to Congress suggesting some form of legislation requiring publicity appears to be very generally approved. The large industrial undertakings can, without legislation, do a great deal in this direction by the publication of complete statements of account, certified by a public accountant appointed by the stockholders.

The United States Steel Corporation, the largest industrial undertaking in the world, has recently adopted this course, and if its example were followed by every honestly managed corporation the publicity thus attained would be of the best kind. It would be free from any Governmental control, which is always to be deprecated in commercial affairs, and often leads to a false feeling of security; and it would entail an endorsement of the accounts by a member of a highly-trained profession free from all suspicion of interested motives, whose reputation is bound up in his certificate. It may well be that legislation will eventually be necessary before complete protection is assured to the public. But all those who are against Government interference with private enterprises, while desiring to compel reasonable publicity in the affairs of commercial undertakings, can direct this legislation into safe channels by using their influence to so firmly establish the principle of independent audits by public accountants that the State will merely have to make compulsory a course of action already adopted by the majority of well-managed enterprises. This has been the experience in Great Britain, where for many years the audit of the accounts of corporations has been a general practice, recommended but not insisted upon by law. On the first day of the Twentieth Century this practice became compulsory by an Act of Parliament, which laid down certain forms of certificate and report to be adopted by the auditors, and provided further that the accounts of every corporation must be examined and certified in this special manner by an independent auditor appointed by the stockholders.

If this short account of the status of the profession of the public accountant, of the duties which he is qualified to carry out, and of the responsibilities which he is prepared to undertake, may lead, in even a small degree, to their fuller appreciation by the public, and to the greater protection of the large number of investors and others who are financially interested in commercial affairs, it will have served the purpose of its author.

THE DEVELOPMENT OF CONTEMPORARY ACCOUNTING THOUGHT

An Arno Press Collection

Baldwin, H[arry] G[len]. **Accounting for Value As Well as Original Cost** *and* Castenholz, William B. **A Solution to the Appreciation Problem.** 2 Vols. in 1. 1927/1931

Baxter, William. **Collected Papers on Accounting.** 1978

Brief, Richard P., Ed. **Selections from Encyclopaedia of Accounting, 1903.** 1978

Broaker, Frank and Richard M. Chapman. **The American Accountants' Manual.** 1897

Canning, John B. **The Economics of Accountancy.** 1929

Chatfield, Michael, Ed. **The English View of Accountant's Duties and Responsibilities.** 1978

Cole, William Morse. **The Fundamentals of Accounting.** 1921

Congress of Accountants. **Official Record of the Proceedings of the Congress of Accountants.** 1904

Cronhelm, F[rederick] W[illiam]. **Double Entry by Single.** 1818

Davidson, Sidney. **The Plant Accounting Regulations of the Federal Power Commission.** 1952

De Paula, F[rederic] R[udolf] M[ackley]. **Developments in Accounting.** 1948

Epstein, Marc Jay. **The Effect of Scientific Management on the Development of the Standard Cost System** (Doctoral Dissertation, University of Oregon, 1973). 1978

Esquerré, Paul-Joseph. **The Applied Theory of Accounts.** 1914

Fitzgerald, A[dolf] A[lexander]. **Current Accounting Trends.** 1952

Garner, S. Paul and Marilynn Hughes, Eds. **Readings on Accounting Development.** 1978

Haskins, Charles Waldo. **Business Education and Accountancy.** 1904

Hein, Leonard William. **The British Companies Acts and the Practice of Accountancy 1844-1962** (Doctoral Dissertation, University of California, Los Angeles, 1962). 1978

Hendriksen, Eldon S. **Capital Expenditures in the Steel Industry, 1900 to 1953** (Doctoral Dissertation, University of California, Berkeley, 1956). 1978

Holmes, William, Linda H. Kistler and Louis S. Corsini. **Three Centuries of Accounting in Massachusetts.** 1978

Horngren, Charles T. **Implications for Accountants of the Uses of Financial Statements by Security Analysts** (Doctoral Dissertation, University of Chicago, 1955). 1978

Horrigan, James O., Ed. **Financial Ratio Analysis—An Historical Perspective.** 1978

Jones, [Edward Thomas]. **Jones's English System of Book-keeping.** 1796

Lamden, Charles William. **The Securities and Exchange Commission** (Doctoral Dissertation, University of California, Berkeley, 1949). 1978

Langer, Russell Davis. **Accounting As A Variable in Mergers** (Doctoral Dissertation, University of California, Berkeley, 1976). 1978

Lewis, J. Slater. **The Commercial Organisation of Factories.** 1896

Littleton, A[nanias] C[harles] and B[asil] S. Yamey, Eds. **Studies in the History of Accounting.** 1956

Mair, John. **Book-keeping Moderniz'd.** 1793

Mann, Helen Scott. **Charles Ezra Sprague.** 1931

Marsh, C[hristopher] C[olumbus]. **The Theory and Practice of Bank Book-keeping.** 1856

Mitchell, William. **A New and Complete System of Book-keeping by an Improved Method of Double Entry.** 1796

Montgomery, Robert H. **Fifty Years of Accountancy.** 1939

Moonitz, Maurice. **The Entity Theory of Consolidated Statements.** 1951

Moonitz, Maurice, Ed. **Three Contributions to the Development of Accounting Thought.** 1978

Murray, David. **Chapters in the History of Bookkeeping, Accountancy & Commercial Arithmetic.** 1930

Nicholson, J[erome] Lee. **Cost Accounting.** 1913

Paton, William Andrew and Russell Alger Stevenson. **Principles of Accounting.** 1918

Pixley, Francis W[illiam]. **The Profession of a Chartered Accountant and Other Lectures.** 1897

Preinreich, Gabriel A. D. **The Nature of Dividends.** 1935

Previts, Gary John, Ed. **Early 20th Century Developments in American Accounting Thought.** 1978

Ronen, Joshua and George H. Sorter. **Relevant Financial Statements.** 1978

Shenkir, William G., Ed. **Carman G. Blough: His Professional Career and Accounting Thought.** 1978

Simpson, Kemper. **Economics for the Accountant.** 1921

Sneed, Florence R. **Parallelism in Two Disciplines.** (M.A. Thesis, University of Texas, Arlington, 1974). 1978

Sorter, George H. **The Boundaries of the Accounting Universe** (Doctoral Dissertation, University of Chicago, 1963). 1978

Storey, Reed K[arl]. **Matching Revenues with Costs** (Doctoral Dissertation, University of California, Berkeley, 1958). 1978

Sweeney, Henry W[hitcomb]. **Stabilized Accounting.** 1936

Van de Linde, Gérard. **Reminiscences.** 1917

Vatter, William J[oseph]. **The Fund Theory of Accounting and Its Implications for Financial Reports.** 1947

Walker, R. G. **Consolidated Statements.** 1978

Webster, Norman E., Comp. **The American Association of Public Accountants.** 1954

Wells, M. C., Ed. **American Engineers' Contributions to Cost Accounting.** 1978

Worthington, Beresford. **Professional Accountants.** 1895

Yamey, Basil S. **Essays on the History of Accounting.** 1978

Yamey, Basil S., Ed. **The Historical Development of Accounting.** 1978

Yang, J[u] M[ei]. **Goodwill and Other Intangibles.** 1927

Zeff, Stephen Addam. **A Critical Examination of the Orientation Postulate in Accounting, with Particular Attention to its Historical Development** (Doctoral Dissertation, University of Michigan, 1961). 1978

Zeff, Stephen A., Ed. **Selected Dickinson Lectures in Accounting.** 1978